D1528144

CONRAD AND RELIGION

Conrad and Religion

John Lester

St. Martins' Press   New York

First published in the United States of America in 1987

Printed in Hong Kong

ISBN 0-312-00979-8

Library of Congress Cataloging-in-Publication Data
Lester, John, 1943–
Conrad and religion.
Bibliography: p.
Includes index.
1. Conrad, Joseph, 1857–1924—Religion.
2. Religion in literature. I. Title.
PR6005.04Z766 **1988**   823′.912   87–14377
ISBN 0-312-00979-8

For My Mother and the Memory of Harry George

Contents

Preface

Any critical work (whether it acknowledges it or not) takes part, not in a debate (that favoured concept of our current predilection for polarities), but in an extended act of consultation whose aim is to bring more understanding and appreciation to the writings of a great artist. The responsibility of the critic is great for he is sometimes privy to the most poignant and intimate emotions of an anguished soul, transmitted to paper at a fevered and unguarded moment and published at a later date so that the confidences of a lifetime can be laid bare before the curious gaze of posterity. Public access to such personal files demands a purity of motive on the part of the beholders, a sympathetic response to the secrets thus revealed and a high degree of integrity among those who would make use of their contents.

This is particularly the case when dealing with the acutely personal area of religious belief, for which we all have our separate quests. Our empathy and understanding are essential if we are to follow the fluctuations of another's search for truth, whatever differences and similarities there may be to one's own path. In Joseph Conrad's case the trail was a tortuous one, involving many agonies of mind and spirit, minutely detailed as to cause and effect (in his later years at least). To observe his pilgrimage is our privilege; to note its results in his many publications is our pleasure; to contribute to the unending appraisal of their value and meaning is our design.

In true consultation what is said is more important than who says it and any clash of ideas (as distinct from the personalities behind them) heralds not conflict but another step towards unravelling yet another fold of the tangled skein of truth. The later critic thus possesses the declared wisdom of his predecessors in the field and where his views collide with previous interpretations the result should be a further evaluation of threatened premises which, in consequence, will either be strengthened or amended. To disagree with a particular approach or critical method is not to deny its contribution to the whole. In the present instance the interpretations with which I have taken issue have led to my own re-evaluations and thoughts. Consultation, properly

performed, creates a pool of collective wisdom in which all may dip.
Conrad's use of religious language seemed to me to be one of the
murkier and neglected areas of that pool. I hope that these few drops
of mine have made it less opaque.

Timaru   JOHN LESTER
New Zealand

Acknowledgements

I first encountered the work of Joseph Conrad in the sixth form where *The Rover* was one of the set novels for A level English. We were also given a supplementary reading list of recommended novels to lead us to a wider experience of English Literature, and this list included *Lord Jim*. My first acknowledgement, therefore, should be to the compiler of that list, J. R. Madell, for, whilst *The Rover* did not make much of an impact, *Lord Jim* did.

In more recent times, I owe a debt of gratitude to the staff of the English Department of the University of Canterbury, whose unfailing encouragement and friendliness made the process of research such an enjoyable one. In particular, I should like to thank Dr P. D. Evans and Dr G. W. Spence for their early enthusiasm, careful supervision, helpful advice and constant patience during the preparation of my doctoral dissertation, upon which this book is based. In addition, Professor K. K. Ruthven, supervisor of graduate studies during the early stages of this work, made many pertinent comments on my initial drafts leading to fruitful areas of investigation. En route, as it were, I feel I should acknowledge the three years of inspiring tuition I received from Professor D. C. Gunby during my earlier days in the university. I am also grateful to the inter-loan section of the University of Canterbury library, who obtained so many important texts for me, and to E. John Neilson who generously allowed me the use of his extensive collection of Conradiana, thus enabling me to have constant access to works which would otherwise have been unobtainable. Since completing the thesis, practical encouragement and advice have also come from Professor Bruce King and from Professor David Leon Higdon, editor of *Conradiana*.

Diane Candy-Karotu typed the thesis with meticulous care; I hope I have approached her achievement in producing the revised typescript for this book. I must also mention the kindly patience, support (and probable forbearance) of my dear wife Barbara during this typing time and the enthusiastic co-operation of Meg Parkin, Director of the Aigantighe Art Gallery, Timaru (New Zealand).

xi

Lastly, it would be remiss of me to omit all reference to the Bahá'í
Faith, whose influence directed my gaze towards the religious aspects
of Conrad's works in the first place and certainly caused me to consider
his treatment of Islām with more than usual interest.

Most of chapter 4 appeared in my essay, 'Conrad and Islām,' in
Conradiana, 13 (1981) 163–79.

List of Abbreviations

With the exception of *The Sisters* (published by U. Mursia in 1968), all references to Conrad's works come from the Dent Collected Edition (1946–54). They are abbreviated as follows:

AF.   *Almayer's Folly – a Story of an Eastern River*
OI.   *An Outcast of the Islands*
NN.   *The Nigger of the 'Narcissus' – a Tale of the Sea*
TU.   *Tales of Unrest*
LJ.   *Lord Jim – a Tale*
Y.   *Youth: a Narrative; and Two Other Stories*
T.   *Typhoon, and Other Stories*
N.   *Nostromo – a Tale of the Seaboard*
MS.   *The Mirror of the Sea – Memories and Impressions*
SA.   *The Secret Agent – a Simple Tale*
ASS.   *A Set of Six*
UWE.   *Under Western Eyes*
PR.   *A Personal Record*
TLS.   *'Twixt Land and Sea – Tales*
C.   *Chance – a Tale in Two Parts*
V.   *Victory – an Island Tale*
WT.   *Within the Tides – Tales*
SL.   *The Shadow-Line – a Confession*
AG.   *The Arrow of Gold – a Story between Two Notes*
Re.   *The Rescue – a Romance of the Shallows*
NLL.   *Notes on Life and Letters*
Ro.   *The Rover*
Sus.   *Suspense – a Napoleonic Novel*
TH.   *Tales of Hearsay*
LE.   *Last Essays*
Sis.   *The Sisters*

Introduction

In 1906, whilst at the height of his creative powers, Joseph Conrad wrote an essay on John Galsworthy in which he concentrated particularly on *The Man of Property*, the earliest part of *The Forsyte Saga*. The manner of his approach to the book is very illuminating, for Conrad speaks of the Forsytes and of their obsession with property as follows:

> The practical faculty of the Forsytes has erected it into a principle; their idealism has expanded it into a sort of religion which has shaped their notions of happiness and decency, their prejudices, their piety, such thoughts as they happen to have and the very course of their passions. Life as a whole has come to be perceptible to them exclusively in terms of property. Preservation, acquisition – acquisition, preservation. Their laws, their morality, their art and their science appear to them, justifiably enough, consecrated to that double and unique end. It is the formula of their virtue. (*LE*, 128)

Soames Forsyte's town house is 'one of the temples of property, of a sort of unholy religion whose fundamental dogma, public ceremonies and awful secret rites, forming the subject of this remarkable novel, take no account of human dignity' (*LE*, 129). The incidents of the book can be viewed 'in the light of the unquenchable fires burning on the altar of property' (*LE*, 131).

The passage in Galsworthy's novel that inspired this kind of treatment seems to have been the following:

> This great and good woman, so highly thought of in ecclesiastical circles, was one of the principal priestesses in the temple of Forsyteism, keeping alive day and night a sacred flame to the God of Property, whose altar is inscribed with those inspiring words: "Nothing for nothing, and really remarkably little for sixpence."[1]

The point is that this is the only passage in the novel that likens the Forsytes' regard for property to a religion and yet it is this one aspect that Conrad has chosen to pinpoint as an illustration of the extent of their preoccupation. Galsworthy made the comparison once within his novel; Conrad makes it five times during his review of that novel. Clearly he found the imagery striking and significant, indicating that such metaphorical use of religious terminology met with his approval, but it is equally evident that he found it important and appealing.

Why this should be so becomes clear when reading Conrad's writings for religion in its literal form (the appearance of a Christian priest, for example) or in a figurative guise (as he saw Galsworthy using it) plays an important role in his works. This has not gone unobserved but has led to some questionable interpretations, mostly archetypal and allegorical in nature. This kind of approach to Conrad's fiction, particularly *The Nigger of the 'Narcissus'*, caused Ian Watt to categorise the varying types of criticism under the major headings of *homeophoric* and *heterophoric*.

According to Watt a *homeophoric* interpretation is a natural extension of the implications of the narrative content and retains a consistent closeness to it whilst a *heterophoric* interpretation goes beyond any demonstrable connection between the literary object and the symbolic meaning it has been given and tends towards allegory. As far as religion is concerned one relevant division of heterophoric criticism is *mythophoric* which depends on allusions to a specific body of mythical, religious or literary knowledge.[2]

A certain restraint is necessary in most heterophoric criticism (a degree of detachment perhaps) since it is not unknown for any deficiencies in such arguments to be attributed to alleged failings on the part of the novelist. This current study, therefore, seeks to achieve a balanced view of Conrad's use of religious language by taking into account all its varied manifestations and by adopting a more homeophoric approach than the subject has received hitherto. Firstly, though, those previous analyses need to be assessed for their validity. Do they indeed lead to new levels of understanding as their supporters claim or is there substance in the complaints of their opponents (such as Tony Tanner) that 'the uniqueness of novelistic detail is lost by reference back to certain rudimentary shapes or outlines which in their generality can subsume the most heterogenous material if the critic so wishes'?[3]

By definition archetypal criticism requires mythical precedents. Human lives, however, which form the intimate concern of literature, follow the same basic outline of birth, procreation and death; thus each work can be seen as a variation of detail within this set pattern. The archetypal critic, therefore, must be aware of the need to distinguish between the deliberate evoking of an age-old myth and the inevitable repetition of a motif. As John J. White comments, 'Such speculations, possibly resulting in the mythological allegorization of novels, take place when it is suggested a certain myth is latent in a text, although in fact all that has been located is an extraneous myth with an archetypal pattern in common with the novel in question.'[4] Northrop Frye, whose *Anatomy of Criticism* seems to have fathered some of these approaches, similarly warns that 'In pointing out the latent apocalyptic or demonic patterns in a literary work, we should not make the error of assuming that this latent content is the *real* content hypocritically disguised by a lying censor. It is simply one factor which is relevant to a full critical analysis.'[5]

Frye's definition of an archetype ('A symbol, usually an image, which recurs often enough in literature to be recognizable as a whole'[6]) is loose enough to be applied to almost any work of literature by an indiscriminate critic. As Tanner complains, 'A man can scarcely get into a boat but he will find himself engaged in a repetition of "a night-sea journey into an ambiguous region either in the dark interior of the earth or below the waters of the sea".'[7]

Even a deliberate allusion to a myth does not indicate that the myth in question can be automatically applied wholesale to the work in which it appears. If we read in a novel that 'People seemed afraid to show their eyes; they averted them swiftly from one another as if they had heard that the gorgon had returned and was even now at large in their streets', this does not mean that we need to seek out a Perseus figure or apply a mythological pattern to the work. The simile could simply show the steadfastness with which the inhabitants of large cities tend to avoid eye contact (and communication) with each other and thus help to build up an atmosphere of mutual suspicion.

Critics have been especially alert to the possibilities of finding Christ figures in the novels, including such victims as Yanko Gooral in 'Amy Foster'[8] and (less obviously) Hirsch, the unfortunate merchant of *Nostromo*.[9] Three major characters are also cited. Thus Lord Jim is 'Christ the Tragic Hero' to Edwin M. Moseley,[10] who explains:

> One almost thinks of the first half of the book as the Old Testament, in which man fails his responsibility and is driven from place to place as if seeking somewhere to hide his guilt. In this half of the book Jim is the archetypal Adam; he is clearly Everyman. Similarly, the

second half of the book is a kind of New Testament, in which the protagonist is no longer Man but a god who assumes the shape of a man to show him by a life of sacrifice the way to redemption. In this half of the book . . . Jim develops as the archetypal Christ; he is clearly the sacrificial scapegoat for Everyman.[11]

To take this view, however, is to lose track of much of Jim's significance. There are undeniable godlike connotations to Jim's position in Patusan but the way one approaches this is a key factor in interpretation. Moseley seems to see him as a deliberately evoked Christ figure. Bruce Johnson, on the other hand, also sees him as godlike but relates him to his milieu – the age of Rajah Brooke and the motif of the white man as god among the natives. Johnson's analysis (embracing the uses of the motif by Rider Haggard, Stevenson and particularly Kipling)[12] seems far more pertinent to *Lord Jim* than Moseley's. For Moseley's emphasis would imply that Conrad's starting point for the novel was Christ; that the purpose of the book, in short, was to re-awaken interest in Christianity. To delineate Jim's role in this fashion is to impose a simplistic notion on a complex book. Podmore, at the height of his attempt to convert James Wait, becomes 'a voice – a fleshless and sublime thing, as on that memorable night – the night when he went walking over the sea to make coffee for perishing sinners' (*NN*, 116); Lingard tells Edith Travers, 'It began by me coming to you at night – like a thief in the night' (*Re*, 398) – both unmistakable echoes of Christ. But this does not make either Podmore or Lingard archetypal Christ figures, though it may indicate that, in their 'supreme conceit' (*NN*, 116) they think or act as if they are. Thus, if Jim is a saviour figure in Patusan it is more because this is what he has aspired to be and he must be seen, not solely in terms of his pretensions but also in terms of character.

It is this kind of equation (that allusion means identification) that seems to lie behind the readings of 'Heart of Darkness' that make Mr Kurtz a perverted form of Christ.[13] But, again, if Kurtz's promise to return is evocative of Christ's promise of a Second Coming, it is also an empty gesture, illustrating the intense egoism of the man. Christ's mission was for three years and Kurtz is also appointed for this period (as Stanley Renner points out)[14] but so is the accountant (*Y*, 74) and, historically, so was Conrad.[15] The accountant says of Kurtz, 'He will be a somebody in the administration before long. They, above – the Council in Europe you know – mean him to be' (*Y*, 70), but connecting this statement to Christ is tenuous, especially since Marlow has been recommended by the same people who sent Kurtz (*Y*, 79). It is also difficult to attach undue significance to Marlow's evocation of the Romans 'nineteen hundred years ago' (*Y*, 47) since it was common practice at the time to compare the situation in the Congo with Britain in Roman times.[16]

The 'pilgrims' with their staves attract attention but here conflicting biblical verses cause problems, for while Mark 6:8 (quoted by W. L. Godshalk)[17] permits the disciples to 'take nothing for their journey save a staff only,' Luke 9:3 (mis-applied by A. M. Hollingsworth to Christ's 'lower apostles')[18] tells them not to take even that. Trying to make a point about the 'pilgrims' having staves (as these two critics do) is thus a hazardous undertaking. Just to add to the confusion, W. B. Stein, who sees the work in the context of Mahayana Buddhism, claims that the 'pilgrims' are 'inversions of the Bodhisattva and his staff.'[19]

In each of these cases the critic seems to have fallen into the dangers of over-specification. Pilgrims have traditionally carried staves; it is the presence of the staves, in fact, that causes Marlow to call the agents 'pilgrims' in the first place. He refers to them as 'faithless' from the beginning; thus to seek out a particular religious source is more likely to obscure than to elucidate a reasonably straightforward point.

The last of these Christ figures discovered by critics in Conrad's work is Axel Heyst; an inevitable choice, perhaps, since he saves a girl who is called Alma and Magdalen. Charles C. Walcutt, however, maintains that 'The Christian symbolism is boldly announced with the name of Heyst. However it might be pronounced in Swedish, it is certainly rhymed with Christ by an English speaking reader.'[20] Walcutt reasons:

> With almost inexhaustible ambiguities and indirection he is iden-
> tified with Christ . . . not directly but obliquely. He is perhaps a
> Christ of the modern world, the world in which the folly of action
> has been so powerfully demonstrated by both secular and religious
> atrocities that this thinking Christ would never undertake to save
> mankind by action or preachment. An ironic version of Christ, then
> — ironic and tangential, and of course partial — in his total commit-
> ment to the ideal of doing no wrong.[21]

An 'ironic . . . tangential, and . . . partial' Christ, suggested by 'ambiguities and indirection' seems to be too hedged in by qualifica-tions to be readily acceptable. Moreover, this commitment to identi-fication leads to some strange assertions, notably in respect of Mr Jones (identified as Satan) when he recoils from Schomberg's mention of a woman. According to Walcutt, 'On the story level, the reaction shows Jones' abhorrence of women; on the symbolic level, it is the devil offended by lack of respect — and also perhaps recalling that the present forms of his angelic followers are the hissing vipers in hell.'[22] But the image of a viper is produced by the narrator to describe the effect of Schomberg's statement on Jones. It does not appear in the conversation between the two men, hence there is nothing for Jones to recall. Walcutt also runs into difficulties with Wang who 'is something of a puzzle in the Christian pattern' and concludes that 'If there is a Christian ideal of service here, it is not really apparent and does not seem to enrich the theme.'[23] In other words the pattern having been imposed, Conrad is now to be criticised for producing a character who does not fit into it. Walcutt cites Heyst's charity as an instance in which he is Christlike but the amount of Morrison's debt is not large and, in fact, it is Morrison's own charity (his feeding of hungry villagers with rice for no return) that is closer to the ideal.

The biblical allusions in *Victory* are many and varied, embracing the whole gamut of Eden, the Deluge, Christ and the Apocalypse. Little wonder that critics who insist on labelling characters have fallen back on such terms as 'an inverted parallel,'[24] or 'mirror image,'[25] though, whilst the first of these statements concerns Christ and Mary Magdalen, the second is about Adam and Eve.

Identification leads to confusion, therefore, principally because it is assumed that the original story to which allusion has been made must either be reproduced, parodied or inverted in some way. Critics applying patterns of the 'Fall of Man' and 'Loss of Eden'[26] to Conrad's work run into similar difficulties and, indeed, their very premise can be questioned, for the story of Eden itself can be taken as a symbol of human experience, illustrating the often disillusioning effects of the acquisition of knowledge. Such an experience is one of the growing pains of life; a transition each of us must make. It is almost impossible, therefore, to write about stages of human existence without describing this important period and, in this light, the use of terms such as 'prelapsarian', 'Fall' and 'Edenic' becomes practically meaningless; any story could be fitted into the scheme. In other words the loss of Eden is itself an allegory of human life, not vice versa. Conrad does refer to the Fall at times, of course, often very directly (as in 'The Return') but this does not indicate a need to denote a pattern or delineate roles. For any such application to have validity it must be discriminating. To assume that biblical allusions or suggestive motifs must point to a biblical pattern, within which a novel's events and characters can, willy nilly, be fitted, is not only to lack this essential discrimination but also to diminish in value those works which do seek to make use of the Bible in this way.

Sometimes these allegorical associations begin with nothing more than names and numbers which, in 'Youth' are taken by William W. Bonney to indicate a crisis of faith:

> . . . in the destruction of the *Judea*, a vessel which to Marlow seems like 'The old village church at home' [*Y*, 18], whose motto is 'Do or Die', whose captain is a feeble and incompetent Beard, steward an aged Abraham, and mate 'Mann' himself, there is figured forth the demise of Judeo-Christian linear metaphysics.[27]

Norman Sherry's investigations reveal that the captain of the *Palestine* was Elijah Beard but this thoroughly biblical name becomes the more neutral 'John' in 'Youth'.[28] The mate's surname also remains unchanged. James W. Matthews mentions the significance of the number 'three' in the story, citing such examples as the number of times the light is out for the *Celestial* and the fact that the storm in the Atlantic abates on the third day, which he sees as a false resurrection.[29] He also refers to the scene where, having prepared the lifeboats, Marlow returns to the ship to find the captain asleep and the crew enjoying their 'last meal aboard' (*Y*, 32–3) as a possible parody of the Last Supper, the ship's complement being thirteen.[30] Since two of the crew remain in the lifeboat Marlow has just left, however (*Y*, 31), there are numerical objections to this last interpretation, and it is pertinent to remember that there were actually thirteen hands on board the historical *Palestine*.[31]

This is not to suggest that the names in 'Youth' are irrelevant but in assessing their importance it is necessary to consider in whose eyes they achieve this status and why. Taken as a whole the names can be said to illustrate the romantic illusions of Marlow as a young man; they are emblems of these illusions. The fact of the historical voyage and its details is in danger of being downgraded if undue significance is sought in the names and numbers within the story. Ian Watt comments of this sort of practice that 'the literary effect of such interpretation is to reduce what Conrad actually created to a mere illustration'.[32]

There are numerous pitfalls awaiting the critic who takes names and numbers as a key to his interpretation. The number 'three' is particularly popular as having special Christian overtones but how does one tell when it carries this significance and when it is just a three? In the early pages of 'The End of the Tether', it is disclosed that Whalley has been captain of the *Sofala* 'for the last three years only' (*Y*, 166) and this is quickly followed by a reference to 'the three palms of the next port of call' (*Y*, 167). It would be tempting to treat this as an allusion to the end of Christ's mission and to suggest that these details indicate that Whalley is nearing the end of his term of office and approaching his Calvary. The *Sofala* remains in port for three days, moreover, but there would be obvious folly in attempting to see resurrection possibilities here. Three palms are also in evidence at the conclusion of 'The Planter of Malata' (*WT*, 72) but if there are echoes of Calvary there they must be simply as an ominous portent for the protagonist; certainly not an indication of a Christlike figure or a Christian pattern.

Patterns can sometimes dominate an entire book and this happens with R. J. Andreach's *The Slain and Resurrected God: Conrad, Ford and the Christian Myth*. Andreach takes 'Heart of Darkness' as delineating 'the archetypal pattern' that Conrad 'continued to refine throughout his career,' this being the pattern of separation – initiation – return undertaken by the mythic quester.[33] He then attempts to fit most of the Conradian canon into this one pattern (with its saving qualification of refinement). This requires some manipulation at times, especially when considering *The Secret Agent*, where he refers to 'Stevie's resurrection in Chapter VIII',[34] (Stevie being 'the archetypal slain and resurrected god'),[35] and sees Winnie as 'the archetypal virgin-mother who offers her brother-son to mankind'.[36]

To regard a Conradian time shift as a 'resurrection' is an example of the way an archetypal approach can be over-extended, for Stevie does not return at all; the story simply goes back in time to trace the steps to his death. On this basis resurrections in literature would be a frequent affair. Similarly, when descriptions of Winnie stress her sensuality, an assertion of her virginal role in the novel seems singularly inapt.

At this stage it might be as well not to discount all the results of archetypal criticism. In many cases the interesting points that are made tend to become submerged beneath some dubiously supported speculations but it would be inaccurate to assert a total absence of archetypes and myths from Conrad's novels. At what point, then, can it be said that the archetypal critic is out of bounds?

A consideration of two comments on *Nostromo* in Claire Rosenfeld's *Paradise of Snakes* could assist here. Having remarked upon the mythic associations that surround the treasure, Rosenfeld continues:

> To extend this distinction between history and tradition, one need only relate both to the concepts of a perfect and of a fallen world.

Sulaco, though its orange groves and isolation suggest Eden, is very different from our conception of paradise. It is inextricably part of the fallen world. Though most of its people are very primitive, a decadent Spanish aristocracy exists to remind us that the equality of Eden has long since been forgotten. Or perhaps we might say that this is a microcosm of the fallen world, possessing within its natural barrier all sorts of evil.[37]

Genesis is invoked here, then, but not on any direct evidence. Orange groves and isolation are not enough to suggest Eden and, surely, if one is to adopt the notion of a Fall, every novel must inevitably deal with a fallen world. Every novel must also be concerned with inequalities; the existence of a privileged class will only give reminders of the 'equality of Eden' if Eden is one's starting point and all things are being regarded in relation to it.

Such an analysis may act as a key to determining admissible and non-admissible assertions; in other words the starting point for interpretation should be the novel which will suggest the myth rather than working from the myth to the novel. Rosenfeld, consequently, seems on firmer ground when discussing the 'paradise of snakes', Don Pepe's term for the San Tomé gorge. To think of Genesis at this stage is clearly appropriate since the starting point is the text. 'Paradise of snakes' indicates a place of destructive temptations and one can hardly argue with Rosenfeld that it is ominously prophetic.

There are thus many snares for the heterophoric critic to avoid. Archetypal criticism is clearly valid at times, though it seems more effective when evoking a general background reference than when it attempts to allegorise a particular sequence of events. Frye's book is in some respects a collation of categories into which literature may be confidently placed. The list is so exhaustive that a work of literature can hardly escape coming within its headings under one form or another. The archetypal critic must beware, therefore, lest he achieve little more than an identification of type and the temptations and pitfalls of this approach are bound to be accentuated by an author's use of a religious lexis.

Perhaps the biggest danger facing archetypal criticism is that of failing to treat the characters of a novel as characters. It is hardly fair to talk of Conrad parodying hero myths because he happens to produce characters with faults that fail to conform to the appropriate pattern. To regard Jim as archetypal Christ or Kurtz as diabolic Christ is, in many ways, to cease regarding them as individual characters. If there are echoes of scripture that suggest these connections, it is important to regard them, not as the end of the investigation (assuming an archetypal pattern forthwith), but as the beginning. What is the purpose of the allusion? What does it tell us about that particular character? By whom is the connection made? Simply to assert a particular pattern and confine a character to a specific role within that pattern is to beg these important questions and this, by and large, is what the more heterophoric of Conrad's critics have tended to do.

1
Religion in Poland, 1820–70

Conrad's earliest religious background was that of Polish Catholicism and the state of religion in Poland during his early years is thus of some importance. Under the oppressive yoke of the occupying powers, particularly Russia, Polish religion became intensely nationalistic (as Conrad himself was later to affirm)[1] and its principal features (notably the influence of the clergy over a largely illiterate and superstitious laity and the elevation of patriotism to a mystical religious belief) frequently appear as elements of his fiction.

The state of Christianity in Poland, certainly during the early years of the nineteenth century, was exposed in an anonymous pamphlet entitled 'Journey to Darktown,' which was published in 1820 to oppose reactionary post-Napoleonic war elements within Poland in which the Roman Catholic bishops were well to the fore. This document was severely critical of the backwardness of the clergy and of their claims of predominance in the fields of religion and culture.[2] The pamphlet was violently condemned yet the conduct of the Polish clergy during the course of the next fifty years did little to refute its strictures. False predictions of a comet in 1857 (the year of Conrad's birth) caused some priests to proclaim the imminent approach of the end of the world, forcing the authorities to send troops to guard the Jewish quarter of Warsaw, 'lest working men, anxious to ensure their passage into heaven, should seek to purchase it by a massacre of the Jews'.[3] This event prompted the British Consul of the time to comment, 'It is curious to observe in the 19th century a movement and its consequences which remind us forcibly of the dark period of the middle ages.'[4] In one small town (Turek) three days' rioting followed attempts by the Christian population to prevent the repair of the synagogue, illustrating the anti-Semitic tendencies that pervaded all classes of Poles and from which Conrad himself was not entirely free.

With an 80 per cent illiteracy rate reported in 1859 (higher still amongst the peasant population),[5] priests had certain responsibilities towards their often ignorant and fanatical flocks; responsibilities they seem not to have discharged satisfactorily, either because of their own ignorance and fanaticism or through a more unscrupulous exercise of

1

power on their part. The period was dominated, in the Russian part of Poland at least, by the two ill-fated insurrections of 1830 and 1863 and the often turbulent years between, during which the clergy used their undoubted influence in varied and sometimes contradictory ways. During the 1863 insurrection, for example, priests in the Ukraine, in conjunction with the police, were instrumental in persuading the peasants there to rise up and slaughter a group of Polish patriots who were hoping to win their support for the uprising.[6] The earlier activities of Father Sciegienny in the 1840s, on the other hand, were an attempt to incite insurrection by claiming the support of Pope Gregory XVI and exhorting the peasants to 'rally round the standard of the Virgin Mary against her enemies and the enemies of the Fatherland and the People'.[7] Both examples illustrate how many of the clergy were not above manipulating the gullibility of their charges by false appeals to their religious fervour. During the crisis-laden years immediately before the 1863 uprising, the clergy did nothing to moderate the passions of their congregations. Angry at the determination of their Polish head of government, Alexander Wielopolski, not to be manipulated by any faction in Poland and to act fairly to all religions, including the Jews, a small body of priests arrogated to themselves the title of 'Catholic Clergy of the Kingdom of Poland' and published a hand bill which maintained that Catholicism was the national religion of Poland.[8] Parish priests came to regard it as a patriotic duty to condemn Wielopolski from the pulpit and, with four times as many priests as schoolteachers in the land, there were few other influences that could counter this.

Wielopolski's stand united both the Catholic hierarchy ('that pillar of Polish conservatism')[9] and the more radical parish priests against him. These two factions of the Church were generally at loggerheads (the bishops tending to support attempts to come to terms with the Russians, the lesser clergy supporting the cause of national independence) but both were adamant that Roman Catholicism (and, by implication, themselves) should enjoy a privileged position among religions in Poland. This is not the place to discuss Wielopolski's political aims, but they do seem to have been those of compromise and moderation and Church support could have helped to avert the impassioned and ill-advised actions that were to come. Instead, the Church's stand seems more appropriate to the days of Innocent III if the views of the Warsaw clergy can be taken as representative. In a letter to their Archbishop (forwarded to Wielopolski and distributed among the population) they maintained that 'We recognize in the church the authority of the successor of St Peter and the authority of the bishops, the successors of the apostles; we know that this authority has been given to them from heaven for the government of the church, that this authority ought to be recognized by everyone who is a member of the church.'[10]

In making such statements the Polish clergy showed themselves to be completely unrealistic as some of their other grievances illustrate. For, like their government, the Polish Catholic Church was not an autonomous entity, able to indulge itself in its every whim, but a restricted body under the close supervision of Russia; a control that became still tighter after the events of 1863. An Orthodox Russian stood at its head, despite Polish protests. Marriage between persons of the Catholic and Orthodox Faiths had to be celebrated in the Orthodox church first and then in the Catholic one and, from 1847, any children of such a marriage had to be brought up in the Orthodox faith. Restrictions were placed on the content of Catholic sermons and (from 1845) direct contact with the Vatican was forbidden, all such communications having to be directed through the government. A gesture of defiance, such as that taken by Archbishop Białobrzeski after Russian troops had cleared Polish churches on 15 October 1861 on the singing of patriotic songs by the congregations, could only be short-lived. Białobrzeski closed the churches in protest at what he regarded as an act of sacrilege but he was quickly exiled to Russia and replaced by a more compliant Archbishop (Felinski) who opened them again. Earlier that year (February 1861) troops fired on the crowd after demonstrators had become mixed up with a funeral procession. During the fracas a man started to use the cross as a club, the breaking of which caused the crowd to cry out that the Russians were defiling holy Catholic objects.[11] Church grievances further included the confiscation of church lands (in return for salaries).[12]

From their official spiritual overlord, the supreme Pontiff in Rome, however, the Polish clergy received little encouragement. After the abortive rising of November 1830, Pope Gregory XVI, in the papal brief 'Impensa Charitas' of February 1831, called upon them to obey their Tsarist superiors, whilst the encyclical 'Cum Primum' of 1832, addressed to the Polish bishops 'in words binding upon their consciences,'[13] enjoined as a duty their co-operation with Tsarist authorities. The spirit of collaboration between Pope and Tsar reached its culmination in the Concordat of 3 August 1847, intended as an alliance between the two powers as forces for restoration. The 1863 insurrection persuaded the Russians that papal attempts to check the

Polish clergy had failed and, after Pius IX had complained abut Alexander II's peremptory reorganisation of the church in Poland, the Tsar revoked the Concordat, broke off diplomatic relations with the Vatican and transferred the spiritual supervision of the Church, previously distinguished from its 'ecclesiastical administration,' to the college at St Petersburg.[14] Though short-lived, the very existence of the Concordat is sufficient to reveal the papacy as an ally of autocracy, the action being seen as part of a process of dogged support for all legitimate monarchs, no matter how absolute they might be, as a reaction to the setbacks the Church had suffered through the French Revolution and Bonaparte.[15] Such alignments are often noted in Conrad's fiction.

It has already been observed, however, that Polish religion tended to be very nationalistic in character, to the extent that the nation itself seemed to become an object of veneration and awe. With such an outlook the failure of the 1830 insurrection was a tremendous blow which historians have seen as having a religious significance:

> Divine intervention did not come. The Poles saw their country, the nation chosen to bear the torch of Christian faith, as they believed, to the eastern frontier of Europe, deserted. They had to adjust their minds to grim reality. God had let the very instrument of His own purposes be destroyed.[16]

By way of her romantic poets, safely escaped to Paris in what became known as 'The Great Emigration', ideas of a Messianic role for Poland began to spread. The Poles had been defeated in 1831; now a greater sacrifice was required. Poland, the Christ of nations, was being crucified for the sins of the world but would rise again on the Third Day as the herald of God's Kingdom on Earth. Thus 'an impassioned patriotism that takes the sacred lineaments of a religion became the basic principle of Poland's romantic literature'.[17]

Ideas such as this appeared in the *Books of the Polish Nation* (1831) by Adam Mickiewicz, greatly influenced by the visions of the mystical Andrzej Towianski.[18] Mickiewicz's works, banned in Poland, were smuggled in to be avidly read in secret and quietly circulated despite threats of punishment by the authorities which simply enhanced their attraction. Their devotees included Apollo Korzeniowski, Conrad's father, whose choice of Konrad as one of the Christian names for his son was undoubtedly influenced by its use by Mickiewicz in *Konrad Wallenrod* (the story of a Lithuanian patriot who becomes Grand Master of the Teutonic Knights so that he can lead them into a trap) and in *Forefathers' Eve III* (where Gustav, a Lithuanian youth, becomes reborn in a Russian prison and assumes the name of Konrad).

Mickiewicz was one of three major romantic poets whose influence and popularity in Poland were widespread. The other figures – Juliusz Słowacki (Conrad's personal favourite)[19] and Zygmunt Krasinski – wrote in similar vein. Słowacki's *Anhelli* (1837) put forward ideas of Poles preparing themselves for martyrdom and of the coming of the great 'King Spirit' who appeared from age to age and would surely come to Poland before long. Krasinski's *Dawn* (1843) was still more explicit:

> . . . and I heard
> A voice that called in the eternal sky:
> As to the world I gave a Son,
> So to it, Poland, thee I give.
> My only Son he was – and shall be,
> But in thee my purpose for Him lives.
> Be thou then the Truth, as he is, everywhere.
> Thee I make my daughter!
> When Thou didst descend into the grave
> Thou wert, like Him, a part of humankind.
> But now, this day of victory,
> Thy name is: All Humanity![20]

Krasinski's death in 1859 caused much re-reading of his greatest work, the enthusiasm for which was fed to some extent by the successful example of Italy, whose famous hero, Garibaldi, also became a popular figure amongst the Poles as a fellow fighter for freedom.[21]

To Poland's Catholic base, therefore, must be added this strange mixture of mystical nationalism if a full picture of Polish religion is to be achieved. Even Polish societies could acquire names with religious overtones (that formed amongst the Polish students of Kiev was called The Trinity, for example).[22] This passionate sense of mystical destiny reached a crescendo in the early 1860s, culminating in the arrival of the long-awaited Third Day (the insurrection of 1863) and failure. To some Polish historians, however, the religious connotations linger on. One reports: 'It had assuredly no chance of success. Nevertheless, this act of despair has left a memory sacred to every Pole. No sacrifice for the national cause had, in fact, ever been so disinterested and of so moving a nature.'[23]

In retrospect, the application of religious terms to their nation's destiny can be seen to have blinded the Poles to the harsh realities of Russian troops and of European politicians, whose sympathies did not extend to active support. Amidst impassioned calls to sacrifice and martyrdom the cooler counsels of moderation were unlikely to be heeded. Irrational religious nationalism had become a fatal obsession and in the days of Conrad's childhood it led the Poles to disaster.

2
Religion in Conrad's Life, 1857–95

Conrad was born in the Ukraine in 1857 as Józef Teodor Konrad Nałęcz Korzeniowski, the son of a father who was deeply imbued with the Messianic visions of Poland's romantic poets. Significantly, Conrad's first sense of identity was that of 'Pole, Catholic, nobleman', expressed by him at the age of five in a letter to his grandmother.[1] Earlier, his baptism had been greeted by Apollo Korzeniowski with verses that exemplify the father's nationalistic beliefs:

> My child, my son, if the enemy calls you a nobleman and a Christian
> − tell yourself that you are a pagan and that your nobility is rot. . . .
> My child, my son − tell yourself that you are without land, without
> love, without Fatherland, without humanity − as long as Poland,
> our mother, is enslaved.[2]

This intense patriotic passion prompted a move to Warsaw where Apollo's fiery political activities led to his arrest in October 1861 and subsequent exile to Northern Russia with his family during the following May. Both Conrad and his mother, Evalina, suffered from severe illness during the journey and for a while the boy was near to death. When death did come, however, it claimed his mother in 1865 and his father four years later. In a sense, then, Conrad's childhood epitomises the fate of Poland during these years. Inspired by a deep religious nationalism, evoked by the great romantic poets, Apollo, unwittingly, led his family to disaster.

As a very young child Conrad seems to have held a simple belief, asking the poor at the church 'to pray for the return of his father from Warsaw'[3] (Apollo, initially, had gone there alone). Certainly the father's letters are full of religious references. During the early days of exile he wrote:

> We have set up and are maintaining a chapel: it is the centre around
> which we live. We pray a great deal, ardently and sincerely. Apart

7

from us, there are people from '30, '46 and '48 who since '56 are
allowed to return but stayed.

For them our arrival was like a few drops of water that have fallen
on to a layer of unslaked lime. They remembered their speech, their
customs, their church. The priests instruct their children; we encourage them to join in common prayer and to take part in the life of
the community, for it would be a shame to let the sheep grow
shabby.[4]

As Evalina's health steadily declined the tone of his letters became
mournful:

We are wretched and unhappy indeed, but thank God that we have
been allowed to bear this fate together. We pray that God remove
the chalice of bitterness from our lips — for we have drunk from it
overmuch, more than enough. But we thank him that our lips
jointly drink up that potion. We should not change it for nectar if
each of us had to drink separately.[5]

After Evalina's death Conrad was left alone with a father whose
state of mind can best be gauged from another letter:

I have passed through heavy and even terrible days of brooding on
God's blessings, and if I survive, it will be thanks not to my own, but
to God's strength. I know I have not suffered and never could suffer
like our Saviour, but then I am only a human being. I have kept my
eyes fixed on the Cross and by that means fortified my fainting soul
and reeling brain. The sacred days of agony have passed, and I
resume my ordinary life, a little more broken but with breath still in
me, still alive. But the little orphan is always at my side, and I never
forget my anxiety for him. . . . I teach him what I know, but that,
unfortunately, is little. I shield him from the atmosphere of this
place, and he grows up as though in a monastic cell. For the *memen-
to mori* we have the grave of our dear one, and every letter which
reaches us is the equivalent of a day of fasting, a hair shirt or a
discipline.[6]

Towards the end of his life Apollo could be found 'sitting motionless
in front of his wife's portrait'. The visitor who found him continues, 'he
did not move and little Conrad, who was coming in behind me, put his

fingers on his lips and said: "Let's go quietly through the room, because father always looks intently at Mother's portrait on the anniversary of her death — all day, saying nothing and eating nothing."'[7]

Apollo's patriotism and the religious fervour he brought to it remained, though. In 1868 he wrote, 'I am a monk and moreover a *frater* in the Polish Order. I have hitherto confined my thoughts in a small cell of patriotism.'[8] His biblical imagery became retrograde when he complained that 'we exert ourselves like Adam and Eve after their expulsion from Paradise. This is an undeserved situation, for it was not from Eden that we came here.'[9] Conrad later confirmed that Apollo was 'withal of strong religious feeling degenerating after the loss of his wife into mysticism and despair.'[10] The young Conrad was thus subject to his father's bouts of gloomy patriotism mixed with periods of almost cultish obsession with the dead Evalina; another example, this time on a very personal level, of religious sentiments being misapplied to no good purpose.

Apollo's last days were spent in Cracow (in Austrian Poland) and Conrad himself has described the religious atmosphere that attended his father's sick-room with its 'noiseless nursing nuns':

> Our domestic matters were ordered by the elderly housekeeper of our neighbour on the second floor, a Canon of the Cathedral, lent for the emergency. She, too, spoke but seldom. She wore a black dress with a cross hanging by a chain on her ample bosom. And though when she spoke she moved her lips more than the nuns, she never let her voice rise above a peacefully murmuring note. The air around me was all piety, resignation, and silence.   (*NLL*, 167–8)

He also describes an attempt (albeit a half-hearted one) on the part of one of the nuns to restrict his reading:

> I read! What I did not read! Sometimes the elder nun, gliding up and casting a mistrustful look on the open pages, would lay her hand lightly on my head and suggest in a doubtful whisper, "Perhaps it is not very good for you to read these books." I would raise my eyes to her face mutely, and with a vague gesture of giving it up she would glide away.   (*NLL*, 168)

The incident may have been trifling but the fact that Conrad could still recall it some 45 years later indicates that it had some impact on the boy, who may have felt that it signified the opposition of religion to the acquisition of knowledge. Certainly this is one of the faces it reveals in his fiction, notably in *Nostromo*.

Apollo's final illness caused his son to experience 'moments of revolt which stripped off me some of my simple trust in the government of the universe' (*NLL*, 168), and the father's death left the boy an orphan. At the funeral Conrad's grandmother described how 'with bitter tears, he prayed for the soul of his father kneeling between the priest and the nuns, until at length Mr Buscznynski took him away and pressed him to his heart'.[11] Soon after this the first of many letters Conrad was to receive from his uncle and guardian, Thaddeus Bobrowski, began thus:

> My dear little Konrad,
>   It has pleased God to strike you with the greatest misfortune that can assail a child – the loss of its Parents. But in His goodness God has so graciously allowed your very good Grandmother and myself to look after you, your health, your studies and your future destiny.[12]

Whether Conrad was able to endorse this view is unknown; it might well have seemed a somewhat perverse pleasure on the part of the Deity to a boy of twelve. There appears to be more than a hint of authorial opinion in the opposing view taken by the external narrator of 'Gaspar Ruiz':

> Some proverbs are simply imbecile, others are immoral. That one evolved out of the native heart of the great Russian people, 'Man discharges the piece, but God carries the bullet,' is piously atrocious, and at bitter variance with the accepted conception of a compassionate God. It would indeed be an inconsistent occupation for the Guardian of the poor, the innocent, and the helpless, to carry the bullet, for instance, into the heart of a father.   (*ASS*, 18)

In fact, as Gustav Morf has pointed out, the proverb in question is not Russian but Polish.[13]

Conrad was later to claim that his dislike of Christianity began two years after the death of his father,[14] whilst Andrzej Busza points out that 'In the Poland of Conrad's childhood "Christian festivals" were first and foremost family occasions. It is therefore not surprising that Conrad, who was an orphan from the age of eleven, developed an early dislike for them. For him they were only painful reminders of his dead parents and his loneliness.'[15] Gustav Morf also feels that Apollo's death marks the end of Conrad's Christian faith:

> The young Conrad had been brought up in the Roman Catholic religion which, especially in Poland, repudiated the "good for the good's sake" principle. He expected . . . that, in this life, every good action shall have its reward, and that every bad action shall be punished. The miserable death of his father (who was a "good" man if ever there was one) shattered his religious belief to its foundations. From that moment, his "pessimistic" outlook was fixed in its main lines.[16]

There are, however, no letters from Conrad to indicate the stages of his declining belief in Christianity. The letters to his uncle are not extant and none of Bobrowski's letters touch on the subject (from which one can only infer that it was never raised). From Catholic Cracow (in 1874) Conrad moved to Marseilles at a time when the Catholic Church was undergoing a deep crisis. The dogma of Papal Infallibility, promulgated by the Vatican Council in 1870, was somewhat rudely followed that same year by the occupation of Rome by Victor Emmanuel II; an act which deprived Pope Pius IX of his temporal power. No longer was there a Papal State and the Pope's self-imprisonment within the Vatican must have seemed little more than a futile gesture to all but the most ardent of Catholics. Conrad was doubtless not greatly affected by these events but he does seem to have had some experience of the Church's vain and unrealistic support for the lost causes of legitimacy if the conduct of his Catholics in *The Arrow of Gold* is any reflection of actual Catholic backing for the Carlist cause.

The crisis of Conrad's career in Marseilles came with his suicide attempt in 1878; an attempt which shows that his faith was certainly waning at this stage. Even if one accepts the story of the duel that Conrad put around, the spiritual position for a Catholic is still not improved for, as Jerry Allen explains, 'The Church in Poland, as in other countries, held that to fight a duel was to commit not one but two major sins: attempted murder and attempted suicide.'[17]

Until 1890, when Conrad's correspondence with Marguerite Poradowska begins, we have only the letters of Thaddeus Bobrowski to Conrad upon which to build a picture of the future novelist (apart from a sprinkling of letters to various Polish correspondents). References to

God are scattered liberally throughout the letters but more, it seems, from habit than from any earnest belief. Thus, on receiving one of innumerable requests from his nephew for money, the uncle accedes, trusting that the sum in question will secure Conrad's career and warning that 'if it serves no purpose, as has been the case up till now — then you will answer for it to your own conscience and to God'.[18] Most other references are of similar brevity; there is nothing in the nature of a theological discussion. Bobrowski's comments on the severe illness (pneumonia) which struck down his brother and left him an invalid, however, may not have met with Conrad's concurrence. According to Bobrowski, 'God has mercy on his servants, and eventually kept him alive',[19] but since this uncle was now functioning on one damaged lung and, with a deteriorating heart, was facing 'a slow prolonged death', his nephew may have experienced some difficulty in tracing the mercy of God in this news. The uncle duly died a month or two later.

From 1878 Conrad's surroundings were generally English — either the country itself or the merchant seamen with whom he had most to do. His sojourns within the land that was to become his home would have enabled him to observe the Protestant wing of Christianity in operation and whilst we are unaware of the extent to which he consciously watched the progress of Victorian religion, it is obvious from his later writings that the hypocritical elements certainly came within his purview. Although his periods of time spent away from England, particularly in the East, clearly enabled him to make some contact with other religions, notably Buddhism and Islām, it seems unlikely that he closely investigated the tenets of these faiths while he was there. Instead, the acquaintance he shows with them in his writings is probably the result of his reading. As will be shown later, there have been suggestions that his knowledge of Buddhism was gained, not from the East, but from the works of Amiel and Schopenhauer. Similarly, much of his information about Islām can be seen to have come from Sir Richard Burton's account of his pilgrimage to Mecca and Medina; a book which would have shown him that the Faith of Muḥammad was experiencing a similar decay to that of Christianity (albeit a more violent one).

Thus, on an extensive scale, religion was in decline and society with it (or so it seemed). The feeling of *fin de siècle* evoked by writers of the decadence, both in France and in England, certainly reflects such a premise, becoming quite explicit in Baudelaire's reference to 'the autumn of ideas'.[20] Historically, such times had seen the birth of new religions, and the formation of various adventist groups (notably the

Mormons and Seventh Day Adventists) towards the middle of the nineteenth century – the same time, incidentally, as that of Polish Messianism which is also adventist in spirit – suggests that some, at least, felt a need for spiritual renewal; the disappointing of their fundamentalist hopes leading frequently to disillusion and doubt.

Religious belief in Victorian England, in fact, had a number of crises to contend with even if, by and large, it did not have early expectations of a dramatic fulfilment of prophecy. To take one's stand resolutely behind a literal interpretation of the Bible, including the Book of Genesis, seemed clearly untenable to many thinking people in the light of the findings of Charles Darwin, and the unrealistic and bigoted fundamentalism exhibited by many of the clergy, notably Bishop Wilberforce during his public confrontation with T. H. Huxley, could only alienate the more impartial observers. This apparent relegation of the long cherished story of creation to the realms of mythology was accompanied by new methods of biblical criticism that made suspect the historical data contained in the Holy Book, not only in its Old Testament, but in the Gospels themselves.

Conrad was doubtless aware of these issues but there are very few signs that he was greatly affected by them. He clearly kept abreast of scientific discoveries and theories, however, for it is a scientific view of the universe (which denied individual man personal immortality in another realm) and the implications of the second law of thermodynamics (which denied mankind as a species immortality in this one) that form the substance of his gloom-laden letters to Cunninghame Graham in the late 1890s.

Conrad's comments on Christian doctrines are mainly to be seen in his correspondence with Marguerite Poradowska, whom Conrad called 'aunt' (she was the wife and then widow of a cousin in Brussels). In September 1891 (a year after his Congo adventure), for example, he refutes the doctrine of expiation by maintaining that 'if these convicts found solace in expiation they would no longer be convicts but angels (Catholic angels) fallen into misfortune' (a view that implies that his aunt has misunderstood human nature just as Lord Jim misunderstands the nature of Gentleman Brown). To Conrad, 'the doctrine (or theory) of expiation through suffering . . . is quite simply an infamous abomination when preached by civilised people. It is a doctrine which, on the one hand, leads straight to the Inquisition and, on the other, discloses the possibilities of bargaining with the Eternal'.[21]

The words in parentheses here – '(or theory)' – are significant; Conrad is not only rejecting the doctrine but also questioning whether it is a doctrine at all. Expiation cannot exist because of the finality and inevitable consequences of each act of life upon which 'all the gnashing of teeth and the sorrow of weak souls' can have no effect. Conrad is here asserting man's full responsibility for his own actions and the need for him to accept those actions. He maintains that 'I shall never need to be consoled for any act of my life . . . because I am strong enough to judge my conscience rather than be its slave, as the orthodox would like to persuade us to be.' Here also, then, is a negative view of orthodoxy, but fictionally it is the likes of Brown and Jones who are in no need of consolation for their deeds in contrast to characters such as Jim, Razumov, Nostromo and Falk, all of whom feel the need to unburden themselves of guilt in some way. Jim should clearly come to terms with his actions on the *Patna* rather than seek absolution for them but Razumov's confession seems to elicit approval since it puts an end to the lie he is living. The attempted confession of Nostromo to Mrs Gould would seem unnecessary according to this code (unless it is seen as an attempt to exorcise the spell of the treasure) and that of Falk would certainly be out of place. But these characters were all in the future at this time and it may be that when he came to write fiction Conrad found his code here too vague or simplistic to be workable in all cases.

In March 1892 he is telling his aunt that she is 'carrying the spirit of self-sacrifice too far' in looking after an elderly relative who lacks 'Charity which is a gift straight from the Eternal to the elect. For Charity is eternal and universal Love, the divine virtue, the sole manifestation of the Almighty which may in some manner justify the act of creation.'[22] The problem is, Conrad feels, that 'abnegation carried to an extreme . . . becomes not a fault but a crime, and to return good for evil is not only profoundly immoral but dangerous, in that it sharpens the appetite for evil in the malevolent and develops (perhaps unconsciously) that latent human tendency towards hypocrisy in the . . . let us say, benevolent'. As a result, 'You have thrown aside dignity, affections, memories! And why? Have you found the peace which is the reward of sacrifices accepted by the Master of our souls?'

The dichotomy evident in this letter – Conrad attacking a Christian doctrine whilst still apparently acknowledging the existence of an 'Almighty' and a 'Master of our souls' – will be noted again more than once in his fictional, non-fictional and private writings. The letter was written from Port Adelaide whilst Conrad was serving on the *Torrens* (and in the process of creating *Almayer's Folly*). An earlier letter, which is sometimes taken as a repudiation of faith, was written in London between berths (just before the *Torrens* offer) and, considering its overall content, has perhaps been taken too seriously. Obviously at a low ebb, Conrad compares himself to Punch being gazed at with frigid astonishment by well-made dolls and remarks, 'Upon my word. I pardon them; once upon a time I was a Christian!'[23] This comment appears more flippant than deeply felt and should be related to the mood of frustration during a period of inactivity and isolation rather than taken as a profound statement of loss of faith. It is usual when joining a religion to make a protestation of belief in one form or another but a declaration of disbelief is rarely called for (especially in Christianity) if that faith should wane in later years. Moreover the extent of belief or disbelief within any human being is likely to be in a state of flux so that even the most devout believer may have periods of doubt, whilst a residue of early faith may still be present in the most outspoken of atheists. Conrad was neither of these and one must take into account the possibility that his comments reflect a particular transitory mood rather than a deliberate philosophy. One must also remember that his letters were written to be read by the recipient only and may have been composed to achieve a particular effect. Zdzisław Najder has shown that one letter to his aunt, protesting a pervading depression on Conrad's part, was written the day after a cheerful note to Emilie Briquel and has suggested an amatory purpose behind both letters, depression being used as an excuse for the aunt whilst Conrad concentrated on the younger girl.[24] It can be unwise, therefore, to consider letters in isolation unless one is also considering the likely purpose of the correspondence.

Basically Conrad's concern in many of these letters seems to be the extent to which a practitioner of Christian virtues (as he saw his aunt to be) could be exploited by others. This concern appears again when he speaks of the 'forgetfulness of wrongs, afflictions, and storms' which is not only 'very Christian' but is also 'most convenient for that troop of worthies which travels about the world poisoning life to right and left, handing you the cup of gall. "Come drink, miserable sinner. It won't kill you. It will only wring your heart − a mere trifle! Come drink − and forget!"' Such forgetfulness could only end 'in a soft crumbling of disappointed hopes, of cheated affections, of righteous indignation that has been outraged, of dignity that has been abandoned, that has been thrown to the winds all for that fatal word uttered with a false semblance of religious feeling'.[25]

Here is a clear awareness of hypocrisy, similar to that encouraged by self-sacrifice, only this time Conrad is suggesting (by the fact that the religious feeling is not just a 'semblance' but a 'false semblance') that the virtue is being deliberately evoked by others for their own ends. Affections and dignity are obviously of importance to Conrad since this is the second occasion one has had cause to note them. Although moved specifically by his aunt's case in this instance (whatever he may have wished their relationship to be), this sentiment is repeated to a large extent five years later in a letter to Miss Watson. This time it is a close friend, E. L. Sanderson, whose unselfishness seems to have led to trouble:

> One hates to preach a lower creed. I have ventured before to do so to him. . . . Abnegation and self-forgetfulness are not always right. They are not always right even in the noblest cause. . . . A man's duties are wide and complex: the balance should be held very even, lest some evil should be done when nothing but good is contemplated.[26]

Conrad had already illustrated this last point with the character of Lingard in *An Outcast of the Islands*. This later letter simply confirms his rejection of the efficacy of certain Christian doctrines, though he was willing to concede to Cunninghame Graham that 'Abnegation – self-sacrifice means something' in comparison with Fraternity which 'means nothing unless the Cain–Abel business.'[27] Clearly Conrad is preaching moderation in such virtues, not their elimination; it is extremes that he seems to oppose.

Most of the letters to his aunt take place between 1890 and 1895, embracing (roughly) the period of gestation of *Almayer's Folly*, the time of Conrad's Congo journey (in which, indeed, his aunt played an important part), his voyages on the *Torrens* and his final arrival as a novelist. The correspondence has some importance, therefore, in cataloguing some of his thoughts and moods whilst at the crossroads of his career. In addition to his comments on Christian doctrines, the main feeling that pervades these letters is one of fatalism, a prime example being when he writes of 'the brutality of the inevitable – since everything is inevitable!' and talks of the poignant sorrows and bitter regrets caused by accidents:

> For here there is always the thought of what might have been, the regret for things unaccomplished, the despair over the useless sacrifice of a love on which depended the happiness of those who re-

mained stunned with astonishment at the inexplicable cruelty of the Invisible that guides inanimate things to destroy a life necessary to the happiness of innocent beings of that being not yet conscious! Truly we are the slaves of fate before our birth, and we pay tribute to misfortune before we have known what it is. Does it, I fearfully ask myself, follow us beyond the tomb?[28]

Again this letter is a reaction to bad news from his aunt and the response is suitably sympathetic. The extract reveals scepticism in a Beneficient Creator who allows apparently 'inexplicable cruelty' to occur. The fears of misfortune following beyond the grave imply a sense of pre-ordained destiny that one is powerless to alter. Clearly, however, it is the decrees of life on earth that cause this scepticism; Conrad needs no other tutor. He is not far away, in fact, from exhibiting the kind of fatalism shown by the Muslims of his early novels, the first of which he was in the process of writing. Later that year (on receiving the berth on the *Torrens*) he writes, 'But what good are plans? Destiny is our master!'[29] This is the kind of outlook Marlow shows in 'Heart of Darkness' when he talks of 'Destiny. My Destiny! Droll thing life is — that mysterious arrangement of merciless logic for a futile purpose' (*Y*, 150).

The legacy of Conrad's Polish experience is plain from these letters. It had cautioned him severely against illusions and the expectation of miracles, against the folly of mis-applied devotion and the dangers of religious obsession, against the prospects of receiving rewards for exemplary Christian conduct; in all probability it constituted the major factor in his undoubted diminution of faith. The events in Marseilles certainly suggest that by the time Conrad reached England his Catholicism was very definitely on the wane. The voyage up the Congo in 1890, during which it is clear that he came upon many Christian missions, could only have revealed to him the ineffectiveness of missionaries in the face of their brutal European companions whose tacit façade of Christianity could not have appeared in a more cynical light. This, then, formed Conrad's religious background as he began to write and it explains, in many respects, the use he was to make of religion and religious terminology within his works. But this needs to be seen also in the light of his later religious outlook, to which we must turn.

3

Conrad's Later Religion

The state of Conrad's religious belief has attracted some vastly differing opinions over the years, from steadfast Catholicism to antagonistic atheism. The evidence (as one would expect) is contradictory. An anecdote of Jessie Conrad illustrates, at least, that Christianity had very little place in the author's household. Conrad, she reveals, alluded to their younger son, John, 'as a little pagan and refused to let him learn any religion until he was turned six years old. Then he chuckled with delight because the boy's first words when he heard of the crucifixion were, "It's disgusting, it ought to be forgotten, it's not a thing to be proud of." ' Jessie comments, 'Possibly such an opinion is unique, but it would not have been possible if the child had been taught any religion whatever.'[1] John Conrad himself, however, recalls a quite different incident with his father in which, during a walk, the pair spent some time in a church:

> We carried on, pausing now and then to look at some tombstone and then, as though thinking aloud, he said, "Profanity is the preserve of the devil." Then as we passed through the lychgate he said, "Don't assume that because I do not go to church that I do not believe, I do; all true seamen do in their hearts."[2]

There were, indeed, times when Conrad would identify himself as a Catholic, as Jessie reveals when describing how J. B. Pinker, aided by Protestant Swiss waiters, parodied a Catholic procession; the fun coming to an abrupt end at the Conrads' sitting-room door when Conrad 'flung it open and said icily: "Yes, and I'm a Catholic, aren't I?"'[3] Jessie continues, 'I heard the singer's voice murmuring insinuatingly. I could not catch what was said, but the effect was a peal of amused laughter from the "Catholic" and I knew the storm was over.' Her use of quotation marks for 'Catholic' and the fact that, clearly, Pinker had forgotten Conrad's religious heritage, suggest strongly that the novelist's Catholicism, at this stage, was nominal only. E. K. Hay shows another instance of this old identity, citing a letter from Conrad in which he is refusing to join a London club:

I was born a R. C. and though dogma sits lightly on me I have never renounced that form of Christian religion. The booklet of rules is so, I may say, theological that it would be like renouncing the faith of my fathers.

Of course you will understand, my dear, that it is not with me any question of the principles but merely a matter of correct conduct. I do not think it would be correct for me to ask you to put my name down, and indeed I do not think it could be done since one of the conditions of membership is to be a Protestant.[4]

In the same letter Conrad also reveals that he had earlier refused to join a Catholic Association because 'I discovered that the members engaged themselves with all their might and power to work for the restoration of the temporal power of the Pope. Conceive you that imbecility! Of course I pointed out that this was a political object, that the accomplished fact had all my sympathy and that I certainly would not lift a finger to re-establish temporal power.[5]

These instances show that, whilst Conrad was not a practising Catholic, he never revoked his faith and he did, indeed, receive a Catholic burial on his death. It is also clear that he was not willing to allow his erstwhile faith to be attacked in his hearing or to join any organisation which would effectively force him to disavow it, though both these factors could be explained as simple defence of heritage. His comments on the temporal aspirations of the Church are interesting when compared with the grievances of the clergy in Poland and the fierce interests of Corbelán in *Nostromo*.

This residue of Catholic identity could explain why Bernard Meyer perceives a difference in religious stance between Conrad's fictional and non-fictional writings and discovers 'powerful and poignant overtones of a deep and abiding devotion to that early Catholic faith' within the fiction and protestations of atheism within his life.[6] The former stance he supports by asserting that Conrad identified himself with Christ in his novels, the latter he bases mainly on two letters to Garnett (to be considered later).

Catholic identity is also claimed for Conrad by certain Catholic writers, one of whom (Patrick Braybrooke) can assert that 'Conrad was both a mystic and a believer in collective worship' who 'sought reality by looking at his own soul but . . . knew also that he could not hope to find it without the aids of the Church,' which 'was for him the means by which the individual was introduced into the presence of God'.[7] Braybrooke maintains that Conrad 'held fast to his religion all through his life' for this 'was the foundation and entire motive of his philosophy',[8] but his support for these statements is scanty and not all Catholic writers agree with him. John K. Ryan, for example, complains of Conrad's treatment of Catholic characters in his novels, especially in *The Arrow of Gold* 'where the characters like Therese and Marquis de Villarel are wretched caricatures, travesties unworthy of the man who wrote "The Nigger of the Narcissus" and "Youth"'.[9] The bias of such comments is obvious, particularly when one considers the character of the bigoted Protestant, Podmore, in the first of the books Ryan cites with approval.[10]

Outside the Catholic circle with its apparent need to know whether Conrad could be considered as 'one of us', most critics feel that he lost his faith at an early age. Certain statements criticising Christianity in Conrad's letters to Garnett and the gloomy world picture emerging from his correspondence with Cunninghame Graham, are usually cited as evidence for this view.[11] Before these can be taken as conclusive, however, they need to be seen in a wider context than hitherto, it being a common failing of mankind to voice only grievances and not satisfactions.

One important and (once disclosed) very obvious piece of evidence is Dwight H. Purdy's deduction that, since Conrad alludes so often to an English translation (the Authorized Version) of the Bible in his writings, he must, therefore, have read it, and read it, moreover, as an adult since he would not have been capable of this before about the mid-1880s. Thus, though his faith may have waned, his interest had not, even if (as Purdy suggests) this was more a literary interest than a religious one.[12] One can follow up this information by adding to it C. F. Burgess's point that the King James Bible was on the Catholic Index in Conrad's time and that Conrad was, therefore, neither a practising nor an obedient Catholic during his adulthood.[13] Burgess reveals that Conrad made appropriate gestures of Catholic belief when writing to Polish Catholic relatives but, in fact, invented such details as Borys's christening in a non-existent church to forestall any awkward enquiries.[14]

What, then, was Conrad's creed? To answer this, one first needs to consider a letter Conrad wrote to Marguerite Poradowska on his return to London from his first voyage on the *Torrens*. Conrad is here giving advice in respect of a nephew of hers:

> . . . one becomes useful only on realizing the utter insignificance of the individual in the scheme of the universe. When one understands

that in oneself one is nothing and that a man is worth neither more nor less than the work he accomplishes with honesty of purpose and means, and within the strict limits of his duty towards society, only then is one the master of his conscience, with the right to call himself a man. [15]

Such work ethics are similar to the advice Conrad himself had often received from his Uncle Thaddeus who, the previous November, had berated his nephew for pessimism and considered that each individual should contribute to mankind, not with dreams of leadership, 'but rather thinking of himself as a modest tiny ant which by its insignificant toil in fulfilling its modest duty secures the life and existence of the whole nest.' [16] Both extracts advocate a sense of vocation and there is much to recommend R. R. Hodges's view that 'Conrad's ideal was that a man's profession, his true work, should also be a vocation, a calling, and some of the old religious meanings cling to the world [sic].' [17]

Certainly it can be said that Conrad had little time for institutionalised forms of religion as his remarks to Edward Noble in 1895 make clear:

Everyone must walk in the light of his own heart's gospel. No man's light is good to any of his fellows. That's my creed from beginning to end. That's my view of life — a view that rejects all formulas, dogmas and principles of other people's making. These are only a web of illusions. We are too varied. Another man's truth is only a dismal lie to me. [18]

Conrad's religion evidently underwent considerable change during the course of his life and his use of religious terminology can be said to indicate the nature of the change. Devotion to an institutionalised belief thus becomes devotion to 'his own heart's gospel' and in Conrad's case this proved to be his vocation to which he would bring his 'few simple ideas,' notably 'the idea of Fidelity' (*PR*, XIX).

The two vocations that (figuratively speaking) acted as Conrad's particular deities were the craft of the sailor with his mystic attraction for the sea, and the craft of the writer; the latter being used many times to describe the former with suitably religious terms. One brief passage in *A Personal Record* brings the two together, in fact:

I had better say that the life at sea . . . is not, upon the whole, a good equipment for a writing life. God forbid, though, that I should be thought of as denying my masters of the quarter-deck. I am not capable of that sort of apostasy. I have confessed my attitude of piety towards their shades in three or more tales, and if any man on earth more than another needs to be true to himself as he hopes to be saved, it is certainly the writer of fiction.   (*PR*, 108)

The tone of this is not entirely serious, of course (though it is not entirely flippant either), but the note is still struck. Soon after this passage Conrad directly compares the initial attraction of the sea with a religious belief:

> In that faint, ghostly sound there live the memories of twenty years, the voices of rough men now no more, the strong voice of the everlasting winds, and the whisper of a mysterious spell, the murmur of the great sea, which must have somehow reached my inland cradle and entered my unconscious ear, like that formula of Mohammedan faith the Mussulman father whispers into the ear of his new-born infant, making him one of the faithful almost with his first breath. I do not know whether I have been a good seaman, but I know I have been a very faithful one.   (*PR*, 110)

Religious images are thus abundant in Conrad's maritime memories and, whilst he is using the terms metaphorically, their very usage indicates to some degree the sense of vocation he felt was necessary. Thus when he compares the captain's state-room to the 'sanctum sanctorum of a temple' (*MS*, 5), there is an underlying seriousness to the apparently playful comparison. In the course of describing a theft on board he wonders 'whether the crime should not be entered under the category of sacrilege rather than theft. Those things belonged to the captain! There was certainly something in the nature of the violation of a sanctuary . . . ' (*NLL*, 186). The incident is regarded as a 'deed of darkness,' for a ship 'has to be respected, actually and ideally; her merit, her innocence, are sacred things' (*NLL*, 188).

Beneath the apparent mocking effect of the inflated language (describing, after all, an instance of petty theft), lies the seriousness of a potential undermining of solidarity; that vital component of shipboard life in Conrad's maritime stories.

Like a literal religion, this creed is invested with its own form of after-life. When remembering a lost shipmate, Conrad remarks, 'may the god of gales who took him away so abruptly between New Zealand and the Horn, let his soul rest in some Paradise of true seamen' (*MS*,

45), whilst, for the wrongdoers, 'I could imagine no worse eternal punishment for evil seamen who die unrepentant upon the earthly sea than that their souls should be condemned to man the ghosts of disabled ships, drifting for ever across a ghostly and tempestuous ocean' (*MS*, 64). It is thus a fitting reminder of the faith that in the episode of the *Tremolino*, Dominic Cervoni should feel (after wrecking the vessel to escape coastguards) that the deed 'lies upon my soul' (*MS*, 179).

Some of the real harshness of the calling is indicated in Conrad's final work, the unfinished 'Legends,' in which he directly contrasts his sailors of the sea with the saints of Christianity. Here he is concerned with the false or fatuous which creeps into worthy or noble stories:

> Or even into a holy story. The Golden Legend itself. The legend of saints and their miracles is an awful example of that danger — as any one who turns over a few pages of it may see. Saintliness is made absurd by the presentation of the miraculous facts themselves. It lacks spirituality in a surprising way. (*LE*, 45)

This, as it happened, was to be Conrad's final tribute to his erstwhile comrades of the sea:

> They did not work miracles, to be sure, but I have seen them repeatedly do all that men can do for their faith — if it was only the faith in their own manhood. And that is something, surely. But there was something more in it, something larger a fidelity to the demands of their calling which I verily believe was for all of them I knew, both afloat and ashore, vocational quite as much in its way as any spiritual call a man's nature has ever responded to. And all that for no perceptible reward in the praise of man and the favour of gods — I mean the sea gods, an indigent, pitiless lot, who had nothing to offer to servants at their shrine but a ward in some hospital on shore or a sudden wedding with death in a great uproar, but with no gilding of fine words about it. *La mort sans phrases.* (*LE*, 45)

His attitude is most explicit, however, in a letter to William Blackwood:

> A wrestle with wind and weather has a moral value like the positive acts of faith on which may be built a doctrine of salvation and a rule

of life. At any rate men engaged in such contests have been my
spiritual fathers too long for me to change my convictions.[19]

These particular aspects span almost twenty years of writing and
show that Conrad was true to his creed. His fictional treatment of it is
most marked in *The Nigger of the 'Narcissus'* (1896) but the Preface to
that work, being not about the sea but about the task of the writer,
indicated a conscious adherence to a new vocation. This transition,
however, was a painful one. *Almayer's Folly* had been worked out at a
leisurely pace whilst Conrad was still at sea and his second novel also
caused him only minor difficulties. But *The Sisters* petered out and its
successor, *The Rescue* (originally *The Rescuer*), was to follow a tortuous passage for over three years, stretching its author on a rack of
despair in the process before being finally put aside.

It was during this time of crisis (1896−99) that Conrad's gloomy
letters to Cunninghame Graham were written and, whilst these have
been frequently cited as evidence of a pessimistic world view held by
the author, the context in which they were written has been generally
neglected. In the course of these letters, Conrad likens the universe to
a knitting machine, knitting unchangeably and remorselessly, and
expresses his despair at the futility of existence in the face of the news
from science that the world would one day perish from cold. He felt
that Graham was too much of an idealist whilst he (Conrad) saw things
as they were. Man was naturally egoistical; no reform of institutions
could improve the situation.

This is melancholy indeed; little wonder that such comments are
thought to indicate a loss of belief, especially since the letter containing
his consideration of final extinction also proclaimed that 'Faith is a
myth and beliefs shift like mists on the shore. . . . As our peasants say:
"Pray brother, forgive me for the love of God." And we don't know
what forgiveness is, nor what is love, nor where God is. Assez.'[20] The
letter ended, 'But salvation lies in being illogical. Still I feel remorse.'

In a way this was a time of religious crisis but it was only incidentally
to do with Christianity and more to do with vocation. To the craft of
literature Conrad brought the same sense of integrity that he had taken
to the art of seamanship and the background to his despair is the soul-
searching that accompanied his doubts of being worthy of his new
profession (or belief). Generally it has been assumed that the despair
shown in his letters is the real Conrad and that this mood has been
transmitted to the novels, whereas there seems to be a case for revers-

ing this assumption to assert that the despair of his letters was caused by the difficulties of composition. In other words, it was not the despair, reflected in the letters, that caused the novels but the writing of the novels that caused the despair. The religious terms Conrad applies to the art of writing show that he had elevated it to the same high position as the calling of the sea. The despair thus reflects, in a very real sense, a spiritual crisis as Conrad reached a state of creative torpor over *The Rescue*. He was failing in his new belief and now, dependent on that belief, were his wife, Jessie, and (from January 1898) a son, Borys. This was no time for authorial paralysis to set in; family responsibilities demanded creativity.

One can see the mood develop in the letters to Garnett, written in 1896. When giving up *The Sisters* (on Garnett's advice) Conrad was almost philosophical in his attitude:

> If one looks at life in its true aspect then everything loses much of its unpleasant importance and the atmosphere becomes cleared of what are only unimportant mists that drift past in imposing shapes. When once the truth is grasped that one's own personality is only a ridiculous and aimless masquerade of something hopelessly unknown the attainment of serenity is not very far off. Then there remains nothing but the surrender to one's impulses, the fidelity to passing emotions which is perhaps a nearer approach to truth than any other philosophy of life.[21]

In this letter Conrad announced his intention of beginning *The Rescue*. Five months later this plan had plunged him into despair, causing him to write, 'I have been living in a little hell of my own; in a place of torment so subtle and so cruel and so unavoidable that the prospect of theological damnation in the hereafter has no more terrors for me. It is all about the ghastly "*Rescuer*".'[22] These lamentations continue for a full page during which the novelist confesses to being 'paralysed by doubt' with 'just sense enough to feel the agony' but 'powerless to invent a way out of it.'[23]

His only solution was to write short stories but this diversion troubled his sense of artistic integrity. His comments to Garnett nine days later reveal a feeling of being unfaithful to a creed, especially with the reference to the 'lost soul'. The image appears several times in his letters with the same connection. Conrad wrote, 'There is only 6,000 words in it so it can't bring in many shekels. . . . Don't you think I am a

lost soul? − Upon my word I hate every line I write. I wish I could
tackle the *Rescuer* again. I simply *can't*! And I live in fear that is worse
than mortal.'[24]

From this state he was rescued for a while by his old belief, the sea,
this time in the fictional form of *The Nigger of the 'Narcissus'*, but
whilst writing the final pages Conrad wrote, 'May the Gods help you. I
am all right − have sold myself to the devil. Am proud of it.'[25] This may
indicate that he still felt his true purpose was his *Rescuer* and that he
was compromising his beliefs in writing anything else. The context is
not too clear, however. What is clear is his comment on the troublesome work a month later: 'The *Rescuer* sleeps yet the sleep like of
death. Will there be a miracle and a resurrection? Quien sabe!'[26]

Whether serious or not, this application of religious terms to his art
shows the development of the new vocation, revealed again by these
comments on *The Nigger of the 'Narcissus'*:

> I am conceited about it − God knows − but He also knows the spirit
> in which I approached the undertaking to present faithfully some of
> His benighted and suffering creatures; the humble, the obscure, the
> sinful, the erring upon whom rests His Gaze of Ineffable Pity. My
> conscience is at peace in that matter.[27]

But the *Rescuer* came to overwhelm him again:

> I trust you are well. I am so so − horribly irritable and muddle-
> headed. Thinking of *Rescuer*; writing nothing; often restraining
> tears; never restraining curses. At times thinking the world *has*
> come to an end − at others convinced that it has not yet come out of
> chaos. But generally I feel like the impenitent thief on the cross (he
> is one of my early heroes) − defiant and bitter.[28]

Two months after this letter, the correspondence with Cunninghame Graham begins, in the midst, it will be noted, of another unavailing attempt to come to grips with the troublesome work. Conrad's
artistic integrity is immediately apparent. Unlike Kipling who 'has the
wisdom of the passing generations − and holds it in perfect sincerity'
but 'squints with the rest of his excellent sort,' Conrad means 'to hold
my beliefs' even though 'Straight vision is bad form − as you know.
The proper thing is to look around the corner, because, if truth is not
there − there is at any rate a something that distributes shekels − And
what better can you want than the noble metals?'[29]

Part of the creed, then, is that any attempt to write for money instead of from conviction attracts the terms of the demonic, but the letter shows also the extent of Conrad's problem and, in many ways, the cause of his gloom. His 'straight vision' was not enticing the 'shekels', nor was it causing enough to be written and it may be that his cynicism towards the 'noble metals' derived, in part, from the fact that he was not receiving many of them. His integrity was proving unprofitable, in short, and he still needed money to live.

The position with *The Rescue* (the title had changed by now) had still not altered. In October he wrote to Garnett, 'I can't get on with the *Rescue*. In all these days I haven't written a line, but there hasn't been a day when I did not wish myself dead. It is too ghastly. I positively don't know what to do. Am I out to the end of my tether? Sometimes I think it must be so.'[30]

By December the position was becoming more and more urgent since Conrad was only one month away from fatherhood and, to add to this additional impending responsibility, was involved in a dispute with Adolf Krieger over a debt; an event that hurt him deeply as his letter to Garnett shows:

> My soul is like a stone within me. I am going through the awful experience of losing a friend. . . . Death is nothing – and I am used to its rapacity. But when life robs one of a man to whom one has pinned one's faith for twenty years the wrong seems too monstrous to be lived down.[31]

This, then, constitutes the background to Conrad's excessively pessimistic letters to Cunninghame Graham, six of which were written in December 1897 and January 1898. The image of the self-evolved knitting machine, knitting remorselessly 'time space, pain, death, corruption, despair and all the illusions',[32] came in the letter of 20 December; the despair over 'humanity condemned ultimately to perish from cold' in a letter of 14 January 1898, coinciding with the birth of Borys.[33] The general tenor of the letters is well known and need not be reproduced here. What they reflect, however, is little more than the morbid thoughts that to some degree are present in everyone and require only a crisis of personal circumstances to bring them to the fore; indeed Conrad confessed that 'this is morbid' at one stage.[34] This crisis was obviously evident in Conrad at the time and it seems likely that it was the religious intensity he brought to the art of writing and his temporary inability to fulfil his new creed that provided the essential background for his despair.[35] The letters to Garnett show 'cause'; those to Cunninghame Graham, 'effect'. To Garnett, he writes:

> I sit down religiously every morning. I sit down for eight hours every day – and the sitting down is all. In the course of that working day of 8 hours I write 3 sentences which I erase before leaving the table in despair. There's not a single word to send you. Not one! And time passes – and McClure waits – not to speak of Eternity for which I don't care a damn. Of McClure however I am afraid.
>
> I ask myself sometimes whether I am bewitched, whether I am the victim of an evil eye? But there is no 'jettatura' in England – is there? I assure you – speaking soberly and on my word of honour – that sometimes it takes all my resolution and power of self control to refrain from butting my head against the wall. I want to howl and foam at the mouth but I daren't do it for fear of waking that baby and alarming my wife. It's no joking matter. After such crises of despair I doze for hours still half conscious that there is that story I am unable to write. Then I wake up, try again – and at last go to bed completely done-up. So the days pass and nothing is done. At night I sleep. In the morning I get up with the horror of that powerlessness I must face through a day of vain efforts.[36]

It is not for nothing that the word 'religiously' is used here, reinforcing his commitment and adding to the extent of his despair. With McClure having purchased the serial rights for *The Rescue* in America, the pressure on the author was greater than ever, and this long extract shows in some detail the dominance the unfinished book had achieved over Conrad's life at this time. Little wonder that he should tell Garnett that 'I am living in a hell of my own'[37] and Cunninghame Graham that 'I would pray to a god made like a man in the City' for 'a little forgetfulness. . . . I would give him my soul for it and he would be cheated. To be cheated is godlike. It is your devil who makes good bargains, legends notwithstanding.'[38] The postscript of the letter to Graham mentions a further demand for material from McClure (a very tangible 'man in the city' in America) and it will be noted that an evocation of the demonic once more accompanies the suspicion of flagging integrity (praying for forgetfulness in this case). Towards the end of the letter he thinks wistfully of his previous vocation, for 'to get to sea would be salvation.'[39]

Conrad was to experience such traumas over most of his books, even to the extent of suffering a nervous breakdown after the writing of

Under Western Eyes (where an antipathy for things Russian may well have assisted), but never again was he to go through such difficulties of composition for such a sustained period of time and it is significant that never again was he to produce such a procession of pessimistic letters. On his recovery from the breakdown that followed the later work he wrote thus to Galsworthy:

> I am thus coming back to the world. Yet that isn't exactly it. It's very much like coming out of one little hell into another. Don't think I am ungrateful to gods and men . . . by saying this. One can't help that feeling. I am glad enough to have changed one hell for another, for I do not feel either helpless or hopeless. On the contrary, there is a sort of confidence — but indeed it may be only the sign of an incipient softening of the brain! However, I am glad enough to feel it on any terms. Anything better than black depression, which may be the sign of religious mania.[40]

If one can take Conrad's vocation as his religion, then his black depressions do indeed indicate religious mania and his recognition of this state in better times suggests an ability to appraise its lack of validity. In this respect it is rewarding to consider one of the earliest letters Conrad wrote to Marguerite Poradowska (in March 1890) before his Congo experience. The occasion of the letter was the recent death of her husband:

> Life rolls on in bitter floods, like the grim and brutal ocean under a sky covered with dark clouds, and there are days when the poor souls who have embarked on the disheartening voyage imagine that never has a ray of sun been able to break through that dreary veil; that never will the sun shine again; that it has never even existed! Eyes that the sharp wind of grief has filled with tears must be pardoned if they refuse to see the blue; lips that have tasted the bitterness of life must be pardoned if they refuse to utter words of hope. . . . I ask you to remember, I beg you to understand, that it is permitted a soul dwelling in a body tormented by pain, exhausted with illness, to have these moments of aberration. Under the stress of physical suffering the mind sees falsely, the heart errs, the soul unguided wanders in an abyss.[41]

Here we have a sympathetic correspondent consoling a bereaved one. The theme is forgiveness and the harshness of existence but the extract seems almost prophetic if applied to its author. Perhaps Conrad could write in such a vein here because he had experienced the feeling (in Marseilles, maybe); certainly he was to reach this state of mind later. More importantly, though, he recognises the falseness of a state of mind akin to that revealed in those letters to Cunninghame Graham at the time of *The Rescue*. In fact, in Conrad's fictional world, the outlook of Axel Heyst, who regards 'Man on this earth' as an 'unforeseen accident which does not stand close investigation' (*V*, 196) and chooses non-involvement as his course of action, would fit very well into those letters, and it may be that *Victory* represents Conrad's fictional rejection of that earlier pessimism. He rejects it directly in an essay on 'Books':

> It must not be supposed that I claim for the artist in fiction that freedom of moral nihilism. I would require from him many acts of faith of which the first would be the cherishing of an undying hope; and hope, it will not be contested, implies all the piety of effort and renunciation. It is the God sent form of trust in the magic force and inspiration belonging to the life of this earth. We are inclined to forget that the way of excellence is in the intellectual, as distinguished from emotional humility. What one feels so hopelessly barren in declared pessimism is just its arrogance. It seems as if the discovery made by many men at various times that there is much evil in the world were a source of proud and unholy joy unto some of the modern writers.   (*NLL*, 8)

The pessimists in Conrad's novels (Heyst and Decoud, for example) find their pessimism self-fulfilling and it is plainly shown that a more hopeful outlook on their parts would have led to happier results.

Conrad is consistent in applying religious terms to his art (as the extract from 'Books' shows), however ironically these may be used. A successful author in his eyes becomes a kind of literary holy man, for example. Conrad reports: 'We live like a family of anchorites. From time to time a pious pilgrim *appartenant à la grande fraternité des lettres* comes to pay a visit to the celebrated Joseph Conrad − and to obtain his blessing. Sometimes he gets it and sometimes he does not, for the hermit is severe and dyspeptic.'[42]

This seems almost sardonic in tone (it follows another battle with *The Rescue* and the beginning of 'Heart of Darkness') but the expansion of such imagery in a letter to Arthur Symons is used to convey a sincere approach; indeed Conrad had used the same set of images in a letter to Garnett the day before:

One thing that I am certain of is that I have approached the object of my task, things human in a spirit of piety. The earth is a temple where there is going on a mystery play, childish and poignant, ridiculous and awful enough, in all conscience. Once in I've tried to behave decently. I have not degraded any quasi-religious sentiment by tears and groans; and if I have been amused or indignant, I've neither grinned nor gnashed my teeth. In other words, I've tried to write with dignity, not out of regard for myself, but for the sake of the spectacle, the play with an obscure beginning and an unfathomable denouement.

I don't think that this has been noticed. It is your penitent beating the floor with his forehead and the ecstatic worshipper at the rails that are obvious to the public eye. The man standing quietly in the shadow of the pillar, if noticed at all, runs the risk of being suspected of sinister designs.[43]

Conrad had reported to Garnett the previous day that, according to Symons, 'I gloat over scenes of cruelty and am obsessed by visions of spilt blood,'[44] thus part of the purpose of this elaborate imagery is to repudiate the charge (which he had, in fact, done far more simply earlier in the month).[45] *The Secret Agent* was his most recent novel at this stage, the pervasive ironic tone of which embraced both the grotesque dismemberment of Stevie and the violent death of Mr Verloc, and can appear to be either callous or detached, according to individual interpretation. For the present purpose, however, it is significant that Conrad chose to defend his art in religious terms and his protestations of 'piety towards things human' were to be repeated six weeks later in a letter which claimed that 'a man who puts forth the secret of his imagination to the world accomplishes, as it were, a religious rite'.[46] Some years later when struggling with *Suspense* it may well be the temple of literature that Conrad has in mind when he writes to Galsworthy:

I can't get my teeth into the novel. I am altogether in the dark as to what is is about. I am depressed and exasperated at the same time and I only wish I could say to myself that I don't care. But I do care. A horrid state. Don't forget me in your prayers. You who have never strayed beyond the precincts of the Temple.[47]

The use of language here is still figurative (Galsworthy having also strayed from orthodox religious belief, holding the ethics of Christianity in high esteem whilst rejecting its dogmas and divine foundations and sharing Conrad's own mistrust of 'glib formulas')[48] and the comparisons are plain. They become extravagant when Conrad reveals his sense of apostasy in writing for magazines (and therefore for money), though the demonic is absent for a change:

> A few days later I saw (and read) in the "Standard" a warm and gentlemanly appreciation of the dumminess of your dummy. Amen! And I beheld the bald summit of my ambition. Some day I shall write a thing that'll be reviewed thus and not otherwise. Then in the dead of night, in the woods about the Cearne, wearing the cope and the pointed mitre of a High Priest in the secrecy of a persecuted faith, by the light of a torch held by David clad in the white vestments − you shall bury my tame and impotent soul. You'll bury it alive − by God − and go home smiling ironically, and sleep no more that night.[49]

The art of literature would seem to be the 'persecuted faith'.

There is a note of self-mockery here, showing that Conrad was aware of the exalted plane to which he elevated his vocation and could see it in a wider perspective at times. But, despite the wry humour of his exaggerated imagery, one can still perceive serious intent beneath. To be universally popular, he seems to say, one must relinquish the essential integrity of the true writer and to do that would be to betray one's creed.

It is against this background that Conrad's comments on Christianity must be set. Two letters to Garnett are frequently cited in this connection but the context requires careful consideration. The earliest of these is chiefly concerned with press reviews of the *Youth* volume before its focus changes:

> J. Bl'wood sent me word that the thing sells decently and that if the Christmas does not kill it or if . . .
> It's strange how I always, from the age of fourteen, disliked the Christian religion, its doctrines, ceremonies and festivals. Presentiment that some day it will work my undoing, I suppose. Now it's quite on the cards that the Bethlehem legend will kill the epic, and the bogie tale, and the touching, tender, noble captain Newcombe − Colonel Whalley thing. Hard. Isn't it? And the most galling feature is that nobody − not a single Bishop of them − believes in it. The business in the stable isn't convincing; whereas my atmosphere (vide reviews) can be positively breathed.[50]

These comments are clearly a reaction to the news that the Christian festival could have effects on his livelihood, not a carefully argued refutation of theological premises. Evident in Conrad's remarks is the exasperation that, because of the religion's hypocritical followers, the fruits of his vocation (the new source of his devotion) could be spoiled. In such circumstances too much can be made of Conrad's professed dislike of the religion since the age of fourteen and of the general tenor of his comments.

The second attack on Christianity is again connected with literature, the catalyst this time being a discussion of Tolstoy (the subject of a book by Garnett that Conrad had just read). Having spoken of the Russian's 'anti-sensualism,' Conrad complains:

> Moreover the base from which he starts — Christianity — is distasteful to me. I am not blind to its services but the absurd oriental fable from which it starts irritates me. Great, improving, softening, compassionate it may be but it has lent itself with amazing facility to cruel distortion and is the only religion which, with its impossible standards, has brought an infinity of anguish to innumerable souls — on this earth.[51]

Such comments pick up the remarks he made on Christian doctrines to his aunt and Miss Watson in the 1890s, but once again this can be seen as a reaction and, in this case, an earlier letter (to Galsworthy) is pertinent. Having pronounced his friend 'a humanitarian moralist,' Conrad writes:

> I don't believe that it will ever lead you into the gratuitous atrocity, of, say, Ivan Illyith [sic] or the monstrous stupidity of such a thing as the *Kreutzer Sonata*, for instance; where an obvious degenerate not worth looking at twice, totally unfitted not only for married life but for any sort of life, is presented as a sympathetic victim of some sort of sacred truth that is supposed to live within him.[52]

Clearly Conrad feels that, within the works he cites, Tolstoy is moralising. The 'anti-sensualism' he spoke of to Garnett is an important ingredient of *The Kreutzer Sonata* and it may well be that Conrad regarded Tolstoy's views as an example of 'cruel distortion'. The cause of the outburst, therefore, would be what Conrad saw as an attempt by a fellow artist to propagate a particularly ascetic view of the religion.

This reading of Conrad's complaint would tend to support E. K. Hay's feeling that too much can be made of these remarks to Garnett (though for different reasons). Hay comments:

> If my subject were Conrad's religion, I should argue that . . . Conrad is himself no mean advocate of 'a purer form of Christianity' and that his religious scepticism goes little deeper than the impasse many reach when finding that the presumptions and commitments necessary to maintaining an active faith, especially in respect to men outside the faith, are odious.[53]

Unfortunately she does not elaborate on this view and, apart from citing Conrad's refusal to join a Protestant club (noted earlier), does not support it. The remarks to Garnett, she feels, 'are not borne out in Conrad's life and other writings.'[54]

This remains to be seen but before moving on one should also consider J. E. Saveson's claim that in the letter which criticises Tolstoy and his Christian base 'Both the substance and the phrasing recall Nietzsche's analysis of spiritualized cruelty and his attack on the ascetic ideal.'[55] Conrad mentioned the philosopher in a letter to Ford in 1903,[56] but before accepting Nietzsche as directing Conrad's thoughts on Christianity, one ought to consider that the views expressed in the 1914 letter to Garnett were not new. Gautier had 'attacked Christianity because it had given mankind sadness and anxiety, with a sense of sin and shame' in the preface to *Mademoiselle de Maupin*,[57] and this was long before the advent of Nietzsche. This is not to say that Conrad had read Gautier's novel (though he may well have done, since he was well read in French literature), but it does indicate that there was nothing exceptional in his strictures on the religion. Conrad concluded his letter: 'However I don't suppose these views of mine can interest you and I only meant to send you a word of thanks. Why I should fly out like this on Xianity which has given to mankind the beautiful Xmas pudding I don't know, unless that, like some good dogs, I get snappish as I grow old.'[58]

This final comment suggests that the attack was a passing impulse rather than the expression of a pervading philosophy, provoked (as has been seen) by the premise of a fellow artist. But he used the argument in his fiction, too, describing the condition of M. George in his obsession with Rita as 'the state like that of some strange wild faiths that get hold of mankind with the cruel mystic grip of unattainable perfection, robbing them of both liberty and felicity on earth.' This comparison, however, signifies not so much an attack on religion as an indication of the extent of George's plight, which is even more serious, in fact, since 'A faith presents one with some hope' (*AG*, 140). That Christianity can be one of these 'strange wild faiths' is shown by the 'big, ascetic, gaunt body' of the old Basque priest (*AG*, 115). But this is encroaching on fictional usage, where purpose is, inevitably, more complex and sustained; and that must await its time in a later chapter.

These two extracts apart, Conrad's comments on Christianity are less direct and less detailed. *The Arrow of Gold*, for example, caused Conrad to write (again to Garnett) in a cynical vein about Christian newspapers, claiming that 'The Church Times (High) the Guardian (Evangelical) and the Methodist Times (2 notices) are most sympathetic and − yes − almost intelligent. I am not joking. Who would have thought it possible. . . . My misfortune is that I can't swallow any formula and thus am wearing the aspect of enemy to all mankind.'[59] Literature again provides the occasion for the remarks. Conrad's professed inability to 'swallow any formula' made him (in his eyes) different from 'the public':

> It will swallow Hall Caine and John Galsworthy, Victor Hugo and Martin Tupper. It is an ostrich, a clown, a giant, a bottomless sack. It is sublime. It has apparently no eyes and no entrails, like a slug, and yet it can weep and suffer. It has swallowed Christianity, Buddhism, Mahomedanism and the Gospel of Mrs Eddy. And it is perfectly capable, from the height of its secular stability, of looking down upon the artist as a mere windlestraw.[60]

The religious references in this statement are frequently quoted but the context (literary again) is usually ignored and it is clear from this that not everything the public swallows is bad since the list includes Galsworthy, to whom the letter was written. There is no evidence to suggest that Conrad disliked Hugo either, whom he had read in Polish as a child (*PR*, 72). If the intention is to show the lack of discernment on the part of the public it may be that Conrad is illustrating this by setting the lesser lights of Hall Caine and Martin Tupper against two writers of whom he approved and, similarly, following the three famous world religions with the bathos of 'Mrs Eddy'. Seen thus, the apparent dismissal of the religions, which seems obvious when quoted out of context, becomes too equivocal for any strong assertion to be made.

Two more of Conrad's better known and often quoted comments

also share the vocational background. The letter to Garnett in which he states 'I would rather grasp the solid satisfaction of my wrong-headedness and shake my fist at the idiotic mystery of Heaven,' also announced the decision to abandon *The Sisters*,[61] whilst a letter to Cunninghame Graham in which Conrad wrote, 'I shall be inexorable like destiny and shall look upon your sufferings with the idiotic serenity of a benevolent Creator (I don't know that the ben. Crea. is serene — but if he is (as they say) then he *must* be idiotic) looking at the precious mess he has made of his only job,'[62] was composed in the midst of traumas about *The Rescue* and, indeed, the day after he had informed Garnett that his friendship with Krieger had ended.

At times he could indulge in sardonic humour at the expense of Christian exclusiveness; an example coming during the Boer War:

> Allah is careless. The loss of your MS. is a pretty bad instance; but look — here's his very own chosen people (of assorted denominations) getting banged about and not a sign from the sky but a snowfall and a fiendish frost. Perhaps Kipling's Recessional (if He understood it — which I doubt) had offended Him.[63]

During the First World War he wrote with similar irony; noting that 'the Yahudi God (Who rules us)' had appeared 'to develop Central European affinities. He's played out as a patron. Why not turn over the whole Establishment and the Non-conf[st] organisations to the Devil and see what'll happen.'[64]

At times a streak of Polish anti-semitism seems evident such as in his expression of regard for 'The Impenitent Thief' who 'was no philistine anyhow — and no Jew, since he had no eye for the shent-per-shent business the other fellow spotted at once.'[65] The comment is also a reminder of his rejection of the doctrine of expiation since it smacked of 'bargaining with the Eternal'. When he again complains about the 'Jewish God' the occasion is literature once more, in this case the non-arrival of Garnett's copy of *Notes on Life and Letters*:

> There must be a special devil with a mission to make trouble between us. As you know the Jewish God (under whom you and I were born) is not direct in his methods. It would have been simpler to put hatred into our hearts without all that low intriguing. But I always suspected him of being a Futile Person . . .[66]

Conrad goes on to cite Garnett and himself as 'incorrigible Gentiles' in a world 'where the seasons of curses and congratulations are still ruled by the Jewish God' and commends him 'to the Merciful, the Compassionate — the same whom I would like to look on me at times. Of course I know He can't do much. Still . . . .'.

Finally, after expressing the difficulties of writing again (*Under Western Eyes* this time), Conrad tells Garnett, 'I wish I could believe in an intelligent, benevolent Supreme Being to whom I could leave the task of paying my debts — such debts as the one I owe you for instance. And perhaps there is one. I don't know . . . .'.[67]

The background to Conrad's comments on religion is important, therefore, and almost exclusively to do with literature, usually his own. This had become his *raison d'être* to such an extent that he would lash out at anything which seemed to be obstructing its progress, be it less talented yet more successful writers or religion. To Cunninghame Graham he once wrote, 'It's a pity my style is not more popular and a thousand pities I don't write less slow. Of such that do is the Kingdom of the Earth. I don't care a damn for the best heaven ever invented by Jew or Gentile. And that's a fact.'[68] Written whilst he was struggling with *Lord Jim*, this at least shows the extent of his aspirations, clearly confined to this plane of existence.

It is when Conrad feels that he is not fulfilling his vocation that pessimism sets in. He was clearly at a low ebb between his return from the Congo and his berth on the *Torrens* (January–November 1891) and his uncle's accusation of pessimism relates to this period, during which, of course, apart from his health problems, he was not following his calling. The creative torpor he experienced over *The Rescue(r)*, which he could easily have regarded as another failure of vocation, provided the occasion (if not the substance) of his gloomy letters to Cunninghame Graham.

For the later Conrad, therefore, the object of intense devotion (akin to that of a faith and demanding, as it were, prodigious sacrifices from its neophyte) was literature, the pursuit of which exercised a controlling influence over the state of his mind and his moods. It attracted, in other words, the kind of devotion his father had given to Poland.

About his attitude towards Christianity, it is clear that Conrad was not a practising believer and, indeed, would not follow institutionalised religion, which would come under the heading of 'formulas' he could not accept. It is not easy, therefore, to accept Cunninghame Graham's view that Conrad held 'the older faith . . . not only as a faith,

but as a bulwark against Oriental barbarism'.[69] When rejecting the
Protestant club, he claimed to hold 'a great regard and sympathy' for
the Church of England,[70] but that may simply have been a tactful
comment to his Protestant correspondent. It may also indicate, however, that it was the *formula* of Christianity that he rejected. Clearly he
doubted its mystical beginnings and disliked certain of its doctrines,
especially if they hinted at a quid pro quo arrangement with the Deity,
encouraged latent hypocrisy, brought about 'anguish' by insisting on
'impossible standards', or led to the exploitation of devoted individual
followers. He seems to have held a low opinion of its clergy (also
reflected in the novels, as will be seen later), and certainly had no liking
for claims of Christian exclusiveness. Some of these are elements of the
formula, some, simply, the faults of the followers. In Conrad's eyes,
then, Christianity needed to be less mystical, less demanding and more
realistic in its appraisal of human frailties and emotions.

This is not a total disavowal of religion, therefore, and complaining
about God when things go wrong is not at all uncommon, even among
the most fervent of believers. Conrad was far from going to the
extremes of disbelief and extolling science and material progress as
substitutes for dwindling spirituality. When a book appeared suggesting that the arts should be enrolled to popularise science as they once
had religion, Conrad was instantly antagonistic and went on in his
review to explain just why arts and science could not merge:

> Many a man has heard or read and believes that the earth goes
> round the sun; one small blob of mud among several others spinning
> ridiculously with a waggling motion like a top about to fall. This is
> the Copernican system, and the man believes in the system without
> often knowing as much about it as its name. But while watching a
> sunset he sheds his belief; he sees the sun as a small and useful
> object, the servant of his needs and the witness of his ascending
> effort, sinking slowly behind a range of mountains, and then he
> holds the system of Ptolemy.   (*NLL*, 73–4)

Conrad felt that the author of the book was 'obsessed by science,
haunted and shadowed by it, until . . . bewildered into awe' (*NLL*, 73)
and he concluded that 'the light of Transfiguration which has illumined
the profoundest mysteries of our sinful souls is not the light of the
generating stations' (*NLL*, 75).

Conrad was also critical of claims that science, through spiritualism,
could prove immortality. In 1908 he ridiculed the idea in 'The Black

Mate' and in his essay 'The Life Beyond' vehemently refuted the whole proposition. As far as Conrad was concerned, 'an immortality liable at any moment to betray itself fatuously by the forcible incantations of Mr Stead or Professor Crookes is scarcely worth having' (*NLL*, 68–9), and he continued:

> And to believe that these manifestations which the author evidently takes for modern miracles, will stay our tottering faith; to believe that the new psychology has, only the other day, discovered man to be a "spiritual mystery," is really carrying humility towards that universal provider, Science, too far. (*NLL*, 69)

The essay concludes:

> We moderns have complicated our old perplexities to the point of absurdity; our perplexities older than religion itself. It is not for nothing that for so many years the priest, mounting the steps of the altar, murmurs, "Why art thou sad, my soul, and why dost thou trouble me?" Since the day of Creation two veiled figures, Doubt and Melancholy, are pacing endlessly in the sunshine of the world. What humanity needs is not the promise of scientific immortality, but compassionate pity in this life and infinite mercy on the Day of Judgement. (*NLL*, 69)

In many ways these final extracts epitomise Conrad's attitude towards religion as well as towards modern progress. There is scorn in the reference to 'modern miracles' but the 'tottering faith', though initially related to the view of the scientist, is obviously applicable to Conrad, as are the two 'veiled figures'. 'Doubt and Melancholy' haunted the course of Conrad's literary vocation just as here he mentions their haunting of mankind. Perplexity 'older than religion itself' implies that religion is a man-made invention (which would be consistent with the 'best known heaven ever invented by Jew or Gentile') but this is then set against the traditional backcloth of 'the day of Creation' and 'the Day of Judgement'. Unable to accept the 'formula' of religion in all its details and doctrines yet similarly unwilling to renounce the concept in its entirety; recognising the validity of scientific discoveries yet sardonically critical of the prominence science was acquiring; aware of a vague allegiance to both and an adherence to neither, Conrad tried to tread a middle path, acknowledging the beneficial aspects of each and condemning their excesses. This precarious balance was affected by the fluctuating state of his vocation into which he pumped all the fervour and devotion of a religious faith. When his creativity was at a low ebb, science's gloomy prognostications loomed powerfully in his mind; when religion encroached on his vocation he would bitterly denounce it; when science attempted a similar intrusion, he would attack its presumption. Truly he could not live according to another's formula and the fate he wryly envisaged through supporting neither Catholic nor Protestant could apply also to his conflict between the spiritual and material worlds. Conrad complained, 'So now you see I have got to stand between the two, a prey to the first inferior devil that may come along. My only hope of escaping the eternal fires is my utter insignificance. I shall lie low on Judgement Day, and will probably be overlooked.'[71]

Conrad seems, therefore, to have established a shifting existence between spiritual and material positions and if the 'great polar ideas of the Victorian period were . . . the idea of progress and the idea of decadence',[72] Conrad was doubtful, not only of the enthusiasm for the former view but also (in his less harrowing literary moments) of the potential despair of the latter. It may, in fact, have been a desire to produce an all-encompassing world view which would accommodate each valid philosophy that prompted him to write:

The ethical view of the universe involves us at last in so many cruel and absurd contradictions, where the last vestiges of faith, hope, charity, and even of reason itself, seem ready to perish, that I have come to suspect that the aim of creation cannot be ethical at all. I would fondly believe that its object is purely spectacular: a spectacle for awe, love, adoration, or hate, if you like, but in this view – and in this view alone – never for despair! Those visions, delicious or poignant, are a moral end in themselves. The rest is our affair. . . . In this view there is room for every religion except for the inverted creed of impiety, the mask and cloak of arid despair; for every joy and every sorrow, for every fair dream, for every charitable hope.

(*PR*, 92–3)

4

The Mirror of Islām

Islām is a prominent presence in Conrad's early fiction yet, surprisingly, has attracted little critical attention. There is need, therefore, to consider the likely sources and depth of his knowledge of the religion before deciding on the uses to which these were put. Conrad's Muslims are usually bigoted, frequently violent, invariably unscrupulous and always complacently exclusive. They constantly accuse the Europeans of being unbelievers, infidels, and sons of Satan, and it is important to ascertain whether Conrad uses them for some more profound purpose than at first appears. If it is accepted that he had specific reasons for producing Christian bigots such as Podmore and Therese, why should this not be the case with his Muslims?

To many Victorians the picture of the Conradian Muslim would have constituted the standard Arab (to some Europeans it still does), and it is worth looking at the Arab with whom Conrad had the closest connection — Syed Mohsin, the owner of the *Vidar* — to see if this was so. Clearly it was not. According to Norman Sherry's sources, Syed Mohsin was 'very well known and liked in Singapore by many of the European community',[1] and there were other Syeds in the city who were equally well regarded.[2] This is not the case with Syed Abdulla in the novels. Sherry reveals that Syed Abdulla was the son of Syed Mohsin but he does not seem to have taken over the trading concerns of his father until after Conrad had left eastern waters for good.[3] Conrad still cites 'Syed Abdulla' as being Almayer's enemy in *A Personal Record*,[4] but the name is such a common Islāmic one that there may have been more than one Arab trader of that name in the region.

Conrad certainly knew about many Muslim practices and laws. It is evident from the novels that a Muslim should not eat the meat of the pig, should not consume alcohol, should pray towards Mecca at certain times of day, and may marry up to four wives. He knew about the pilgrimage to Mecca and the title — Hadji — that goes with it. Whether he knew more or was aware only of the many corrupt practices that have bedevilled Islām is an intriguing question. In *An Outcast of the*

41

Islands, for example, Abdulla and Omar are horrified at the idea of a Christian — an unbeliever — living in their midst, yet this does not contradict Qur'ānic prescriptions. On the other hand Islām proscribes theft and murder — the very activities in which Omar has been most proficient. If it could be proved that Conrad knew this — and he would surely have known that murder and robbery were not part of Muḥammad's scheme of things — one can look at the conduct of his Muslims with a different attitude than if one assumes that he shared the common European prejudices. Perhaps the attitude depends on the reader, but, judged against a knowledge of the religion, Conrad's Muslims can be seen to achieve a much greater significance.

In his essays and correspondence, however, there is no indication of how deeply Conrad had investigated the faith. Occasionally he would give Cunninghame Graham an Islāmic greeting such as 'Istaghfir Allah! O! Sheik Mohammed! I take refuge with the One the Invincible',[5] in which he adopts an air of familiarity with the subject, and we have already seen how he likens his attraction for the sea to 'that formula of Mohammedan faith the Musselman father whispers into the ear of his new-born infant, making him one of the faithful almost with his first breath' (*PR*, 110), but there is little else.

What knowledge he did have could have come from first-hand experience during his time in the East Indies when working for Syed Mohsin in Singapore, but this seems unlikely when one considers Sir Hugh Clifford's accusation (admitted by the novelist) that Conrad knew nothing about Malays (*PR*, iv). If he knew nothing (or very little) about Malays, what did he know of Arabs?

Conrad's only other direct opportunity would have come during his stay at Stanley Falls, when, as he relates in 'Geography and Some Explorers', he was surrounded by 'the yet unbroken power of the Congo Arabs' (*LE*, 17). Certainly, at Stanley Falls he could have heard of Islāmic fanaticism for he was there only five years after the death of General Gordon at Khartoum and only one year after rumours had reached Nicholas Tobback at the Falls that there were plans to kill all the Europeans and establish a Central African Empire with its centre in the Sudanese city.[6] This last notion was scarcely feasible, there being nearly 1000 miles of almost impenetrable jungle between Stanley Falls and the Sudan, but it may well have seemed a real threat to the isolated Europeans. Tobback would have been at Stanley Falls during Conrad's visit.[7]

It seems more likely, though, that Conrad's information was derived from his reading, which, in many cases (especially if the press formed any part of it), would have supported the picture of Muslims being

violent, intolerant and fanatical. Gordon's death was greatly publicised and news of the Jihad (Holy War) against the infidel, called by
the self-proclaimed Mahdi (a Messianic figure for Islām), would thus
have reached many Victorians. Similar tales of Islāmic fanaticism
(though rather less publicised) were coming out of Iran, with the
persecutions of Bahá'ís, recorded by E. G. Browne[8] and from Morocco, with the intimidation of Christian travellers, mentioned by Cunninghame Graham.[9] Thus the equation of piety with violence, frequently encountered among Conrad's Muslims − Omar (*OI*), the men
of Sherif Ali (*LJ*) and Daman (*Re*), for example − would be well
understood by Victorian readers and could be the kind of behaviour
they would expect from a Muslim. Would they know, however, that
this was not the way a Muslim was supposed to be? What did they, or
could they (and Conrad) know about the precepts of Islām?

In fact, they could have learned a great deal. By 1880 there were
three full translations of the Qur'ān in print in addition to numerous
books about the religion, whose tones ranged from Christian condemnation to thoughtful appraisal. Even some of the former kind could
admit that 'Mahomet speaks of the Christians much more tenderly
than the Jews,'[10] and that the idea of predestination, the source of
Islāmic fatalism, was 'more extreme in the opinion of the followers
than in actual doctrine'.[11] Islāmic images of the afterlife were regarded
as possessing elements of 'grossness and possible impurity',[12] (a judgement which reflects Christian preoccupation with sex as sin), and
charges of sensuality were levied against Muḥammad.[13] There were
complaints that Islām kept people away from Christianity,[14] but some
writers proved more sympathetic; so much so that one author could
comment of Muslims: 'Notwithstanding the unfavourable opinion entertained by many − principally in the Christian world − against their
religious principles, I must, in strict justice, add that I have found these
persons liberal and intelligent, sincere, and most faithful friends.'[15]
Elsewhere, the same writer comments: 'It is worthy of remark that the
Prophet, as well as his direct successors, had Christian and idolatrous
servants in their service,and that it is nowhere mentioned that any
violence was ever used to induce them to become Moslems.'[16] Others
seemed to share this view since, at the end of the century, the editor of
the posthumous publication of Sir Richard Burton's essay, 'El Islām',
could write that since the essay had been written (in the 1850s), 'a
change has taken place among thinking men in the estimate of El Islām
among the religions of the world', and could go on to cite writers who
had 'cleared away many misconceptions concerning the "Saving Faith",

and discussed its merits as a humanizing creed'.[17] Some Victorians, in fact, painfully aware of the shortcomings of Christianity, began to see Islām in a new light. Wilfred Scawen Blunt, who wrote a series of articles about the future of Islām in 1882 and was later to become a friend of Cunninghame Graham, was one who became increasingly attracted by its doctrines.[18]

Thus there were sympathetic writers among those who wrote of Islām and its Prophet; writers who could dispel the ideas of proselytisation by force being part of the creed. Burton commented: 'The protégé of El Islām paid a small capitation tax, and was allowed to practise his faith and to worship his God as his law directed.'[19] The Qur'ān, in fact, would have been found to prohibit forcible conversion.[20]

The only book of this kind that Conrad is known to have read is Cunninghame Graham's *Mogreb-El-Acksa*, which, being published in 1898, could only have influenced *Lord Jim* and parts of *The Rescue* of those novels which contain Muslim characters. Graham's dedication of his book to a Muslim travelling companion revealed his belief that Muslims thought they could attain paradise by killing unbelievers (just as was noted earlier, Polish peasants thought that killing Jews was similarly rewarded) and also showed a widespread superstition, amongst the Moroccan believers at least, that Christians could cast spells. The first of these observations may explain why Jim 'was to be murdered mainly on religious grounds. . . . A single act of piety (and so far infinitely meritorious)' (*LJ*, 310). Cunninghame Graham's condemnation of the Sherifs in his book − hypocritical parasites who 'occupy a semi-religious, semi-political position'[21] and who cadge from the rich 'for Allah and His Holy Prophet's sake'[22] − may have contributed to the character of Sherif Ali in *Lord Jim* (at least to the extent of making him a Sherif); whilst his criticism of the Christian missionaries as living in a 'dream world'[23] (conversions being a rarity), may have helped in forming the gullible missionary who thinks he is converting Gentleman Brown. Cunninghame Graham, whilst remaining a Christian, felt that 'With a fair field, without the adventitious aids of Christian goods the Muslim wins hands down', because of the contrast between the racial equality of Islām and the white supremacy of Christianity.[24] He also revealed the Arab belief that 'the official Christian's God is money'.[25]

A more potent source for Conrad's knowledge of Islām seems to have been Sir Richard Burton's *Personal Narrative of a Pilgrimage to El-Medinah and Meccah*.[26] This is certainly the kind of book he would have read, given the fascination he had with explorers such as Livingstone, Mungo Park, Tasman, Cook and Burton himself, revealed in the essay 'Geography and Some Explorers'. Conrad mentions the work in a letter to Mrs Bontine in the course of praising *Mogreb-El-Acksa*:

> It is a glorious performance. Much as we expected of him. I, and two men who were staying with me when my copy arrived, have been astonished by the completeness of the achievement. One said: "This is *the* book of travel of the century." It is true. Nothing approaching it had appeared since Burton's *Mecca*. And, as the other man pointed out, judging the work strictly as a book − as a production of a unique temperament − Burton's Mecca is nowhere near it . . . [27]

The most telling evidence that Conrad read the book, however, is textual. There are too many close correspondences between Burton's narrative and Conrad's novels to be explained by coincidence as the following examples illustrate:

> To the invalid you say, 'There is nothing the matter, please Allah, except the health.' (Burton, I, 77)
> 'There is no misfortune − please God − but the sight?' (*OI*, 122)

> Allah makes all things easy! (Burton, I, 253)
> 'Allah makes everything easy,' interjected Babalatchi, piously, from a distance. (*OI*, 131)

> 'Repentance: I take refuge with Allah.'* (Burton, I, 107)
> * A religious formula used when compelled to mention any thing abominable or polluting to the lips of a pious man.
> (Burton, I, 107*n*.)
> 'Penitence! I take refuge with my God. . . . How can he live under my eyes with that woman who is of the Faith? Scandal! O abomination!' (*OI*, 120)

> The generous is Allah's friend. (Burton, I, 242)
> He was largely charitable because the charitable man is the friend of Allah. (*OI*, 110)

> After touching the skin of a strange woman, it is not lawful in El Islām to pray without absolution. For this reason, when a fair dame shakes hands with you, she wraps up her fingers in a kerchief or in the end of her veil. (Burton, II, 47*n*.)

Abdulla glanced at her swiftly for a second, and then, with perfect good breeding, fixed his eyes on the ground. She put out towards him her hand, covered with a corner of her face-veil.   (*OI*, 131)

'A Jew. May his lot be Jehannum!'   (Burton, I, 161)
'We gave it to the white woman − may Jehannum be her lot!'
                                                                  (*Re*, 450)

'Glorified be the Lord my Lord, and glorified be the faith, my faith. . . . We pray thee for safety in our goings forth and our standings still, in our words and our designs, in our dangers of temptation and doubts, and the secret designs of our hearts.' [A prayer for safety at sea, recited on the pilgrim ship taking Burton to Yambo.]   (Burton, I, 312)
. . . and for a time nothing was heard above the crackling of the fire but the intoning of Omar glorifying the God − his God, and the Faith − his faith.   (*OI*, 106)
[The Arab] recited aloud the prayer of travellers by sea. He invoked the favour of the Most High upon that journey, implored His blessings on men's toil and on the secret purposes of their hearts.
                                                                  (*LJ*, 15)
[Burton's description of the horrors of the sun's heat on board the pilgrim ship and the relief of the nights (Burton, I, 305−6) seems also to have influenced a similar description on the *Patna* (*LJ*, 16).]

Pilgrims, especially those from Turkey, carry a 'Hamail', to denote their holy errand. This is a pocket Koran, in a handsome gold embroidered crimson velvet or red morocco case, slung by red silk cords over the left shoulder.   (Burton, I, 352)
The Koran in a velvet case hung on his breast by a red cord of silk.
                                                                  (*Re*, 293)

After vainly addressing the pilgrims . . . the boy Mohammed collected about half a dozen stalwart Meccans, with whose assistance, by sheer strength, we wedged our way into the thin and thin-legged crowd. . . . After thus reaching the stone, despite popular indignation . . . we monopolised the use of it for at least ten minutes. Whilst kissing it and rubbing hands and forehead upon it I narrowly observed it.   (Burton, III, 210)
[Babalatchi] . . . had even struggled in a pious throng for the privilege of touching with his lips the Sacred Stone of the Holy City.
                                                                  (*OI*, 52)

There are many other, less direct, correspondences that could also be considered. Burton reveals, for example, that 'Those who tread the hallowed floor are bound, among many other things, never again to walk barefooted, to take up fire with the fingers, or to tell lies' (Burton, III, 293–4), which may be a source for Babalatchi's habit of playing with the live embers of a fire (*OI*, 122); the prohibition would apply to him since, as seen above, Babalatchi has been a pilgrim.

Conrad's Muslims act like Arabs of the desert, it appears, although their environment is the East Indian jungle. For his knowledge of this environment, Conrad was again much indebted to books, as Norman Sherry has shown; notably to A. R. Wallace's *The Malay Archipelago*, from which, among other things, the novelist seems to have discovered the Muslim burial procedures. Wallace describes how 'The body was wrapped up in a new white cotton cloth,'[28] whilst in *The Rescue*, one of Lingard's followers is buried at sea, 'wrapped up decently in a white sheet, according to Mohammedan usage' (*Re*, 74). Wallace also speaks of the possible influence of Arab priests or Hadjis returned from Mecca, spreading strange ideas of Islāmic might among Muslim villages,[29] which may be another factor prompting the presence of Sherif Ali in the Patusan of *Lord Jim*. Certainly another piece of information given by Wallace, that '"Orang Sirani", or Nazarenes, is the name given by the Malays to the Christian descendents of the Portuguese',[30] seems peculiarly relevant to *Lord Jim* where Tamb'Itam says of the Malacca Portuguese, Cornelius, 'Here comes the Nazarene' (*LJ*, 284).

It was probably from other travel books that Conrad learned of the Padris, a Muslim sect which began in the 1820s with a group of Hadjis zealously desiring to discipline their lax countrymen into conforming more closely to the requirements of their faith. They succeeded in beginning a war as well as a reform and were defeated by the Dutch.[31] In the manuscript of *The Rescue* (though not in its final form), such Padris are to be found within Belarab's camp; followers of the old chief's father who was 'full of fight and religion – just the man for the Padris' (f. 183). The historical demise of the movement appears in the characterisation of these followers who are devoted to 'a flag known in the deserts of central Arabia' which 'proclaimed Belarab's puritanical belief, the memory of a lost cause, the fidelity of the man who understood the meaning of the banner' (f. 193). The old men 'with the fire of belief in their hearts and with austere faces would lift in a moment their downcast eyes to the fluttering emblems of a purified faith' and they are apt to taunt 'their chief with the laxity of his principles' (f. 194). The way Conrad brings different sources together is seen by the way the Padris revere the grave of Belarab's father:

> And there was something ironically pathetic summing up the futility of belief and teaching in this tribute paid to the memory of a wandering and fierce leader to whom reverence for the dead was a heathenish superstition and who all his life inculcated sword in hand and pious quotations on his lips that there is no God but God and that in the matter of graves the best are those that are forgotten.
>
> (f. 195)

Burton is again a likely source here, for he reveals a saying of Muhammad – 'O Allah cause not my tomb to become an object of idolatrous adoration! May Allah's wrath fall heavy upon the people who make the tombs of their prophets places of prayer!' – and contrasts it, in a footnote, with other sayings which encourage Muslims to visit graveyards, especially those of parents (Burton, II, 71).

This deleted section serves as an example of how Conrad's Muslims are generally neglected by critics. Thomas Moser is one of the few people to consider the passage and he simply dismisses its deletion by relating it to the 'exotic' writing of Conrad's early period and deciding that the author recognised the limitations of such elements when he came to revise the novel.[32] But, if one works on the assumption that Conrad had a purpose behind his Muslim characters, another reason becomes evident. The impact of the original is to emphasise the inability of these old men to live in the present; they are still stirred by 'the memory of a lost cause' and waste much of their time in remembrance for the dead. Their presence would thus act as a further warning to Lingard about the futility of pursuing lost causes and trying to right the past. What the passage would also achieve, however, is an undermining of Belarab's position, for his act of withdrawing from his village 'to pray at his father's tomb' (*Re*, 176) could then be construed as filial disobedience. It would also be inconsistent for him to be able to outweigh Tengga's power whilst still at the tomb on the grounds that Tengga 'was not a professed servant of God famed for many charities and a scrupulous performance of pious practices, and who also had no father who had achieved a local saintship' (*Re*, 281), if he was also being 'taunted with the laxity of his principles'. Belarab's standing in the village is important for Lingard's enterprise, and the fact that even the old chief has faith in the Rajah Laut gives a still greater boost to the sailor's prestige. To have this standing undercut by the discontent of the old followers of his father would be clearly inappropriate.

On the whole, though, Malay Muslims were less fanatical. Sir Frank Swettenham remarked in his *Malay Sketches* (1895) that the real Malay 'is a Muhammadan and a fatalist, but he is also very superstitious. He never drinks intoxicants, he is rarely an opium-smoker.'[33] He stressed that 'Though the Malay is an Islām by profession, and would suffer crucifixion sooner than deny his faith, he is not a bigot; indeed, his tolerance compares favourably with that of the professing Christian.'[34] Swettenham entitled one of his sketches 'Malay Superstitions', which included the belief that familiar spirits could enter into and plague an enemy but could be exorcized by certain native priests.[35] This may have had some influence on 'Karain', although a belief in ghosts among the Malay believers is also evident in *Almayer's Folly* and *An Outcast of the Islands*, both written by the time Swettenham's book came out.

Overall, it seems that the well-read Victorian had ample opportunity to read about Islām from both antipathetic and sympathetic bases. The incidence of a large number of reprints and publications in the 1870s and 1880s (coinciding with an increased interest in the Middle East caused by the opening of the Suez Canal in 1869 and the British occupation of Egypt in 1882) suggests that books about Islām would have a ready readership. If Conrad read Burton's account of his pilgrimage (and the evidence indicates strongly that he did) he would have known not only the way Muslims behaved but also, to some extent, the way they ought to behave. It would be reasonable to suppose that some of his readers would know this too. The disparity between precept and practice could be utilised, therefore, not to display stereotyped Arab fanaticism to an ill-informed Victorian public, but to illustrate and indicate some of the central issues in Conrad's early fiction; a circumstance that makes the presence of Islām a more important ingredient of these novels than has been generally acknowledged.

Given this background, Conrad's Muslims appear in a more purposeful light. Their familiar and apparently bigoted accusations, for example, can be seen to have relevance if applied closely to the conduct of Conrad's Europeans. The cunning Babalatchi has more than dogma to guide him when he makes the following comments:

> The fate of the Believers is written by the hand of the Mighty One,
> but they who worship many gods are thrown into the world with

smooth foreheads, for any woman's hand to mark their destruction
there. Let one man destroy another. The will of the Most High is
that they should be fools. They know how to keep faith with their
enemies, but towards each other they know only deception.   (*OI*, 60)

This common Islāmic accusation that white men worship many gods is
borne out by European obsessions throughout the novel, highlighted,
indeed, by religious terms. The statement has obvious relevance to
Willems who, as a 'consistent worshipper in the "temple of self"',[36] is
easily overcome by his sexual passion for Aïssa and serves to make
Babalatchi's remark prophetic. The most explicit example, however,
is that of Almayer in his adoration of Nina:

> And as he stood in the still night, lost in his enchanting and gorgeous
> dreams, while the ascending, thin thread of tobacco smoke spread
> into a faint bluish cloud above his head, he appeared strangely
> impressive and ecstatic: like a devout and mystic worshipper, ador-
> ing, transported and mute; burning incense before a shrine, a
> diaphanous shrine of a child-idol with closed eyes; before a pure and
> vaporous shrine of a small god – fragile, powerless, unconscious
> and sleeping.   (*OI*, 320)

In *Almayer's Folly*, where Almayer's wife also accuses Europeans of
having 'many gods' (*AF*, 151), such conduct leads him to disaster.

The charge of Europeans being 'unbelievers' or 'infidels' is also
shown to have some point. Jim is thus regarded by the Muslim passengers of the *Patna*, who, having 'surrendered to the wisdom of white
men and to their courage, trusting the power of their unbelief and the
iron shell of their fire-ship' (*LJ*, 17), are proved right about the 'unbelief' only. The indictment has particular pertinency when applied to
Jim for, by jumping from the steamer, he proves unfaithful to those
dreams of heroism which are said to have 'carried his soul away' (*LJ*,
20). As far as his romantic egoism is concerned he is truly an 'unbeliever'.

On two occasions the Muslims are said to be 'pilgrims of an exacting
belief' (*LJ*, 15, 17–18) and this is also relevant to Jim. If he is to be true
to his exalted conception of himself, he must be aware of it as an
exacting belief. Had he been so aware, the invocations of the Arab for
'blessings . . . on the secret purposes of their hearts' (*LJ*, 15) would
have been fulfilled on the *Patna* and Jim would not have missed his
chance. But Jim's heroic beliefs are unexacting, like the comfortable

rural Christianity of his youth, and are heedless, therefore, of Islāmic blessings, valid only for followers of an exacting belief. As a result the blessing simply precedes his disgrace. Similarly the blessings of Jim's father, a clerical representative of rural Christianity, are relevant only to the followers of an unexacting faith and (for the reader) come immediately before the disaster in Patusan which they are powerless to prevent because Jim's belief has now become an exacting one.

One role of the Muslims, then, is to indicate European failings by their bigoted yet, in reality, perceptive accusations. In their other comments and deeds they reflect, in an exaggerated form, the short-comings of their Christian counterparts. In *The Rescue*, for example, the Malay chief, Tengga, complains that he has been forbidden to loot the stranded yacht of Mr Travers because 'their skin is like yours and to kill them would be wrong, but at the bidding of you whites we may go and fight with people of our own skin and our own faith — and that is good' (*Re*, 173). Later in the book, Belarab, the head of the village, reveals similar considerations, feeling that 'It would be even in a manner a sin to begin a strife in a community of True Believers' (*Re*, 435). Both comments, however, can be seen to echo those of Lingard's Christian mate, Shaw, in the opening pages:

> My grandfather was a preacher and, though my father served in the navy, I don't hold with war. Sinful the old gentleman called it — and I think so, too. Unless with Chinamen, or niggers, or such people as must be kept in order and won't listen to reason; having not sense enough to know what's good for them, when it's explained to them by their betters — missionaries, and such like au-tho-ri-ties. (*Re*, 22)

Thus Muslim exclusiveness on the grounds of religion becomes equated with racial exclusiveness on the part of some of the Euro-peans; a point that is exemplified by Belarab's denial of paradise to the white man (*Re*, 113) — which smacks also of Christian claims to exclusive salvation — and Shaw's attempt to eject the Malay Prince Hassim and his sister from the cuddy on the grounds that they are 'niggers' (*Re*, 239). This equation is not peculiar to *The Rescue*; there are many other instances in the early eastern stories.

Muslim exclusiveness is loudly proclaimed and its religious observ-ances are ostentatiously performed. In contrast, the Europeans are relatively quiet about their beliefs which are brought forth, it seems, only to stress their hypocrisy. Thus the 'Protestant wing of the proper Mrs Vinck' (*AF*, 41) proves unaccommodating to Almayer's half-caste

daughter when Nina is found to be more attractive than the Vinck girls
to potential suitors (*AF*, 30), and Willems remembers appropriate
Christian doctrines on marriage (*OI*, 26, 349) and suicide (*OI*, 278)
when these seem to work to his convenience.

Islāmic protestations, however, are just as suspect. Syed Abdulla's
acceptance of the will of God in *Almayer's Folly*, for example, is shown
very ironically, for 'Where was the use to wonder at the decrees of
Fate, especially if they were propitious to the True Believers? And
with a pious ejaculation to Allah the Merciful, the Compassionate,
Abdulla seemed to regard the incident as closed for the present' (*AF*,
109). Such overt piety is seen to be at odds with Abdulla's dealings as a
businessman (*AF*, 28) and his ill-treatment of the slave girl, Taminah
(*AF*, 110); the latter action going against Burton's statement that 'The
laws of Mahomet enjoin his followers to treat slaves with the greatest
mildness, and the Moslems are in general scrupulous observers of the
Prophet's recommendation' (Burton, I, 89). Abdulla's professed
absorption in the delights of the next world also does not prevent his
appreciation of more earthly issues. When suggesting to Almayer that
Reshid should marry Nina, he presents such a union as a profitable
alliance, since Reshid will be the first Arab in the islands when his
uncle has been 'called to the joys of Paradise by Allah the All-merciful'
(*AF*, 45). But the inducements he offers are material luxuries and
worldly position and his calling upon Allah to give Almayer 'many
more years to gladden the eyes of his friends by his welcome presence'
(*AF*, 44) is produced either as part of a meaningless ritual or to achieve
an effect, but certainly not as an expression of sincere regard.

Conrad's first novel ends with Abdulla gazing on the dead Almayer,
'this infidel he had fought so long and bested so many times. Such was
the reward of the Faithful!' The Arab leaves the scene, clicking his
prayer beads, 'while in a solemn whisper he breathed out piously the
name of Allah! The Merciful! The Compassionate!' (*AF*, 208). In
giving instructions for the translation of this work into Polish, the
author emphasised that 'Abdulla recites the well-known formula
mechanically,'[37] a word that is also used to describe Belarab's recital of
formula in *The Rescue* (*Re*, 443), and which obviously denotes habit
rather than conviction. In a later novel, Rita de Lastaola suspects that
priests recommend repentance from the same unthinking cause (*AG*,
116).

Hypocrisy also exists in the lesser Muslims. Thus Mahmat, who fears
he may have defiled himself touching the body of a possible unbeliever
before eating, finds that his greed outweighs a belief in witchcraft when

confronted with a gold anklet, claiming that 'I have a charm against the ghosts and am not afraid. God is great!' (*AF*, 96). There is superstition involved here, too, little different from the knowledge of Christianity possessed by Mrs Almayer, who regards the little brass cross around her neck 'with superstitious awe'; a feeling 'connected with some vague talismanic properties of the little bit of metal and the still more hazy but terrible notion of some bad Djinns and horrible torments invented, as she thought, for her especial punishment by the good Mother Superior in case of the loss of the above charm' (*AF*, 41).

Such comparisons (or, rather, exaggerated reflections) are made more emphatically in *An Outcast of the Islands* with the description of the blind Omar at prayer (*OI*, 106) for Omar's 'ostentatious piety' (*OI*, 58) has been accompanied by a life of robbery and murder that serves to belie the precepts of the Faith he so loudly professes. Nevertheless, this ostentation leads to him being regarded as a 'holy man' by Mahmat later in the book (*OI*, 354). The narrator adds his own assessment of Omar's life after his death as Babalatchi sits in the hut 'from which the fierce spirit of the incomparably accomplished pirate took its flight, to learn too late, in a worse world, the error of its earthly ways' (*OI*, 214).

Babalatchi and Lakamba are similar characters. Babalatchi, as noted earlier, has been a pilgrim, 'and after attaching himself to Omar el Badavi, he affected great piety (as became a pilgrim), although unable to read the inspired words of the Prophet' (*OI*, 52). He too has engaged in 'the manly pursuits of throat-cutting, kidnapping, slave-dealing, and fire-raising, that were the only possible occupation for a true man of the sea' (*OI*, 52). Here, then, is another professing a belief that his actions belie; one who is quick to produce the appropriate pious phrase at the right time. To Patalolo, then Rajah, he remarks that 'Charity was a virtue recommended by the Prophet' (*OI*, 55); to a doubting Lakamba he cries 'verily our only refuge is with the One, the Mighty, the Redresser of . . . ' (*OI*, 48); to Willems and Abdulla he comments 'Allah makes everything easy' (*OI*, 131). This is especially appropriate when Abdulla is present. Faced with the possibility of the great Syed establishing his trade in Sambir and challenging Lingard's monopoly, 'Lakamba and Babalatchi have no doubt — if Allah wills. They are in the hands of the Compassionate' (*OI*, 136).

In the cases of Omar and Babalatchi, the divergence between religious profession and actual practice is extreme and such cynical manipulation of belief is to appear again in *Lord Jim*; utilised this time by Sherif Ali and his men, one of whom 'leaning on the long barrel of a rifle, exhorted the people to prayer and repentance, advising them to

kill all the strangers in their midst, some of whom, he said, were
infidels and others even worse – children of Satan in the guise of
Moslems' (*LJ*, 295). Superstition is thus to be encouraged to perpetuate one's power or to ensure exclusiveness. The latter reason seems to
lie behind the old jurumundi's discourse to 'a small knot of unsophisticated citizens of Sambir' that Almayer's books are 'books of magic . . .
that makes them [the white men] great, powerful, and irresistible while
they live, and – praise be to Allah! – the victims of Satan, the slaves of
Jehannum when they die' (*OI*, 299–300).

Abdulla, however, is presented more subtly in Conrad's second
novel. As a Syed he holds a special place among Muslims, being
regarded as a direct descendent of Muḥammad,[38] and he appears as an
apparently exemplary Muslim who for more than forty years 'had
walked in the way of his Lord':

> Allah had made it his fate to become a pilgrim very early in life. This
> was a great favour of Heaven, and it could not have been bestowed
> upon a man who prized it more, or who made himself more worthy
> of it by the unswerving piety of his heart and by the religious
> solemnity of his demeanour.   (*OI*, 109)

He seems to acquire virtues:

> He bore himself with the humility becoming a Believer who never
> forgets, even for one moment of his waking life, that he is the
> servant of the Most High. He was largely charitable because the
> charitable man is the friend of Allah, and when he walked out of his
> house – built of stone, just outside the town of Penang – on his way
> to his godowns in the port, he had often to snatch his hand away
> sharply from under the lips of men of his race and creed; and often
> he had to murmur deprecating words, or even to rebuke with
> severity those who attempted to touch his knees with their finger-
> tips in gratitude or supplication.   (*OI*, 110)

This picture of Abdulla's piety and his successful progress is carried
along by Conrad's mocking of Islāmic fatalism with such comments as
'the book of his destiny contained . . . ' or 'the writing on his forehead
decreed . . . ' (*OI*, 109). The possible sources of his name have already
been noted. 'Abdullah' was also, however, the alias under which
Burton travelled during his pilgrimage (Burton, I, 20*n*.). Burton explains that the name means 'servant of God,' which would be very

appropriate for the pretensions of the character and gives extra weight
to the phrase 'the servant of the Most High' which is applied to him.

Thus far there is little to criticise since there have been no suggestions of dishonesty in the building up of his business. But Abdulla is
overwhelmed by a mania (the desire to triumph over Lingard) which
becomes 'the paramount interest of his life, the salt of his existence'
(*OI*, 111). This mania appears to interrupt his role as a 'servant of the
Most High' and induces him to use force to impose his position in
Sambir once his ship is safely in the river and to assist Lakamba to
become the new ruler, though it should be noted that Lingard would
also use force to restore his own position if he could (*OI*, 173). Abdulla's preoccupation persuades him to accept the relationship between
Willems and Aïssa, though not without many misgivings:

> But Omar is the son of my father's uncle . . . and all belonging to
> him are of the Faith . . . while that man is an unbeliever. It is most
> unseemly ... very unseemly. He cannot live under my shadow. Not
> that dog. Penitence! I take refuge with my God. ... How can he
> live under my eyes with that woman who is of the Faith? Scandal! O
> abomination!   (*OI*, 120)

Marriage with Christians is actually permitted by the Qur'ān[39] but since
Willems is already married, Abdulla is condoning adultery, which is
proscribed by both Islām and Christianity. But it is the fact that
Willems is an outsider that troubles Abdulla most and it illustrates the
power of his obsession that the apparently scrupulous Muslim Syed is
thus willing to compromise his sense of exclusiveness. We do not see
his reaction to Babalatchi's offer of poisoning Willems, except to note
that he does not take advantage of it, preferring instead to hand the
outcast over to Lingard. Abdulla's word is suspect at this stage as he
shows when commenting to Babalatchi, 'I have promised everything. I
mean to keep much' (*OI*, 134).

What is not clear from this portrait is whether Abdulla's faith has
been corrupted by his mania to get the better of Lingard or whether
this has been his conduct all along. Almayer reports that 'Abdulla sat
amongst them like an idol, cross-legged, his hands on his lap. He's too
great altogether to eat when others do, but he presided, you see' (*OI*,
176). This observation certainly suggests that Abdulla's humility has
dissolved. Earlier, however, Abdulla has commented that he refuses
food because 'his habits are ascetic and his temperament inclines to
melancholy (*OI*, 135). One has the choice of believing Almayer (in

which case the image of the Arab as an idol amongst iconoclastic
Muslims would comment potently on his state of faith), or the Syed.
There is also the question of what is to happen to the deposed rajah.
Patalolo leaves on Abdulla's ship to go on a pilgrimage but Almayer
believes that he goes to his death. In *Almayer's Folly*, he departed this
life 'by a convenient decree of providence' (*AF*, 27), but that is still
enigmatic, and Almayer is not a reliable commentator.

In varying degrees, therefore, Conrad's Muslims show their hypocrisy, from a cynical disregard of all religious precepts (Omar, Lakamba
and Babalatchi) to the less cynical but still egotistical Abdulla. Even
the source of their fatalism is suspect, for the narrator reveals that
'Fatalism is born of the fear of failure, for we all believe that we carry
success in our own hands, and we suspect that our hands are weak' (*OI*,
126).

Such shortcomings succeed, once more, in reflecting in an exaggerated way the European and, by implication, Christian society that
banishes Willems out of jealousy and pride. Hudig, in plotting to have
Willems marry his half-caste daughter by dangling the bait of riches
and, by involving a priest in the plot (*OI*, 35), obtaining the tacit
approval of the church, can thus be equated with Babalatchi, who uses
Aïssa's sexuality to tempt Willems into betraying the secret of the
river. There is, in fact, a similar pattern to each plot: Willems seduced
(first by wealth, then by sex), Willems triumphant (before his mis-
appropriation at Hudig's and at the time of his revenge over Almayer),
and Willems in decline (after his dismissal by Hudig and his disen-
chantment with Aïssa). Willems is, therefore, the victim of two sets of
schemers, Europeans and Muslims, and it is the enormous gap between the ostentatious profession of religion and its actual practice on
the part of the latter group that reveals the empty reality of the
protestations of the former.

Perhaps the most explicit comparison of Muslim with European
comes in 'Karain' where the accusation of unbelief is placed in the
centre of the story. To Karain, haunted by the ghost of a companion he
killed long before, unbelief in his religion means a lack of belief in
spirits also; an outlook he shares with the seaweed-gatherers of 'The
Idiots' who, when regarding the distraught Susan as an evil spirit of
some kind, consider that 'Millot feared nothing, having no religion,
but it would end badly some day' (*TU*, 80). In fact, Hollis's box reveals
that, though the haunting is of a different nature, the European also
has his ghosts, 'the homeless ghosts of an unbelieving world' (*TU*, 49).

But European and Muslim are also linked in the method of keeping the avenging spirit of Matara at bay. Earlier this protection has been achieved by the presence of an old man, regarded by Karain's followers as 'the old wizard, the man who could command ghosts and send evil spirits against enemies' (*TU*, 16). The ruler explains:

> When I met him he was returning from a pilgrimage, and I heard him intoning the prayer of sunset. He had gone to the holy place with his son, his son's wife, and a little child; and on their return, by the favour of the Most High, they all died . . . and the old man reached his country alone. He was a pilgrim serene and pious, very wise and very lonely. I told him all. For a time we lived together. He said over me words of compassion, of wisdom, of prayer. He warded from me the shade of the dead. I begged him for a charm that would make me safe. For a long time he refused; but at last, with a sigh and a smile, he gave me one. Doubtless he could command a spirit stronger than the unrest of my dead friend, and again I had peace. (*TU*, 42)

This may be some of Conrad's irony at the expense of Islāmic fatalism again (death as a favour from God), not unconnected, perhaps, with the way Thaddeus Bobrowski used to write to him about death and sickness in the family. The phrase may also be connected with Burton's comment that 'Those who die on a pilgrimage become martyrs' (Burton, III, 253*n*.). The most important part of this passage, however, concerns the manner in which the charm is given ('with a sigh and a smile') for this suggests that it is given in the same spirit as Hollis's jubilee sixpence. Swettenham's *Malay Sketches* revealed the antipathy of learned Muslims for such superstitions and the wise old man may have been drawn as just such a Muslim, hence his reluctance to fall in with Karain's wishes.[40] Karain, indeed, compromises his faith by wearing the portrait of Queen Victoria on the sixpence since, as Hollis points out, Muslims are not permitted to wear 'an engraved image' (*TU*, 48).

If *The Rescue* can be regarded as belonging to Conrad's early period, then Islām virtually disappears from his works after *Lord Jim*, presumably because its purposes had been fulfilled or had been taken over by something else. Once one has accepted the likelihood that Conrad knew enough about Islām to realise the shortcomings of its adherents and made deliberate use of the disparity between precepts and practice, numerous possibilities unfold. Islāmic exclusiveness is pronounced but even the likeable Padre Román of *Nostromo* has the feeling of

compromising his Catholic exclusiveness by his admiration of the
heretical Emilia Gould (*N*, 399), whilst, like the Muslims, the Autocracy of *Under Western Eyes* brands those who oppose it as 'perfect
unbelievers' (*UWE*, 51). Many of Conrad's novels reveal the hypocrisy, superstition and often blind fanaticism abounding within institutionalised religions, and it may be that Islām is used in the early works
not only to give an exaggerated reflection of Christian failings but also
to act as a surrogate for the European's belief; a way of presenting the
faults of religion without incurring the wrath of Christian Victorians.
Christian hypocrisy and bigotry are dealt with very obliquely in the first
two novels — there are no fervent representatives centre-stage, as it
were — but the corrupt practices of European Christianity come to the
fore thereafter. 'The Idiots' reveals a complacent and self-seeking
clergy living off French peasant villagers who are every bit as superstitious as their Malay counterparts; indeed, the unfortunate Susan dies
because she fears that the husband she has killed has come back to
haunt her, and she has, therefore, much in common with Karain. In
The Nigger of the 'Narcissus' Conrad felt able to present an ostentatiously professing Protestant (the bigoted Podmore), but at least one
of his friends felt that the portrait of the cook was irreverent.[41] In other
words, whilst bigoted Muslims were acceptable, Podmore was coming
rather too close to home.

The Muslims, therefore, can be said to act as harbingers of these and
other Christian inadequacies. For the manipulation of religion by
people such as Omar and Sherif Ali is on a par with its cynical utilisation by Guzman Bento or its subtle subjugation by the material interests of *Nostromo*. If the creed is different, the outlook is much the
same. Islāmic fatalism may be suspect but it stands the Muslims in
better stead than the inaccurate presumption of Captain Whalley to
know the workings of Providence, and Lingard would do well to heed
Hassim's cry that, as to what is written, 'Nobody knows' (*Re*, 77). The
author's note for *Almayer's Folly* warned against dividing humanity
into distinctive categories (*AF*, vii–viii), hinting, perhaps, that the
Muslims and their religion were not to be regarded in isolation. The
note implied that their bigotry and cunning served a deeper purpose;
one that the well read Victorian would have been well able to appre-
hend.

5

Idols and Edifices

The apparent neglect of Islāmic elements of Conrad's work by critics cannot be said to extend to Buddhist references, although these are far less pervasive. Comments vary from an arbitrary application of very basic Buddhism (The Noble Eight Fold Path) to 'Heart of Darkness',[1] to assumptions of a much closer acquaintance with its doctrines on Conrad's part in this and other works. These latter readings require Conrad to have possessed a detailed knowledge of Buddhist iconography (W. B. Stein)[2] or the traditions of Zen Buddhism (Jerry Wasserman)[3] when describing Marlow's Buddha poses in 'Heart of Darkness', a familiarity with Buddhist parables in *Almayer's Folly* and *An Outcast of the Islands* (Stein again)[4] and extensive information about Tantrik Buddhism and a Buddhist holy city − Patna − in *Lord Jim* (William W. Bonney).[5] Others (notably R. O. Evans)[6] think it unlikely that Conrad knew much about eastern religions at all.

Neither Stein nor Bonney claims that Conrad had any direct contact with the religion. Stein feels that he was influenced by Henri-Frederic Amiel, who had a 'hesitant, remorseful surrender to the fatal charm of Hindu-Buddhist pessimism,' and claims that Conrad's use of Amiel's *Journal Intime* for the epigraph to *Almayer's Folly* 'directly admits his capitulation to the Eastern view of existence,'[7] even though the passage in question actually refers to Moses.[8] Bonney suggests that Conrad could have learnt of Buddhism and Hinduism from the writings of Arthur Schopenhauer 'for Schopenhauer discusses at length the philosophies of the Orient in *The World as Will and Idea*.'[9] Bonney's evidence of Conrad's interest in Schopenhauer is Galsworthy's remark that 'Of philosophy he had read a great good deal. Schopenhauer used to give him satisfaction twenty years and more ago.'[10] From this beginning, Bonney proceeds to discuss most of the references to eastern religion in the novels (including some rather oblique ones), working from the assumption that, like Schopenhauer, Conrad was favourably impressed by the nothingness to which eastern thought suggested man was progressing.

Both Stein and Bonney assume that Buddhist theology (if applicable) is cited by Conrad with approval. Critics not so committed to

Buddhist interpretations have pointed out other possibilities, such as
the ironies C. T. Watts spies in 'Heart of Darkness' where 'Like
Buddha Marlow instructs by means of paradoxes; he offers eloquent
warnings against eloquence, while describing the snares of the
appetite; and he indicates the impermanence and possible illusoriness
of the phenomenal world.'[11]

Bruce Johnson sees a different aspect to the possible Schopenhauer/
Buddhist connections, explaining that Schopenhauer saw art and asce-
ticism (based on a Buddhist model) as ways of escaping from Will. He
suggests that the Buddhist allusions in 'Heart of Darkness' may reflect
this, the Will in question being 'the grotesque Will of Kurtz (which is in
Marlow as well, and in all life)'.[12] Johnson thus agrees with Bonney on
the source for Conrad's Buddhist allusions but, whereas Bonney seems
to take Schopenhauer as source and Buddhism as influence, Johnson
takes Schopenhauer as both source and influence. Johnson, in fact,
explicitly refutes any ideas of Conradian sympathy for Buddhism when
comparing the manuscript of 'Falk' with the finished story and quotes
the following (manuscript) passage:

> . . . and my good friend Hermann upright in his chair in the cabin
> door, his thick hands resting on his round knees had a staring
> serenity of aspect (a bit vacuous perhaps) as though he had that very
> moment issued all complete out of Buddha's thigh – or whatever
> part of Buddha's the honorable caste of skippers comes out of.
> (MS., pp. 15–16)[13]

Johnson remarks, interestingly, 'Apparently the myth Conrad retails
represents a popular grafting from the Brahmanic tradition on to a
Buddhism generally uncongenial to the whole idea of caste.'[14] This may
indicate that Conrad's knowledge of eastern philosophy was, in fact,
only superficial; that he did not know that what he was writing was a
'popular grafting'. It may, however, simply illustrate typical western
ignorance of eastern doctrines on the part of the narrator to indicate
inadequacies in his perception.

In the event, of course, the passage was cancelled, but it enables
Johnson to make a further point about Buddhism in Conrad's works,
claiming that 'Conrad's word "Annihilation" sums up his distaste for
this religion's rejection of the ego. Falk is in refreshing contrast to both
Hermann and Buddhism, for he intuitively accepts the ugly basis of
life. . . . Conrad did not like Buddhism, and . . . if he saw a certain
vacuity in Hermann, he also saw it, by way of evaluation, in Buddha.'[15]

Conrad's Buddhist allusions are most apparent in two stories, there-fore: 'Heart of Darkness' and 'Falk'. In 'Heart of Darkness', the first of these references comes when the frame narrator is describing his companions. 'Marlow,' he says 'sat crossed-legged right aft, leaning against the mizzen-mast. He had sunken cheeks, a yellow complexion, a straight back, an ascetic aspect, and, with his arms dropped, the palms of hands outwards, resembled an idol! (*Y*, 46). Here is a vague evocation of the East, clearly distinguishing Marlow from the others, but the image is not precise and is formed, one must remember, in the mind of the narrator. The second reference is more specific. Marlow begins to speak again, 'lifting one arm from the elbow, the palm of the hand outwards, so that, with his legs folded before him, he had the pose of a Buddha preaching in European clothes and without a lotus-flower . . . ' (*Y*, 50). The paragraph ends with an echo of its beginning with 'An idea at the back of it; not a sentimental pretence but an idea; and an unselfish belief in the idea — something you can set up, and bow down before, and offer a sacrifice to . . . ' (*Y*, 51).

It will be noted here that, whilst Marlow continues to resemble an idol with a particularly eastern appearance to the frame narrator, he himself is likening the rationale of European interests, similarly, to an idol. In western eyes, Buddhism would seem futile and superstitious; especially since it appears to offer only eternal nothingness (something atheism promises, though without the rigour). Here, then, it is equ-ated with European motivation, by implication, just as futile and, if one thinks of the ill-health of the agents of progress, just as rigorous. When one considers the frame narrator's earlier romantic enthusiasm for his nation's history and its heroes, 'bearer of a spark from the sacred fire' (*Y*, 47), it is clearly appropriate for his casual likening of Marlow to a Buddha to be thrown back at him in this way, illustrating that idols, which have negative theistic connotations in the west, are usually regarded as the deities of others. Conrad is carefully structur-ing Marlow's tale at this point, for he knows (and probably Marlow does too) that belief in an idea is held by the frame narrator at least, if not by the others, and that equating such a belief with idolatry is likely to provoke a sense of vague uneasiness in his hearers. David Ketterer points out that there is a connection here with Kurtz's position as idol for the natives (Marlow makes this explicit by maintaining that 'Mr Kurtz was no idol of mine' [*Y*, 132])[16] but the 'idea' as idol is best exemplified at the Central Station where the agents have the appear-ance of faithful pilgrims praying to ivory in Marlow's eyes (*Y*, 76).

There are two ways of interpreting the word 'pose'; the first being simply that this is how he appears to the frame narrator, the second that Marlow is deliberately adopting the position. The fact that he seems to be 'a Buddha preaching in European clothes' indicates his universality. He is, in reality, as thoroughly English as his audience (at least, there are no suggestions that he is not) but he also appears to embody something eastern too, uniting, perhaps, the wisdom of both east and west. There is, indeed, irony in the frame narrator's comment but it is, to some extent, a double irony since the experience Marlow is to relate belongs neither to east nor to west but to mankind as a whole. Marlow's 'regular dose of the East' is pretty varied, too, embracing the Indian and Pacific Oceans and the China Seas (*Y*, 51), and the part of the world to which he goes is 'Dead in the centre' (*Y*, 56). He sets off after a spell of 'invading your homes, just as though I had got a heavenly mission to civilise you' (*Y*, 52) which not only links Marlow's view of past activities with the frame narrator's view of his present pose, but also appears ironically similar to Kurtz's initial attitude to the natives later on (*Y*, 118). There is a later reminder of Marlow's ascetic appearance during a break in his narrative when he feels that he is not being understood:

> There was a pause of profound stillness, then a match flared, and Marlow's lean face appeared, worn, hollow, with downward folds and dropped eyelids, with an aspect of concentrated attention; and as he took vigorous draws at his pipe, it seemed to retreat and advance out of the night in the regular flicker of the tiny flame. The match went out.   (*Y*, 114)

Marlow's face thus reveals his experience compared to the innocence of his listeners, exposed by their obtuse reactions. The illusory nature of appearances is emphasised here with the apparent mobility of Marlow's face through the flicker of the match. That Marlow's is a universal experience is shown by the vagaries of time and place and the great diversity of religious, classical, literary and historical allusions that are evoked.

When his story is over, the frame narrator reports that 'Marlow ceased and sat apart, indistinct and silent, in the pose of a meditating Buddha' (*Y*, 162), and one can agree with Seymour Gross that the less optimistic view of this narrator at the end, seeing the river now as leading 'into the heart of an immense darkness,' indicates that he, at least, has been enlightened to some extent.[17] The final pose is also a reminder of the misguided idolatry revealed in Marlow's story; idolatry from which, it is to be hoped, the frame narrator is now free.

In fact, since Marlow's final position is similar to his initial one, the structure of the work can be said to be circular. Marlow meditates and, having likened him to an idol, the narrator romanticises England's colonial history; Marlow speaks and, having again been likened to an idol (this time, specifically, Buddha), he equates idols with ideas and supports this by his references to the pilgrims and to Kurtz, thus illustrating the falsity of the narrator's romantic notions; Marlow meditates again and, once more likening him to Buddha, the narrator broods on darkness.

The Buddhist presence in 'Falk' is represented by its religious edifices, the first of which appears during the narrator's pursuit of a thief. Hermann joins the chase:

> Realizing the situation as though he had eyes in his shoulder-blades, he joined us with a leap and took the lead. The Chinaman fled silent like a rapid shadow on the dust of an extremely oriental road. I followed. A long way in the rear my mate whooped like a savage. A young moon threw a bashful light on a plain like a monstrous waste ground; the architectural mass of a Buddhist temple far away projected itself in dead black on the sky. We lost the thief of course . . .
> (*T*, 158)

Here the temple and the moon appear as aloof spectators of the excitement going on beneath them, diminishing its apparent importance. As far as the narrative is concerned their appearance serves to terminate the chase; the light of the moon reveals only barrenness whilst the 'dead black' of the Buddhist temple emphasises the nihilism with which Conrad (or his narrator) seems to equate the religion in this story. The temple also confirms the futility of the chase, already hinted at by the evident effort and noise that marks the progress of the Europeans in contrast to the apparently noiseless, effortless speed of the oriental. The narrator's excitement animates both moon and temple but their combined presence puts an end to the action.

The second reference serves to explain why the shallow bar exists at the mouth of the river, for 'the authorities of the State were piously busy gilding afresh the great Buddhist Pagoda just then, and had no money to spare for dredging operations' (*T*, 164). Buddhism again has the effect of negating action, therefore, in this case by diverting the

energies of the State. The irony of 'piously' reflects the views of the
narrator; there are no doubts about where he thinks their priorities
should lie. Once out of the river, he comments:

> There was nothing to look at besides but a bare coast, the muddy
> edge of the brown plain with the sinuosities of the river you had left,
> traced in dull green, and the Great Pagoda uprising lonely and
> massive with shining curves and pinnacles like the gorgeous and
> stony efflorescence of tropical rocks. You had nothing to do but wait
> fretfully for the balance of your cargo, which was sent out of the
> river with the greatest irregularity.   (*T*, 165–6)

The Pagoda, whose presence has indirectly caused the problem,
thus continues to dominate the scene; its size and apparent indifference again contrasting with the urge for action possessed by the
narrator. Its comparison with rocks and its evident isolation are far
from comforting attributes. For to a sailor (like the narrator and
author), rocks are destructive and perilous; clearly a nihilistic view of
Buddhism is again being projected. This view is continued when the
narrator finds that his ship would be 'very awkwardly ashore at a spot
two miles below the Great Pagoda' if he tried to sail her away from
harbour without Falk's help (*T*, 203).

The last and longest reference precedes Falk's revelation that he has
eaten man:

> During the afternoon I looked at times at the old homely ship, the
> faithful nurse of Hermann's progeny, or yawned towards the distant
> temple of Buddha, like a lonely hillock on the plain, where shaven
> priests cherish the thoughts of that Annihilation which is the worthy
> reward of us all. Unfortunate! He had been unfortunate once.
>   (*T*, 210)

Here is a juxtaposition that can either be said to indicate a choice
(domesticity opposed to annihilation) or (if one follows Johnson's
deductions from the initial manuscript connections between Hermann
and Buddha) different aspects of the same thing. There is obvious
irony in the narrator's attitude towards the religion here; whilst he
looks towards the ship, he *yawns* towards the temple, and the use of
'cherish' and 'worthy' make the effect emphatic. But the next juxtaposition is between Buddhist Annihilation and Falk's misfortune; what
can be unfortunate in the face of inevitable annihilation?

Falk's misfortune has been caused because he has refused to accept annihilation and has fought for life; he is now fighting for domesticity. Hermann's horror on behalf of outraged decency does indeed reflect a negative attitude to the affair, though he refuses to suggest what Falk should have done. Indeed his main horror is caused by the fact that the tug-master should have thought it necessary to reveal the fact (*T*, 222); clearly he wishes the innocence of his ship to remain. The narrator (whose own innocence has been mentioned once or twice but who is able to hear Falk's story), seems to approve of a struggle for life as opposed to the doctrines of Buddhism. These doctrines only prevail, therefore, if one accepts the narrator as unreliable; that his irony, in other words, simply betrays his ignorance of reality and his clinging to western teleology. But his description of a 'mute and unhearing heaven' as a backdrop to the fateful last days of the *Borgmester Dahl* shows no religious optimism in his make-up and there are no perceptible signs that he does not have his creator's approval.

In each of their appearances, Buddhist temples are seen to negate action, being seen as 'dead black' in opposition to the 'bashful light' of the moon, as a diversion from needful action by the authorities, as rocks, treacherous and deadly to seamen, as an indication of a place of probable shipwreck and finally as a symbol of annihilation. A lust for life may well be futile (Falk will obviously perish one day anyway) but whilst the Buddhist references clearly reflect this, such an outlook is rejected by the narrator and there are no signs that this nihilism is not similarly condemned by Conrad. The Pagoda appears again, dominating the horizon at the beginning of 'The Secret Sharer', but it is far less pervasive in the later tale which again contains a fight for life on the part of one of its protagonists (Leggatt). In *The Shadow-Line*, its one appearance seems to signify little more than a landmark, though one could say more about the 'temples, gorgeous and dilapidated' that are seen soon afterwards (*SL*, 48), since they could serve as a warning of the uncertainty of fate to the newly-appointed master in that tale.

Unless one is to apply the same kind of interpretations as Bonney and Stein, there are very few other instances of Buddhism or Hinduism being a feature of Conrad's work, and these are too isolated to carry any deep significance. In *Lord Jim*, there is the Hindu policeman Marlow sees 'who looked up at me with orientally pitiful eyes as though his migrating spirit were suffering exceedingly from that unforeseen — what d'ye call 'em — avatar — incarnation' (*LJ*, 157), the Hindu with 'a bright yellow caste-mark above the bridge of his nose' whose case follows Jim's (*LJ*, 158) and the child in attendance at

Brown's death-bed 'naked and pot-bellied like a little heathen god' (*LJ*, 345). The reference to the policeman may have relevance to Jim's situation (Jim has, in a sense, been incarnated into a character which he feels is false); the triviality of the assault case may serve to put Jim's into a wider perspective, and the apparent mocking effect of the small boy emphasises the futility of Brown's egotistical gestures − but one could say little else. Similarly, in *Victory*, the strange view of Ricardo, who 'Crossed-legged, his head drooping a little and perfectly still . . . might have been meditating in a bonze-like attitude upon the sacred syllable "Om"' (*V*, 267), may indicate that he is a kind of fate (or Karma) for Heyst's attempt at total withdrawal; but, again, this is an isolated reference. When Heyst turns the bungalow into a funeral pyre for himself and Lena, he may be said to be reversing the custom of certain fanatical Hindu sects in which the wife must perish with the husband in this way. This reversal reveals his devotion to Lena; indeed his very despair at losing her acts as a repudiation of non-involvement as a viable doctrine to live by. His participation in the death rite has a purifying effect, as Davidson makes clear (*V*, 411), but, in the absence of any other definite eastern religious imagery, these two scenes can only be taken as a small element of the whole.[18] In the eye of a hurricane, Captain MacWhirr, consulting his barometer 'resembled a booted and mis-shapen pagan burning incense before the oracle of a Joss' (*T*, 84) and here the religious reference is used to illustrate man's dependence on the instruments of his fashioning. The Hindu term 'avatar' is used to denote the transformation of de Barral into Mr Smith in *Chance* (*C*, 377, 382) and, since the concept of the word is that of the same body in a different form, its use here indicates that Anthony's hopes that all problems will be solved by being at sea are doomed to failure since these are still present under a different name.

Essentially then Buddhism and Hinduism are used sparingly in Conrad's work and his knowledge of the latter faith especially seems very peripheral if his comment to Cunninghame Graham about the 'potbellied gods . . . gods with more legs than a centipede and more arms than a dozen windmills' is a fair sample of his attitude.[19] It is echoed, fictionally, by old Peyrol when considering Arlette's adoration of Réal:

> "She sat and stared at him as if he had been gilt all over, with three heads and seven arms on his body" − a comparison reminiscent of certain idols he had seen in an Indian temple. Though not an iconoclast, Peyrol felt positively sick at the recollection. (*Ro*, 179)

These are not positive comments but, more importantly, nor are they informed ones and, overall, the deeper wells of eastern mysticism appear to remain untapped, yielding only some familiar physical images to contribute towards the greater pattern of religious allusions.

6

Conrad's Christians

It will be recalled that the enormities of Conrad's Muslims in his early works provide an exaggerated reflection of the faults of his Christians, particularly in the areas of exclusiveness, superstition and hypocrisy. As we have seen, Conrad hovered uneasily between belief and disbelief and attempted to fulfil himself spiritually in his literary career. To convey 'things human' in 'a spirit of piety' would clearly involve him with the whole human being, including what may be called man's spiritual side; an intangible component from which, at least, the reaction to art is drawn (or so he suggests in 'The Ascending Effort'). 'A moralist,' he writes to Galsworthy, 'must present us with a gospel – he must give counsel, not to our reason or sentiment, but to our very soul.'[1]

Theologically, of course, man's 'very soul', the seat of his spirituality, should find the fulfilment of its aspirations within religion but this had not happened in Conrad's case and is denied to most of his major characters. The parlous state of Christianity at the turn of the century receives eloquent expression within the pages of his fiction and few of its clerical representatives appear in a positive light.

His first such character (the Basque priest of *The Sisters*) is fanatical and ignorant:

> His brother, the genius of the family, had become a priest and now was in charge of a hamlet full of fiery Basque souls which he endeavoured to keep in the path of godliness with fierce denunciations, with menacing words, with gloomy fanaticism, knowing nothing of the world, hating it, for it was the hospitable playground of the devil, hardly able to bring himself to tolerate the impious sunshine that, by an inexplicable oversight of the Creator, shone indiscriminately upon the believing and upon the wicked. A tall lean priest with . . . an ascetic yet coarse face. . . . A mystical fanatic who . . . saw visions . . . heard voices; who living amongst simple men and women felt clearly that he was living in a world inhabited by damned souls. (*Sis*, 68–9)

The egoism inherent in this point of view is also emphasised, for 'He believed in the wickedness of mankind with all the innocence of his soul. . . . In the appalling desert of human sinfulness the blood of his race flowed pure like a miraculous stream' (*Sis*, 72). He is a monarchist for 'With the rightful monarch the fear of God would reign in the land' (*Sis*, 73).

In *The Arrow of Gold*, Conrad's reworking of the fragment, the priest is similarly described as 'The saintly uncle in his wild parish' (*AG*, 40) and as a 'stern, simple old man' who will only accept a gift of snuff, 'the only gratification his big, ascetic, gaunt body ever knew on earth' (*AG*, 141), when he thinks it has come from the king. His niece, Rita, however, poses interesting questions:

> As I mounted my mule to go away he murmured coldly: "God guard you, Senora!" Senora! What sternness! We were off a little way already when his heart softened and he shouted after me in a terrible voice: "The road to Heaven is repentance!" And then after a silence, again the great shout "Repentance!" thundered after me. Was that sternness or simplicity, I wonder? Or a mere unmeaning superstition, a mechanical thing? If there lives anybody completely honest in this world, surely it must be my uncle. And yet — who knows? (*AG*, 115–16)

Use of the word 'mechanical' by Rita reminds us of Conrad's description of Abdulla's reciting of Islāmic formula, the sense of unthinking ritual. In appearance, this priest is very similar to the abbé in *The Rover*, 'a gaunt man with a long, as if convulsed face' (*Ro*, 147) who has similar Royalist sympathies (*Ro*, 152) and who also prescribes repentance when confronted by a concerned Arlette (*Ro*, 156). Both Rita and Arlette are regarded as being 'for no man' (*AG*, 135; *Ro*, 225) but whilst Rita confirms this by leaving George, Arlette prays for the furtherance of her love affair with Réal with whom she finally forms a life-fulfilling relationship in contrast to the life-denying advice offered by the abbé. *The Rover* also shows the negating effects of the doctrine of celibacy which blights the life of Catherine (Arlette's aunt) when she falls in love with a priest and acquires the nickname of 'la fiancée du prêtre' (*Ro*, 89), causing her to feel 'cast out from the grace of God' (*Ro*, 232). It may be significant that when Arlette visits the priest, the view of the presbytery is not a hopeful one:

She pushed open the little gate with the broken latch. The humble
building of rough stones, from between which much mortar had
crumbled out, looked as though it had been sinking slowly into the
ground. The beds of the plot in front were choked with weeds,
because the abbé had no taste for gardening.   (*Ro*, 147)

Here is an immediate feeling of decline, almost as if the building has
no place in the present. In the light of what follows it is tempting to
regard this picture as being symbolic of the doctrines and character of
its incumbent; the beds of Christianity being stifled by the weeds of
outmoded dogmas that the priest is unwilling to relinquish. The abbé's
advice draws forth an appropriate comment from Peyrol when the old
seaman is told of it by Catherine:

"He wanted to shut her up from everybody," and the old woman
clasped her meagre hands with a sudden gesture. "I suppose there
are still some convents about the world."
    "You and the patronne are mad together," declared Peyrol, "All
this only shows what an ass the curé is."   (*Ro*, 230)

One mould for a priest is thus that of a 'gaunt' ascetic whose mind is
fixed upon sin and repentance and who reflects his Church's support
for absolutist and little-wanted monarchies. This kind of priest possesses an acute awareness of the dignity of his position, combined in some
cases with a sense of condescension; traits that are best illustrated by
the abbé of *The Rover* who 'had accepted, without a word, the charge
of this miserable parish, where he had acquired influence quickly
enough. His sacerdotalism lay in him like a cold passion. Though
accessible enough, he never walked abroad without his breviary,
acknowledging the solemnly bared heads by a curt nod' (*Ro*, 148). The
sense of pride and ambition revealed by the use of 'miserable' to
describe his parish is taken up on a larger scale with Father Carpi in
Suspense. There are also obvious affinities between these priests and
the more exalted figure of Father Corbelán in *Nostromo*.
    This picture of the clergy is grim and forbidding but, except for
Rita's question (which is unresolved), there is no reason to suspect that
the fanaticism and superstition they exhibit is not genuine nor that
their intentions are not good. Conrad's second type of priest is of a very
different kind. He first appears in 'The Idiots', a story which derives
from an incident of Conrad's honeymoon in Brittany whilst he and
Jessie were being driven by a friend (Prijean). Jessie Conrad reports

that they saw the actual idiots during the ride and that 'the story had its origins in Prijean's remark just after we had passed them sprawling in the ditch. "Four — hein. And all in the same family. That's a little too much. And the priests say it's God's will!" '[2] The implications of an unfeeling clergy, inherent in this statement, are taken up more explicitly in the story, in which the birth of idiot twins and a further idiot boy to Jean-Pierre and Susan Bacadou causes the local priest 'to deliver himself with joyful unction of solemn platitudes about the inscrutable ways of Providence' to 'the rich landowner, the Marquis de Chavanes.' The priest, likened to 'a black bolster' and gesticulating 'with a fat hand,' is 'exulting and humble, proud and awed' (*TU*, 64–5).

These contrasting emotions constitute the priest's reaction to the decision of Jean-Pierre — 'the enraged republican farmer' — to attend mass and to offer 'to entertain the visiting priests at the next festival of Ploumar! It was a triumph for the Church and for the good cause' (*TU*, 65). Clearly evident here are the lack of compassion on the part of the priest and the sense of well-fed indolence he enjoys; both aspects tending to support Jean-Pierre's habit of comparing the clergy with scavenging crows. The marquis shares the priest's joy since he sees the conversion as a matter of political advantage.

Jean-Pierre, however, regards his act as a decision to 'sacrifice his convictions', proceeds to show hospitality 'when a black soutane darkened his doorway' and feels 'like a man who had sold his soul' (*TU*, 67). Though seen from Jean-Pierre's point of view, such inversions stress the negativity of the arrangement. Jean-Pierre's conversion is for a specific purpose — a non-idiot child — and, like the expiatory advice given by the abbé to Arlette, this is another attempt at spiritual bargaining; the practice Conrad so abhorred. In *The Sisters*, the father, dismayed at the departure of his son, Stephen from his native land, 'made a solemn vow to build a church in which the misguided son could have his peace with God by painting, on a gold background, a gorgeous altar-piece' (*Sis*, 48), only for the narrator to remark that 'Providence, unlike the powers of this earth, was impervious to the effect of a splendid bribe' (*Sis*, 49). The father's earlier attempts to enlist 'the help of renowned saints' has been answered only 'by the meaningless stare of naïve art' (*Sis*, 47). Use of the word 'bribe' gives an unpleasant perspective to the act (and seems very much in line with Conrad's view); whilst 'naïve' is an indication of the futility of the old man's belief in miracles.

Both these aspects have been transferred to 'The Idiots'. When the condition for Jean-Pierre's conversion is not fulfilled (his fourth child is

also an idiot), he recants his faith by shouting at the church and
receives a similar response to the 'trustful prayers' of Stephen's father;
in this case 'The song of nightingales' beating 'on all sides against the
high walls of the church', and flowing back 'between stone crosses and
flat gray slabs, engraved with words of hope and sorrow' (*TU*, 69).
When, fearful of conceiving a fifth idiot, Susan has killed him she
complains at the injustice of Heaven which seems not to distinguish
between blasphemy and prayer (*TU*, 75–6) and does, indeed, remain
'high and impassive' during her final cry for help (*TU*, 84). This
indicates the falsity of a belief which regards misfortune in this life as
punishment for sin and felicity as the just reward for piety.

The unpleasant influence of the priest intrudes again since Catholic
theology prohibits the burial of a suicide in holy ground. But the
Marquis agrees to 'speak to the curé' since it would strengthen his
position if Susan's mother administered the farm (*TU*, 85). The
priests, therefore, can be seen as subservient to wealthy interests and
material concerns.

In *Nostromo* the familiar elements of a superstitious laity influenced
by a powerful clergy (the epitome of the Church in Poland) are quickly
introduced with the legend of the wandering sailors who disappeared
during a search for treasure:

> The impious adventurers gave no other sign. The sailors, the Ind-
> ian, and the stolen burro were never seen again. As to the mozo, a
> Sulaco man – his wife paid for some masses, and the poor four-
> footed beast, being without sin, had been probably permitted to
> die; but the two gringos, spectral and alive, are believed to be
> dwelling to this day amongst the rocks, under the fatal spell of their
> success. Their souls cannot tear themselves away from their bodies
> mounting guard over the discovered treasure. They are now rich
> and hungry and thirsty – a strange theory of tenacious gringo ghosts
> suffering in their starved and parched flesh of defiant heretics,
> where a Christian would have renounced and been released. (*N*, 5)

This legend signifies more than a simple reflection of superstition but
the beliefs that it reveals are worthy of note. Evident in this extract are
the religious concerns of the simple Catholic laity of Sulaco: a preoccupation with sin, a belief in ghosts, the regarding of all non-Catholics as
heretics (and, thus, non-Christians) and the need to pay for masses to
aid the progress of a dead man's soul – all of which indicate a
combination of primitive superstition and priestly indoctrination. The

need to pay for masses necessarily enhances the prestige of the clergy and augments their income as well.

The pervading nature of this heritage is illustrated later by the way Nostromo is affected by his refusal to bring a priest to Teresa's deathbed. Despite his disbelief in the 'sacerdotal character' of priests, he feels 'uneasy at the impiety of this refusal' (*N*, 255). Once 'the admired publicity of his life' has gone, he is ready 'to feel the burden of sacrilegious guilt descend upon his shoulders'. The cause of this vulnerability is cited as lack of scepticism, whose absence delivers the masses 'to the wiles of swindlers and to the pitiless enthusiasm of leaders inspired by visions of a high destiny' (*N*, 420). Scepticism, one recalls, was extolled by Conrad to Galsworthy (to whom *Nostromo* was dedicated), as 'the tonic of minds, the tonic of life, the agent of truth — the way of art and salvation'.[3]

The superstitious nature of the Costaguanan masses is deliberately perpetuated by the clergy in such instances as the stories of the infamous dictator Guzman Bento who 'reached his apotheosis in the popular legend of a sanguinary land-haunting spectre whose body had been carried off by the devil in person from the brick mausoleum in the nave of the Church of Assumption in Sta. Marta. Thus, at least, the priests explained its disappearance to the barefooted multitude that streamed in, awestruck, to gaze at the hole in the side of the ugly box of bricks before the great altar' (*N*, 47).

Three priests are specifically named. The first to appear is Father Román and he too can be seen to be encouraging ignorance and superstition (and may be also revealing his own) by purporting Europe to be 'a country of saints and miracles' (*N*, 103). Román is the pastor of the silver miners and has spent much of his past serving in wars during which he 'had shriven many simple souls on the battlefields of the Republic.' This violent background seems to be encouraged by the representation of the Resurrection in the miner's chapel, which has 'a figure soaring upwards, long-limbed and livid, in an oval of pallid light, and a helmeted brown legionary smitten down, right across the bituminous foreground' (*N*, 103).

Román is a likeable character who enjoys his game of cards and is apparently genuinely fond of his charges. But the concern he shows for their fate during the revolt of Montero reveals other aspects of his character that are not so endearing:

He entertained towards the Indians of the valley feelings of paternal scorn. He had been marrying, baptizing, confessing, absolving, and burying the workers of the San Tomé mine with dignity and unction for five years or more; and he believed in the sacredness of these ministrations, which made them his own in a spiritual sense. They were dear to his sacerdotal supremacy. Mrs Gould's earnest interest in the concerns of these people enhanced their importance in the priest's eyes, because it really augmented his own.   (*N*, 399)

What is evident from this passage is the sense of importance Román feels, deriving from his feelings of superiority over his flock. The more important his flock becomes, the more important he becomes and it is also self-evident that this power will be greatly diminished if Montero should succeed. He has, therefore, a vested interest in seeing that the status quo should be maintained. Despite the influence of dogma, however, Román is still able to appreciate Emilia Gould, though not without this causing some inner confusion for 'Padre Román was incapable of fanaticism to an almost reprehensible degree. The English senora was evidently a heretic; but at the same time she seemed to him wonderful and angelic.' This disparity in the Catholic claim to exclusive saintliness causes him to 'shake his head profoundly' but he does not question further.

In reality, though, Román is serving the San Tomé mine; a position that is made clear by the cynical but perceptive Dr Monygham after the crisis has passed:

And the heroic Father Román – I imagine the old padre blowing up systematically the San Tomé mine, uttering a pious exclamation at every bang, and taking handfuls of snuff between the explosions – the heroic Padre Román says that he is not afraid of the harm Holroyd's missionaries can do to his flock, as long as *he* is alive.
(*N*, 507)

Román's duty to God and his flock is thus confused with his devotion to the San Tomé mine, that symbol of material interests which to some extent will claim the allegiance of almost every character in the book. His egotistical sense of control over the simple souls of the miners is also evident in the last few words of the passage which refer to the arrival of Protestantism in the area. Though a Catholic priest (as his name helps to emphasise) Román is really an illustration of how, in a subtle way, religion can be manipulated to serve other ends, in this case those of material interests.

Father Corbelán, the most dominant religious figure in the novel, first appears through the eyes of the sceptically observant Martin Decoud whose analysis is perceptive. Decoud reports how the priest 'said Mass for the troops' before 'an altar of drums' with 'wooden saints' standing 'militarily in a row . . . like a gorgeous escort attending the Vicar-General'. Corbelán 'glittered exceedingly in his vestments with a great crimson velvet cross down his back. And all the time our saviour Barrios sat in the Amarilla Club drinking punch at an open window' (*N*, 187–8).

This first dramatic appearance shows Corbelán as one who is acutely conscious of the trappings of the Church and very keen to perpetuate them. The wooden saints seem to recognise in him a member of the Church Militant but Decoud's ironical reference to Barrios as 'our saviour' helps to undercut this sense of importance and Corbelán's harangue of the general soon afterwards is a quick reaction to Barrios's apparent flouting of ecclesiastical (and Corbelán's) authority. The ill-fated journalist is also perceptive enough to realise where the priest's true passions lie:

> But I know him, too, our Padre Corbelán. The idea of political honour, justice, and honesty for him consists in the restitution of the confiscated Church property. Nothing else could have drawn that fierce converter of savage Indians out of the wilds to work for the Ribierist cause! Nothing else but that wild hope! He would make a pronunciamiento himself for such an object against any Government if he could only get followers! (*N*, 188–9)

Corbelán's view of 'an outraged Church waiting for reparation from a penitent country' (*N*, 195) causes the less informed citizens of Sulaco to murmur that the greater part of the land will be taken from the people and 'go to the padres'. Earlier, indeed, Don Pepe has confirmed that in the past 'it was everything for the Padres, nothing for the people; and now it is everything for these great politicos in Sta. Marte, or negroes and thieves' (*N*, 89). Church and corrupt government are thus clearly linked. Even at the end Corbelán is described as 'everlastingly worrying the Government about the old Church lands and convents'; conduct which Mitchell believes is approved of in Rome (*N*, 478).

Corbelán fails to see that his temporal demands are anachronistic. The ruined convent in which he meets Nostromo (*N*, 196) and the battered 'moss-stained effigy of some saintly bishop' which adorns premises that were 'once the residence of a high official of the Holy

Order' (*N*, 98) are clear indications that the days of ecclesiastical splendour in Sulaco belong to the past; a fact that is confirmed by the exchange between Emilia Gould and Sir John in the early stages of the novel (*N*, 35–6).

Román and Corbelán are the cream of the priests, however, and their fearlessness is in marked contrast to the characteristics of their fellow clergy. When Teresa is dying, Nostromo reveals that 'the populace are much incensed against the priests. Not a single fat padre would have consented to put his head out of his hiding-place to-night to save a Christian soul, except, perhaps, under my protection' (*N*, 268). The phrase 'fat padre' implies that the priests have been living well off the people, in a similar way to those of 'The Idiots'.

Under the notorious regime of Guzman Bento, they have appeared in a still more unfavourable light, from the 'trembling, subservient Archbishop of his creation' who celebrates solemn Masses of thanksgiving on his behalf 'in great pomp in the cathedral of Sta. Marta' (*N*, 139), to the slovenly army chaplain in attendance at executions (*N*, 138),[4] to the sadistic Father Beron whose exhortation to prisoners – 'Will you confess now?' (*N*, 373) – is a clear perversion of the confessional. Under Bento, the 'power of Supreme Government' becomes 'an object of strange worship, as if it were some sort of cruel deity' (*N*, 137). This easy manipulation of the clergy and its subservience to whatever power is predominant is seen, in a symbolic sense, when Pedro Montero enters Sulaco to the peal of Cathedral bells and those of 'every church, convent, or chapel in town' (*N*, 381). The clergy are in hiding at this stage, but the utilisation of religious edifices is a reflection of their own pliability. Little wonder old Giorgio should consider that 'the sea, which knows nothing of kings and priests and tyrants, is the holiest of all' (*N*, 341), and should advise Giselle to pray 'not to the God of priests and slaves, but to the God of orphans, of the oppressed, of the poor, of little children' (*N*, 533); a concept that sounds much closer to the ideals of Christianity as advocated in the Gospels than the version current in Sulaco.

There is, therefore, much scope for a 'purer form of Christianity' that pet dream of the American financier, Holroyd (*N*, 240). But this proves to be little more than an adjunct to material interests and its introduction into Sulaco simply starts a sectarian battle for souls. Indeed, Corbelán's elevation to Cardinal is thought to be 'a counter move to the Protestant invasion of Sulaco organized by Holroyd' Missionary Fund' (*N*, 509). The term 'invasion' again denotes a powe struggle and seems, once more, to connect the outlook of institutional-ised religion with that of governments.

In effect, Holroyd is attempting to replace Corbelán's religious autocracy with his own and the arrogant assumption he holds of his country's future control over all aspects of life in the continent, includ-ing religion (*N*, 77), reveals the extent of his egoism and his vanity. The combination of 'the temperament of a Puritan and an insatiable imagi-nation of conquest' (*N*, 76) has bred a self-righteous dictator whose prime concern is actually 'silver and iron' (*N*, 71), just as Corbelán's seems to be land. To Holroyd, evidently, the ways of God are not mysterious but financial and assist in the establishing of his religious reputation, for 'his lavish patronage of the "purer forms of Christian-ity" (which in its naïve form of church-building amused Mrs Gould) was looked upon by his fellow-citizens as the manifestation of a pious and humble spirit' (*N*, 80). Emilia considers this to be as much 'idol-atry' as 'the tawdriness of the dressed up saints in the cathedral' which has caused 'Mr Holroyd's sense of religion' to be 'shocked and dis-gusted' and prompted him to call it 'the worship . . . of wood and tinsel' (*N*, 71). She undercuts Holroyd's dogmatism and echoes more closely the spirit of the Gospels by commenting that 'A poor Chulo who offers a little silver arm or leg to thank his god for a cure is as rational and more touching' (*N*, 71).

Nostromo, in fact, is Conrad's most comprehensive consideration of Christian inadequacies, embracing not only the Church of his native land but also one akin to that of his adopted country. The Catholic laity is shown to be suffering under a heritage of persistent and insidious superstition and also to be harbouring resentment against their clergy, the main purveyors of this heritage. Their priests prove to be either subservient to or even willing allies of ruthless tyranny and, under milder regimes, either fight for Church power (Corbelán), live lives of ease at their flocks' expense ('fat padre'), or are subtly manipulated by material interests (Román). The Protestant wing of the religion is still more closely linked with materialism and offers no hope of succour for the oppressed masses. The literal religious language of *Nostromo*, therefore, reveals a spiritual void and we shall see later on how attempts to fill this void prove to be just as unsuccessful.

Conrad's treatment of Catholicism rarely strays from the pattern laid down in 'The Idiots' and *Nostromo*. Even his unfinished *Suspense*, written in the early 1920s, contains a simple villager whose beliefs extend to the efficacy of exorcism and the inevitability of all Englishmen (heretics) having their 'wickedness written on their faces' (*S*, 160); this is a further indictment of priestly influence, although Father Román was seen to have similar problems in assessing Emilia Gould. It also contains a calculating priest in Father Paul Carpi whose 'first stirrings of ambition' cause him to be judiciously perceptive and subservient when in the presence of the powerful Count Helion (*S*, 163) who, however, shows an awareness of priestly pretensions to power by equating 'the reign of God' with the reign of the clergy (*S*, 162). When confronted with the problem of the troublesome Clelia, Father Paul proves to be a master of evasion:

> To gain time he smiled, a slight non-committal smile.
> "We priests, M. le Comte, are recommended not to enter into discussion of theological matters with people who, whatever their accomplishments and wisdom, are not properly instructed in them. As to anything else I am always at Monseigneur's service."
> He gave this qualification to Count Helion because it was not beyond the bounds of respect due from a poor parish priest to a titled great man of his province.   (*S*, 164)

This is clear hypocrisy since, after a comment by Helion 'that the only thing which seemed to put a limit to the power of God was the folly of men,' the priest is seen to have 'too poor an opinion of Count de Montevesso to be shocked by the blasphemy' (*S*, 165). He also possesses an enduring capacity to swim with the current as his treatment of the likely suicide of Clelia's mother shows:

> He had consented to bury her in consecrated ground not from any compassion but because of the revolutionary spirit which had penetrated even the thick skulls of his parishioners and probably would have caused a riot and shaken the precarious power of the Church in his obscure valley.   (*S*, 166)

Lack of 'compassion' and contempt for his flock are uppermost here, together with a willingness to compromise with supposedly sacred principles if this will maintain the 'power' of the Church. Faced with the (to him) inexplicable behaviour of Clelia and the 'sense of his own powerlessness' (*S*, 166), he is reduced to futile (and unsuccessful) threats of exorcism.

The mysterious Attilio links the clergy with Austrian spies or Piedmontese police (*S*, 11) and with the 'old tyrannical superstitions of religion' which are allied to 'the oppression of privileged classes.' He respects all religions 'but despised the priests who preached submission' (*S*, 257). There is also corruption within the Church. Catholic laws can be circumvented at times, it seems, not only when inconvenient to enforce (as seen above) but also when wealth or position is involved. Madame de Montevesso describes how, on the early breakdown of her marriage, 'Some of these good friends offered him [Helion] their influence in Rome for the annullation of the marriage, for a consideration of course' (*S*, 139), which would effectively side-step the Catholic prohibition on divorce. *Suspense* thus adds deliberate cunning to the composite picture of a Conradian priest and reveals the easy corruption of Catholic doctrines where material advantage is involved.

This unpleasant picture of Catholicism in Conrad's novels is completed by two characters in *The Arrow of Gold*, members of the laity this time. The introduction of Therese at once sounds the chord of ostentatious religion and likely hypocrisy, for J. M. K. Blunt comments not only on the 'rosary at her waist' but also on her love of money (*AG*, 40). M. George describes her as 'Therese of the whispering lips and downcast eyes slipping out to an early mass from the house of iniquity into the early winter murk of the city of perdition, in a world steeped in sin' and as being afraid of the 'impious streets' as if of a 'contamination', but despite her 'really nun-like dress' (*AG*, 40), her inner passions are less ascetic and are made explicit at the end when she runs off with the wounded Ortega. Therese proves to be miserly (*AG*, 155), vain (*AG*, 156), and hypocritically complacent, as when she masters 'the feelings of anger so unbecoming to a person whose sins had been absolved only about three hours before' (*AG*, 157). Indeed, part of her animosity towards Rita seems to stem from her feelings that salvation is less assured in the sinful city than in the country, 'serving a holy man, next door to a church, and sure of my share of Paradise' (*AG*, 160). She is capable of displaying 'a distracting versatility of sentiment: rapacity, virtue, piety, spite, and false tenderness' (*AG*, 289) but when she confronts George and Rita, who have spent the night together after the dramatic scene with Ortega, her claim that she will never desert her sister brings the perceptive comment from Rita, 'What is it . . . my soul or this house that you won't abandon?' (*AG*, 335). Knowingly or unknowingly, Therese's bigotry acts as a mask for her selfish desires and may, indeed, be used as a means to attain them.

The picture of Don Rafael de Villarel, on the other hand, not only emphasises the fanatical side of the Church but gives reminders of its past cruelties too:

> Of him I had only heard that he was a very austere and pious person, always at Mass, and that sort of thing. I saw a frail little man with a long, yellow face and sunken fanatical eyes, an Inquisitor, an unfrocked monk. One missed a rosary from his thin fingers. He gazed at me terribly and I couldn't imagine what he might want. I waited for him to pull out a crucifix and sentence me to the stake there and then.   (*AG*, 82)

This is Rita's description but George confirms the impression later in the book (*AG*, 250–3). This, then, is the man who equates service to the deposed monarch with service to religion – accompanying his references to the king with the pious words 'whom God preserve' (*AG*, 250, 251) – and who crosses himself whenever he makes mention of 'our Holy Mother the Church' (*AG*, 251, 252).

Villarel seems like a figure from the past, reflecting the Church's inclinations to move back in time instead of forward. Support of the Carlists in *The Arrow of Gold* and of the monarchy in *Suspense* can be seen in the same light as Corbelán's fixation with the restoration of Church lands; these are examples of an unrealistic and reactionary intransigence.

Roman Catholicism is not alone in being an ally of autocracy. In *Under Western Eyes* the Orthodox Church in Russia appears in a similar light, causing Mrs Haldin to remark, 'With us in Russia the church is so identified with oppression, that it seems almost necessary when one wishes to be free in this life, to give up hoping for a future existence' (*UWE*, 103). This view is later endorsed by another revolutionary, Sophia Antonovna, who explains, 'As I could not go to the Church where the priests of the system exhorted such unconsidered vermin as I to resignation, I went to the secret societies' (*UWE*, 263).

Even those priests who have good intentions are forced to adhere to the system, unless they actively rebel like Father Zosim, 'the priest democrat' (*UWE*, 136). The old priest who reveals to Natalia Haldin and her mother that he has 'been ordered to watch and ascertain in other ways too (such as using his spiritual power with the servants)' all that goes on in their house, fears that his deacon will 'make the worst of things to curry favour' if he disobeys:

He did not wish to spend the evening of his days with a shaven head
in the penitent's cell of some monastery — "and subjected to all the
severities of ecclesiastical discipline; for they would show no mercy
to an old man," he groaned.   (*UWE*, 139)

Here is a picture of the clergy as a network of spies and of Christianity as being in league with the secular government to such an extent
that non-cooperation with the autocracy is regarded as a sin meriting
strict penance. That priests could be so punished if they strayed from
autocratic prescriptions is confirmed by Conrad in *A Personal Record*,
though here he gives due credit to the Greek Orthodox priest who
vainly attempted to prevent an unruly mob of peasants from ransacking the home of the author's great-uncle, Nicholas Bobrowski. The
immediate promise of gold, however, outweighed the more distant
prospect of salvation for these country-folk and there is a bitter irony in
the fact that 'a small ivory crucifix' was all that remained after the
priest's efforts had proved unavailing (*PR*, 61–2).[5] This event seems to
form the basis for an incident in *The Rover* where Scevola, the fervent
supporter of revolution, is rescued from irate villagers by the speedy
intervention of their newly restored abbé (*Ro*, 42).

Conrad's Protestant clergy are less pervasive in his fiction but are
also generally inadequate and unworldly. The easily flustered curate of
'Typhoon' is a mild example of this, his misunderstanding of 'Solomon
says . . . ' being a source of humour in the story (*T*, 16). Having a
grandfather who was 'a preacher' (*Re*, 22) does not prevent Shaw
(Lingard's mate in *The Rescue*) from being a bigoted advocate of racial
superiority. In *The Secret Agent* the Professor, the ultimate anarchist,
ready to destroy at a moment's notice, is the son of 'an itinerant and
rousing preacher of some obscure but rigid Christian sect — a man
supremely confident in the privileges of his righteousness' (*SA*, 80) and
here it is suggested that the fanaticism and bigoted egoism of the father
has contributed to that of the son and thus proved destructive.

The most extended example of an inadequate clerical parent comes
in *Lord Jim*, introduced as early as the fourth paragraph:

Originally he came from a parsonage. Many commanders of fine
merchant-ships come from these abodes of piety and peace. Jim's
father possessed such certain knowledge of the Unknowable as
made for the righteousness of people in cottages without disturbing
the ease of mind of those whom an unerring Providence enables to

live in mansions. The little church on a hill had the mossy greyness
of a rock seen through a ragged screen of leaves. It had stood there
for centuries, but the trees around probably remembered the laying
of the first stone.   (*LJ*, 5)

The red front of the rectory is said to possess 'a warm tint' exuding a
sense of cosiness, but two inadequacies are immediately evident. The
parson keeps noticeably silent about the privileged among his flock,
suggesting that his truths stay a comfortable distance away from home.
The other hint of inadequacy is given in the comparison of age between
the church and the trees. The church gives the impression of being
older than it really is but nature is older still; the implication being that
there is an ancient wisdom not possessed by the comfortable rural style
of religion practised by Jim's family who have had the living for
generations. Marlow's picture of the old man, 'grey haired and serene
in the inviolable shelter of his book-lined, faded and comfortable
study, where for forty years he had conscientiously gone over and over
again the round of his little thoughts about faith and virtue, about the
conduct of life and the only proper manner of dying' (*LJ*, 341), reveals
how out of touch the parson is with the harsh realities confronting Jim,
who, indeed, believes his father 'wouldn't understand' (*LJ*, 79). The
father's 'little thoughts' are shown to be combined with a pretentious
assumption of exclusive wisdom which is, ironically, shown to be
derived from ignorance.

Just as unrealistic is the missionary who thinks he is converting
Gentleman Brown 'to a better way of life' when, in fact, that notorious
robber, who is giving him such hopes of 'a remarkable conversion,' is
preparing to seduce the missionary's wife (*LJ*, 384). Both the missionary and Jim's father (and, by implication, the church they represent),
for all their book learning, are incapable of realising the perfidy that
exists among the human race. This dangerous innocence is shared by
Jim, whose treatment of Brown is, indeed, comparable to the missionary's and leads to disaster.

Conrad's Protestant laity show up in no better light as the shortcomings of Holroyd and his American brand of Christianity have revealed.
In *Almayer's Folly*, the hypocritical and racial character of the proper
Mrs Vinck's 'Protestant wing' is a factor in alienating Nina Almayer
from white society. In *The Nigger of the 'Narcissus'*, Podmore is
complacent (being assured of his own salvation), bigoted (being equally assured of the ultimate damnation of his shipmates), and fanatical,
and his egotistical conviction that he will save the soul of the dying

James Wait succeeds only in provoking a near-mutiny on board the ship. His Christian fundamentalism − a belief in 'lilies, gold harps − and brimstone' (as Conrad observed to Cunninghame Graham)[6] − creates only disruption, therefore, and it is made clear that his duty towards the ship is not to preach but to cook.

The shortcomings of religion among Conrad's adopted countrymen are at their most pervasive in his fiction between 1896 (*The Nigger of the 'Narcissus'*) and 1902 ('The End of the Tether'). 'Amy Foster' (1901) is a damning indictment of Christian practice in an English village. The churches of Brenzett and Colebrook − one with its 'spire in a clump of trees,' the other with its 'square tower' (*T*, 105) − are both prominent features of their respective villages, but the early mention of a Martello Tower (built to thwart invasion) is a reminder of a heritage which has not been overtly welcome to those from overseas. The unfortunate shipwrecked foreigner, Yanko Goorall, is regarded with suspicion by the villagers so that their response to his appeal 'in God's name to afford food and shelter' (*T*, 120) is to shut him up as a dangerous lunatic; the action being performed by a Mr Smith whose name may serve as a cynical reflection of English normality. It may be indicative of the test that Goorall's presence creates for the community that Kennedy, the narrator, should liken the ship's rigging to 'another and slighter spire to the left of Brenzett Church', and an indication of the community's response that the dead bodies should be 'laid out in a row under the north wall of the Brenzett Church' (*T*, 123). It may also be significant that the only person to aid Yanko and render him sustenance (as all Christians are enjoined to do) should be Amy Foster whose subsequent love for the man is described as primitive and pagan (*T*, 110).

Once Yanko begins to settle, his observations act as a telling exposé of Christian hypocrisy. After noting that 'the aspect of the people, especially on Sunday, spoke of opulence' he is moved to wonder 'what made them so hard-hearted and their children so bold' (*T*, 128), and confesses that, but for 'the steel cross at Miss Swaffer's belt he would not . . . have known whether he was in a Christian country at all' (*T*, 129). The emphasis on Miss Swaffer (with her reputation for piety) being 'Church − as people said (while her father was one of the trustees of the Baptist Chapel)' (*T*, 128), adds an element of sectarianism to the scene.

Yanko's unconscious exposure of hypocrisy becomes still more incisive as time passes whilst the concern of the villagers is simply to convert him to their own sect of Christianity:

He became aware of social differences, but remained for a long time surprised at the bare poverty of the churches among so much wealth. He couldn't understand either why they were kept shut up on week-days. There was nothing to steal in them. Was it to keep people from praying too often? The rectory took much notice of him about that time, and I believe the young ladies attempted to break the ground for his conversion. They could not, however, break him of his habit of crossing himself.   (*T*, 131)

Yanko, then, retains his simple Catholicism and, after the manner of his father, recites the Lord's Prayer every evening 'in incomprehensible words'; a phrase that illustrates the prejudiced and ignorant view of the villagers, unable to see that his 'slow fervent tone' implies sincerity. Amy later objects to his praying habits and his expectation of his son repeating the prayer after him (*T*, 137). Eventually she deserts him when, during a fever, he asks for water in his own language, and he dies in Doctor Kennedy's arms, perplexed and miserable, knowing only that 'She had left him − sick − helpless − thirsty. The spear of the hunter had entered his very soul. "Why?" he cried, in the penetrating and indignant voice of a man calling to a responsible Maker. A gust of wind and a swish of rain answered' (*T*, 141).

Yanko receives a familiar empty response from the heavens and, faced with the heartlessness of man, Kennedy, at least, can see no evidence of supernatural intervention. The emptiness of the heavens reflects the emptiness of the villagers' religious protestations which, together with the Christian echoes attached to Yanko himself, are a reminder of Christian charity (in this case effectively withheld).

A final unsatisfactory aspect of Christian conduct is considered in 'The End of the Tether'. Captain Whalley, initially, appears to be a fine exemplar of the faith he professes but his belief extends to a fatal presumption of continuing good health, inconsistent with his age, when he enters into partnership with Massy:

"Let that go," Captain Whalley had said with a superb confidence in his body. "Acts of God," he added. In the midst of life we are in death, but he trusted his Maker with a still greater fearlessness − his Maker who knew his thoughts, his human affections, and his motives. His Creator knew what use he was making of his health − how much he wanted it.   (*Y*, 271)

Though Whalley claims to expect 'no miracles' (*Y*, 291), this presumption causes him to ignore certain ominous signs, for life has not been as he would have planned. Thoughts of his dead wife, for example, frequently distract him from his Bible reading and indicate that death or misfortune can come between the man and his faith. Hints of earlier delusion follow:

> It was like an article of faith with him that there never had been and never could be, a brighter, cheerier home anywhere afloat or ashore than his home under the poop-deck of the *Condor*, with the big main cabin all white and gold, garlanded as if for a perpetual festival with an unfading wreath. (*Y*, 172)

But the festival has not been perpetual, nor has the wreath been unfading and, whilst this has only been 'like' an article of faith with him, it has not proved enduring. The passage reveals Whalley's failure to understand the transitoriness of life and should make him question his blithe assumptions. Later, during his conversation with Captain Eliott, the cathedral in the background symbolises his situation:

> The sacred edifice, standing in solemn isolation amongst the converging avenues of enormous trees, as if to put grave thoughts of heaven into the hours of ease, presented a closed Gothic portal to the light and glory of the west. The glass of the rosace above the ogive glowed like fiery coal in the deep carvings of a wheel of stone. (*Y*, 198)

This is especially ominous for the 'light and glory of the west' is the sun setting on the day that has gone (just as Whalley's glory belongs to the day that has gone) and to this light the cathedral presents a 'closed Gothic portal' amidst its sense of age and opulence. The building seems to belong to the past also and gives no hint that it (or what it represents) will be of any service to Whalley; the implication, in fact, is that it will not.

Whalley's belief (an expectation of earthly favours for faithful conduct) is a subtle variation on the 'bargaining with the eternal' theme that Conrad had exposed in 'The Idiots'. Consequently when Whalley's sight fails, he regards it as a 'punishment' which is 'too great for a little presumption, for a little pride' and begins to question his faith (*Y*, 324–5). In the end he feels 'forgotten' by God (*Y*, 338) and the mercy of the death he prays for comes only by his own hand.

Whalley's plight, however, has been the saving of Mr Van Wyk who comes out of seclusion to re-enter the affairs of the world. Whether Whalley's daughter will thank 'a God merciful at last' (*Y*, 338) seems unlikely but, materially, her position is also improved by her father's death. Nevertheless, the practice of treating belief in God as a kind of charm that will ward off misfortune is condemned here as totally invalid. Though one of the most humane of Conrad's practising Christians, Whalley's outlook on life is still shown to be based on a false premise.

Wherever it exists and whatever its institutionalised form, therefore, Christianity, as practised in Conrad's fiction, is shown to be inadequate to the needs of the human race. In their dogged support of legitimacy, Conrad's Churches uphold tyranny and this alliance, together with the acute consciousness of their own power, brings oppression instead of relief to the people by perpetuating mediaeval superstition. Their priests, with a very few exceptions, are either grim fanatics, proclaiming outworn shibboleths to a credulous populace, or indolent self-seekers, prospering at their parishioners' expense. Very few of the clergy exhibit the signs of compassion, understanding and love that should be the hallmark of their calling. Both the Catholic and Protestant Faiths are shown to be riddled with hypocrisy and bigotry; true to the trappings of belief but false to its spirit. Their uninformed laity seeks in vain for earthly bounties to reward righteous conduct – an example of the 'shent-per-shent' business that Conrad condemned. Whalley apart, the virtues lacking in the clergy are also absent from their more obtrusive laity and we generally have to look elsewhere, to those who do not make loud proclamations of belief, for the most humane of Conrad's characters. All in all, the state of Christianity within the Conradian canon is pitiful and it is little wonder that, faced with such a background, bewildered souls, such as Flora de Barral in *Chance*, should find no consolation at religion's door (*C*, 164). Little wonder, too, perhaps, that the real gods to whom mankind pays homage should be shown to be outside religion altogether.

7

Devil and Soul

THE DEVIL AND THE EGO

Two aspects of Conrad's religious lexis merit special attention; his use of the demonic and its natural prey, the soul. Both seem to have meanings beyond their traditional theological ones and their usage is frequently closely connected with the novelist's major themes.

There are warnings to be heeded in any analysis of Conrad's use of the demonic. When an age-old concept of a Satanic scapegoat, at whose door may be laid all the wrongdoings of mankind, has been so firmly embedded in the consciousness, one has to be careful to distinguish between deliberate usage for a specific effect and the mere repetition of common phraseology. Terms such as 'poor devil' and the use of 'infernal' as an adjective were frequently in use at the turn of the century (appearing regularly within Conrad's correspondence) and one could make too much of their presence. The cry of 'Not a pice more! You go to the devil!' from an unnamed member of the crew of the 'Narcissus', for example (*NN*, 4), is unlikely to have meaning beyond its obvious colloquial abuse. When, however, the term is used with definite meaning – literal or figurative – there is a need to probe further. The questions posed earlier have now to be answered. What makes a character 'Satanic'? Is he Satanic because demonic terms are associated with him or because he possesses Satanic attributes? What are Satanic attributes? If a character has been 'possessed', what has possessed him? Presumably the devil. But what is the devil?

To answer these questions, one must consider the actions and attributes of those characters with whom the demonic associations have been made. Conrad, clearly, had no firm belief in the traditional depiction of Hell and its overlord; his use of the term must surely be taken to indicate some fault, some destructive mode of behaviour in a character that exerts a pernicious influence upon all around it.

Such a character is James Wait who is regarded as Satanic because of the effect he has over the crew of the 'Narcissus' and it is through their eyes that the associations are made. There are two narrators in *The Nigger of the 'Narcissus'* – one omniscient, the other an unnamed seaman – which produces the dual effects of involvement and detachment.[1] Demonic images become attached to Wait either by the seaman–narrator or the cook but not by the more knowledgeable officers or the omniscient narrator (or, indeed, by the patriarchal Singleton), to whom he is just a dying man.

Wait is demonic in the sense that he brings disruption to the essential orderliness of life at sea. Devotion to the ship is the necessary creed, the true religion of the 'Narcissus', and is so equated by the omniscient narrator. Destiny for the sailor is controlled by 'the immortal sea' which is described as a kind of presiding deity, possessed of a 'disdainful mercy,' conferring 'in its justice the full privilege of desired unrest' as an example of 'the perfect wisdom of its grace' (*NN*, 90). Existence on its surface depends on the solidarity of a crew in their working of the ship. This devotion, this solidarity is undermined by Wait who, in thus opposing true religion (in the nautical sense at least), can be considered demonic.

The build-up of demonic imagery associated with Wait has been carefully noted from time to time but noted without its referent. Podmore comments of him, 'I thought I had seen the devil' (*NN*, 19), which, initially, tells us more about the cook and his fundamentalism that it does of Wait. Obviously his thought is dictated by Wait's colour; the immediate association of blackness with darkness and evil. When Belfast steals the pie, the cook decides that 'Satan was abroad amongst those men' (*NN*, 38), whilst the seaman narrator speaks of 'the infernal spell which that casual St Kitt's nigger had cast upon our guileless manhood' (*NN*, 37). Later he affirms: 'Had we been a miserable gang of wretched immortals, unhallowed alike by hope and fear, he could not have lorded it over us with a more pitiless assertion of his sublime privilege' (*NN*, 47). From their different standpoints, therefore, cook and crew are now in essential agreement; fundamentalistic assertion and observable effect thus concur.

During the fury of the storm, Jimmy is forgotten, but once the ship is on her side and there is nothing more that can be done, he is remembered and has to be rescued. As four of the sailors attempt to reach him, their endeavours are accompanied by an image of hell, for 'Wamibo . . . remained glaring above us – all shining eyes, gleaming fangs, tumbled hair; resembling an amazed and half-witted fiend gloating over the extraordinary agitation of the damned' (*NN*, 66). The true religion here, it must be remembered, is the devotion towards the proper running of the ship. Wait's presence takes the men away from that essential belief. Thus, during the rescue, the seamen hand nails up to the boatswain who 'as if performing a mysterious and appeasing rite, cast them wide upon a raging sea', and Belfast sets to 'cursing the Clyde shipwrights for not scamping their work' (*NN*, 68). Both are acts of blasphemy in this particular religious context giving point to the demonic image that preceded this.

Finally Wait is seen in the light of 'a black idol, reclining stiffly under a blanket,' which 'blinked its weary eyes and received our homage' (*NN*, 105). Traditionally Satan was guilty of the sin of pride which has its roots in an immoderate egoism that causes Wait to become a disruptive force of such potency that, with Donkin's aid, he almost succeeds in creating a mutiny. Wait's egoism brings to the fore the egoism of others; nor is he the only one to be accused of possessing Satanic attributes.

The catalyst for the revolt is the attempt of Podmore to convert Jimmy to Christianity before he dies, thus ensuring his salvation. But if one applies the association of devil and egoism to Podmore, he too can be seen as demonic.[2]

Podmore is one of the few men on the ship who realises that Jimmy is dying, but the cook simply aggravates the situation through his own sense of mission. Already he has appeared frequently in the pages of the story, self-righteous and bigoted in the exclusiveness of his belief. His complacent assurance, that 'I am ready for my Maker's call . . . wish you all were,' causes Belfast to rage 'You holy fool! I don't want you to die. . . . You blessed wooden-headed ould heretic, the divvle will have you soon enough. Think of Us . . . of Us . . . of Us!' (*NN*, 20). It is unlikely that Belfast is really consigning all non-Catholics to Hell, though this is a comic inversion of Podmore's own attitude. The comment should, however, make Podmore consider that there are contrary views concerning his salvation and lead him to give more thought to others and less to himself.

The cook's fanatical Christianity, therefore, serves as a harbour for his own excessive egoism and threatens his devotion to the ship and to the rest of the crew. He is described as 'beaming with the inward consciousness of his faith, like a conceited saint unable to forget his glorious reward' (*NN*, 32). He does his duty according to the creed of the sea by making the coffee which warms the crew, but instead of regarding this action as part of his devotion to the ship, he declares himself 'to have been the object of special mercy for the saving of our unholy lives' (*NN*, 83). His prayer during the 'fiendish noises' of the storm, when he implored 'the Master of our lives not to lead him into temptation' (*NN*, 61), and seemed, incidentally, not to have been so ready for his Maker's call as he had claimed, has not been answered. The crew's good opinion of themselves after the storm, persuaded by Donkin, is thus already evident within the cook. When he decides to 'save' Jimmy, his mind is filled up with traditional images of heaven and hell, but that decision has been influenced by 'the pride of possessed eternity' (*NN*, 115) and his true emotions are made explicit a moment later. He hesitates because 'A spark of human pity glimmered yet through the infernal fog of his supreme conceit', a statement that links very clearly the demonic and the ego. This 'supreme conceit' finally causes the cook to identify himself with Christ. Podmore 'had prayerfully divested himself of the last vestiges of his humanity. He was a voice – a fleshless and sublime thing, as on that memorable night – the night when he went walking over the sea to make coffee for perishing sinners' (*NN*, 116).

Wait gasps afterwards that 'he talked about black devils – he is a devil – a white devil' (*NN*, 119) and, in the terms of the devil/ego equation, he is right. The pride of an excessive egoism is a Christian vice not a Christian virtue and it is essentially an opposition of egos that causes the commotion in Wait's cabin.

The strange alliance between Podmore and Donkin that follows is fully appropriate since both have acted as disruptive elements challenging the essential devotion of seamen for their ship. Podmore's Christianity, if properly applied, should be able to prevent the crew from falling under Jimmy's spell; the cook, at least, has correctly gauged the state of Wait's health. But the hypocrisy, bigotry and sheer egocentricity of the application of his religion has prevented any possibility of this knowledge being conveyed to the crew whilst the wisdom of Singleton and Allistoun is prevented from having any impact on the men by the machinations of Donkin (*NN*, 43, 101). The true faith of the sea, held unflinchingly by the officers and by Singleton, is thus attacked by the forces of egoism inherent in Podmore and Wait and indicated by demonic imagery; forces that are orchestrated by the virulent negativity of Donkin, attain their peak, appropriately enough, in the darkness of night and are dissipated meekly in the light of day. It is indeed an 'infernal spell' that James Wait casts upon the crew; undermining their solidarity, drawing out the egotistical fanaticism of the cook and compelling devotion that, for their own safety, should be directed elsewhere.

Two things link Podmore and Wait: their association with the demonic, made by each other, and by different narrators (it would be beyond the limited perspective of the seaman-narrator to discern infernal attributes within the prayerful cook), and their deistic connections (Wait with a 'black idol', Podmore with Christ). Here, then, are two means by which Conrad reflects an excessive egoism; either or both are used frequently within his early works. Thus, in the early pages of *An Outcast of the Islands*, the state of Willems' ego is quickly indicated by his relations with the De Souza family, for 'That family's admiration was the great luxury of his life. It rounded and completed his existence in a perpetual assurance of unquestioned superiority. He loved to breathe the coarse incense they offered before the shrine of the successful white man' (*OI*, 3–4). His egoism is quickly connected with the Devil (*OI*, 21), thus, when Aïssa tells him, 'You taught me the love of your people which is of the devil' (*OI*, 144), the best definition of devil would again be self or ego. Almayer claims that the outcast 'appeared in this courtyard as if he had been jerked up from hell – where he belongs' (*OI*, 165), and the question of demonic possession is mentioned more than once. Thus, Babalatchi tells Lingard, 'I was glad; for a white man's eyes are not good to see when the devil that lives within is looking out through them.' Lingard's response is '"Devil! Hey?" . . . half aloud to himself, as if struck with the obviousness of some novel idea' (*OI*, 228).

Later, Lingard does indeed suggest to Willems that he has been 'possessed of a devil' (*OI*, 273). Willems seems to agree, claiming that 'After the thing was done, I felt so lost and weak that I would have called the devil himself to my aid if it had been any good – if he hadn't put in all his work already' (*OI*, 274).

These admissions and accusations have some point for Willems has indeed been possessed but possessed by his passion for Aïssa; the fate, as Babalatchi has already remarked, of those who worship many gods. This again derives from the fact that Willems never thinks beyond himself; the egoism that has caused his first downfall leaves him incapable of resisting Aïssa's spell despite his struggles. Even when Lingard is taking him to Sambir, Willems' response to the information he is given is simply the feeling that it has come to him too late since he could have used it profitably before (*OI*, 43). In betraying Lingard's secret, therefore, Willems is acting consistently; instead of betraying it to Hudig to satisfy his ambition, he betrays it to Abdulla to satisfy his passion. The specific goal may be different but the motive remains essentially the same – personal advancement, of which the root is an excessive egoism.

Willems' fellow white men also run into difficulties. Lingard's 'absurd faith in himself' (*OI*, 13) is an early indication of this failing

which results in the wrecking of his ship (*OI*, 173). He too is likened to
a deity, his judgement of Willems being accompanied by sympathetic
climatic elements to which he is closely compared:

> This last thought darkened Lingard's features with a responsive and
> menacing frown. The doer of justice sat with compressed lips and a
> heavy heart, while in the calm darkness outside the silent world
> seemed to be waiting breathlessly for that justice he held in his hand
> – in his strong hand – ready to strike – reluctant to move.
>
> (*OI*, 224)

After he has given judgement an apocalyptic storm breaks with 'violent louder bursts of crashing sound, like a wrathful and threatening
discourse of an angry god' (*OI*, 283). His egoism is reflected not only in
this manner but also in the way he regards his betrayal, which causes
him to be confronted 'with a situation that discomposed him by its
unprovoked malevolence, by its ghastly injustice, that, to his rough but
unsophisticated palate tasted distinctly of sulphurous fumes from the
deepest hell' (*OI*, 235–6). This is a more serious consideration of
demonic elements than the use by Muslims and Europeans of such
terms as 'Satan the Stoned' (*OI*, 103) or 'that hellish crowd' (*OI*, 164)
to refer to each other and, as has just been noted, Lingard does tell
Willems that he has been possessed. To assume demonic opposition,
then, can be taken as another indication of excessive egoism since it
elevates the importance of the person being opposed.

In a sense, though, Lingard himself can be regarded as demonic by
the hold he claims over the course of people's lives, as an accusation of
Willems makes clear:

> "You talk like that! You, who sold your soul for a few guilders,"
> muttered Willems, wearily, without opening his eyes.
>   "Not so few," said Almayer, with instinctive readiness, and stop-
> ped, confused for a moment. He recovered himself quickly, howev-
> er, and went on: "But you – you have thrown yours away for
> nothing; flung it under the feet of a damned savage woman."
>
> (*OI*, 91)

Almayer's consideration of his office furniture repeats the thought as
he reflects on having 'sold himself to Lingard for these things' (*OI*,
300).

Almayer's own ego is similarly enlarged. The outrage upon him is a 'fiendish outrage' in his words (*OI*, 180) because it violates his dignity (and thereby his ego). This reading of the word could also be applied to *Almayer's Folly* where the 'devil of gin' (*AF*, 135, 137), which makes Almayer curse and shout, is a devil because it reinforces the disappointed ego of its consumer.

In these early novels, therefore, the demonic is used principally to reveal excessive egoism (or passions that have the ego as their root) that proves destructive and disruptive. Whilst writing 'Heart of Darkness', however, whose Mr Kurtz is both deified and demonised in the now familiar fashion (though to a greater extent), Conrad wrote '*C'est l'egoisme qui sauve tout – absolument tout, tout ce que nous abhorrons, tout ce que nous aimons. Et tout se tient.*'[3] Kurtz, of course, had egoistic intentions of pervading the natives with '*tout ce que nous aimons*' and ended, instead, by bringing '*tout ce que nous abhorrons*'. Conrad's letter was chiefly concerned with International Fraternity (about which he was cynical) and implies that in his view egoism stands alone. A letter to the *New York Times* in 1901 gives a more modified opinion:

> Egoism, which is the moving force of the world, and altruism, which is its morality, these two contradictory instincts of which one is so plain and the other so mysterious cannot serve us unless in the incomprehensible alliance of their irreconcilable antagonism. Each alone would be fatal to our ambition. For in the hour of undivided triumph one would make our inheritance too arid to be worth having and the other too sorrowful to own.[4]

The topic of this letter (written to be published, of course) is *The Inheritors* but the view of egoism that it contains is more easily applicable to the novels than the extreme (and better known) view that precedes it. When ego is denoted by the demonic, therefore, it indicates that 'the incomprehensible alliance' has not taken place and it stands fatally alone (in Wait, in Podmore and in Willems, for example). Conrad told H. G. Wells that 'An enlightened egoism is as valid as an enlightened altruism – neither more nor less.'[5] Here, then, is a further modification: egoism is valid when it is enlightened (which it clearly is not in Wait, Podmore and Willems). One could consider Lingard here, too. He is both egoist and altruist; since both seem to be unenlightened, both are invalid. The combination of enlightened egoism and enlightened altruism would produce an angel, therefore; unenlightened egoism produces a .devil or suggestions of demonic possession; unenlightened egoism combined with unenlightened altruism produces, unwittingly, effects that can be demonic.

In 'Heart of Darkness' (whose very title suggests demonic habitation) Marlow gives new definitions for devil during his time at the outer station:

> I've seen the devil of violence, and the devil of greed, and the devil of hot desire; but, by all the stars! these were strong, lusty, red-eyed devils, that swayed and drove men — men, I tell you. But as I stood on this hillside, I foresaw that in the blinding sunshine of that land I would become acquainted with a flabby, pretending, weak-eyed devil of a rapacious and pitiless folly.   (*Y*, 65)

The demonic here has become a set of immoderate human passions (violence, greed, hot desire) which Marlow considers are being taken to unprecedented lengths. All are manifestations of unenlightened egoism. But devil is also equated by Marlow with 'a rapacious and pitiless folly' where the selfish (and cruel) connotations of the two adjectives are what make an unenlightened state demonic. This kind of devil comes not from an immoderate and egoistical passion but from an immoderate and egoistical folly (or mania) that causes Africans to die in a place likened by Marlow to 'the gloomy circle of some Inferno' (*Y*, 66).[6] Little wonder that 'big flies buzzed fiendishly, and did not sting but stabbed' (*Y*, 69), this place is clearly a kind of hell; a hell that, at the Central Station at least, has the 'flabby devil' in charge of it (*Y*, 72) causing the bewitchment of its pilgrims.

The (now familiar) deistic elements are there too, not only in the attitude of the 'faithless pilgrims' to the ivory, whose name 'rang in the air, was whispered, was sighed' so that one 'would think they were praying to it' (*Y*, 76), but also in their reaction to the Eldorado Expedition which 'came in sections during the next three weeks, each section headed by a donkey carrying a white man in new clothes and tan shoes, bowing from that elevation right and left to the impressed pilgrims' (*Y*, 87). This scene seems to echo Christ's entry into Jerusalem, but Marlow refers to it as 'an invasion, an infliction, a visitation'; language more appropriate to the seven plagues of Egypt. Indeed, he has already made an ironical reference to that section of Exodus with his comment about the brickmaker who 'could not make bricks without something, I don't know what — straw maybe' (*Y*, 77). In fact Conrad directly stated that 'the Belgians are worse than the seven plagues of Egypt' in a letter to Roger Casement in 1903.[7] In this case

Marlow has already undercut the self-importance of the expedition by referring to the donkey first, as if that beast is the leader.

Hell has been caused here by a particularly destructive kind of folly and within this environment it is not surprising to find many demonic terms which invite close scrutiny. Kurtz refers to a presumably debilitated assistant as a 'poor devil' (*Y*, 89) and, whilst this is a common and usually meaningless phrase (it is the 'poor' that generally carries the meaning not the 'devil'), it is tempting to interpret 'poor' as 'inadequate' here. On the journey upriver Marlow considers the noise of the natives as a 'fiendish row' (*Y*, 97). This is a case of the demonic being used to describe a European attitude to primitive rites but it is also 'fiendish' because it has appeal. On board the steamer the demonic is evoked by Europeans to control the native fireman who tends the boiler in the belief that there is an evil spirit within. When, soon after, Marlow comments that 'the boiler seemed indeed to have a sulky devil in it' (*Y*, 98), though this is simply a simile on one level, on another it indicates that Marlow is beginning to empathise with the natives; an empathy that seems complete when he throws his blood-filled shoes 'unto the devil-gog of that river' (*Y*, 114), and can later accept that the steamer appears as a 'fierce river-demon' (*Y*, 146). This reflects both the primitive superstitions of the natives and the cold reality of European progress, for the steamer is the means of transportation (and therefore a significant tool) for the controlling 'flabby devil'. Darkness is equated with ignorance as a rule; here the superstitious ignorance of the natives is equated with the folly of the Europeans. Each has its tempter, resisted by Marlow; the appeal of the drums being the one, the papier-mâché Mephistopheles representing the other (*Y*, 81).

At the Central Station Kurtz's name attracts contradictory adjectives. To the brickmaker he is 'a prodigy . . . an emissary of pity, and science, and progress, and devil knows what else' (*Y*, 79) and a later comment by the same speaker that 'he feared neither God nor devil, let alone any mere man' (*Y*, 84) reinforces the effect. Marlow himself has observed that 'I could see a little ivory coming out from there, and I had heard Mr Kurtz was in there. I had heard enough about it too – God knows! Yet somehow it didn't bring any image with it – no more than if I had been told an angel or a fiend was in there' (*Y*, 81). Whether Kurtz turns out to be angel or fiend seems to depend on the extent to which his egoism and altruism become enlightened. Marlow, already aware of the two types of temptation (savagery and folly) considers the vulnerability of mere human beings:

Of course you may be too much of a fool to go wrong – too dull even
to know you are being assailed by the powers of darkness. I take it,
no fool ever made a bargain for his soul with the devil; the fool is too
much of a fool, or the devil too much of a devil – I don't know
which. Or you may be such a thunderingly exalted creature as to be
altogether deaf and blind to anything but heavenly sights and
sounds. Then the earth for you is only a standing place – and
whether to be like this is your loss or your gain I won't pretend to
say. But most of us are neither one nor the other.   (*Y*, 116–17)

The first part of this comment seems to look forward to the advent of
the harlequin who, having been told to 'go to the devil' by his Dutch
employer (*Y*, 124), appears to have done just that in coming to Kurtz,
but continues to be ruled by 'the absolutely pure, uncalculating, un-
practical spirit of adventure' (*Y*, 126). Fool is equated with dullness
here; it could hardly apply to the kind of folly engaged in by the
pilgrims since that has already been connected with the demonic.
Kurtz is clearly neither fool nor 'a thunderingly exalted creature',
though his problems may stem from believing that he is the latter.
Kurtz's report for the Society for Suppression of Savage Customs
argues that the Europeans must appear to the natives 'in the nature of
supernatural beings – we approach them with the might of a deity' (*Y*,
118). Instead, Marlow considers that Kurtz 'had taken a high seat
amongst the devils of the land – I mean literally' (*Y*, 116). Kurtz is
'literally' a devil to the natives (from Marlow's viewpoint) since he has
succumbed to the temptation of being deified; the manifestation of an
enormous, unrestrained egoism, indicated also by the echoes of Christ
given by Kurtz's promise to return (*Y*, 137). Kurtz has reached this
position, Marlow surmises, by way of 'the inconceivable ceremonies of
some devilish initiation' (*Y*, 115), but Kurtz is also demonic in the
'flabby devil' sense since his conduct is the logical extension of a
'rapacious and pitiless folly' whose ivory deity he has come to resemble
(*Y*, 115).

    'Heart of Darkness', then, makes use of the demonic more exten-
sively than earlier works. Ego is still at the root but its heartless
manifestations take the form of folly as well as passion. The demonic
also functions to link primitive natives and civilised Europeans, emphasising the similarities between superstitious savagery and the cause of
progress. This cause has been described with glowing, positive religious imagery in the early pages of the story (especially by Marlow's

aunt); the negative imagery of the demonic reveals in religious terms its true reality.

Lord Jim continues the pattern of usage in these early tales. The extent of Jim's romantic egoism is indicated by the assumptions of demonic opposition – the *Patna* incident being a 'joke hatched in hell' (*LJ*, 108) – and by the deistic associations with Jim in Patusan which end with his willingness to take the blame on his own head (*LJ*, 415) to the background of an apocalyptic sky. As a water clerk, Jim is describ-ed as 'a regular devil for sailing a boat . . . a yelling fiend at the tiller . . . more like a demon than a man' (*LJ*, 194), which reflects the way his ego pushes him to become the foremost water clerk. Marlow makes mention of the 'Dark Powers' whose 'tremendous disdain' has caused the events on the *Patna* (*LJ*, 121). Demonic opposition seems indi-cated once more but 'Dark' also suggests the unknown or the unfore-seen (fate perhaps) rather than evil since 'disdain' implies callous indifference rather than active malevolence. In Patusan, Jim is undone by Gentleman Brown, 'a blind accomplice of the Dark Powers' (*LJ*, 354), whose enormous egoism gives him 'a blind belief in the right-eousness of his will against all mankind' (*LJ*, 370). In a milder form this could apply to Jim but, unlike Brown, Jim is not totally self-seeking, desiring, instead, the welfare of Patusan and justice for all. He is, like Lingard, an example of unenlightened egoism and unenlightened altruism. His ego extends only to a belief that his will is the best way of achieving justice, but he does not have the monstrous egoism of Brown that would seek unlimited and ruthless power. Perhaps it is this factor that causes Brown to comment, 'Rot his superior soul! He had me there – but he hadn't devil enough in him to make an end of me' (*LJ*, 344). Indeed, in regarding Brown on his death bed, Marlow directly connects evil and egoism as he reflects 'how much certain forms of evil are akin to madness, derived from intense egoism, inflamed by resist-ance, tearing the soul to pieces, and giving factitious vigour to the body' (*LJ*, 344).

It is Brown's excessive egoism that destroys Jim. Brown has 'a satanic gift of finding out the best and the weakest spots in his victims' and is so successful that it is 'as if a demon had been whispering advice in his ear' (*LJ*, 385–6). He desires, demon-like, 'to get in and shake his twopenny soul around and inside out and upside down – by God' (*LJ*, 384). Here, then, is demonic opposition (in Marlow's eyes this time) to deistic pretensions; the devil in Brown (intense egoism) opposing and awakening the devil in Jim (unenlightened romantic egoism). The resultant empathy this produces in Jim proves fatal.

The evocation of the demonic by Brown thus pre-figures disaster, just as, earlier, a similar evocation preceded disgrace. On the *Patna*, shortly before the collision, the dreamy cosmic lyricism of the narrator is abruptly terminated by more practical reality:

> The ship moved so smoothly that her onward motion was impercep-
> tible to the senses of men, as though she had been a crowded planet
> speeding through the dark spaces of ether behind the swarm of suns,
> in the appalling and calm solitudes awaiting the breath of future
> creations. 'Hot is no name for it down below,' said a voice.
>
> $(LJ, 21-2)$

This sudden descent (from the heavens to hell) is effected by the second engineer who makes the polarity more explicit by commenting that 'he did not mind how much he sinned, because these last three days he had passed through a fine course of training for the place where the bad boys go when they die — b'gosh he had'. This is prophetic as far as Jim is concerned for he too is musing (just as the narrator seemed to be) and an unpleasant fact from down below is about to turn his life into a kind of hell, as Marlow, by the implications of his own first-mate's behaviour, begins to realise *(LJ*, 156). Hell and an engine-room are easily compared, of course, but in the light of what happens, the possible function of the demonic as an evil portent is clearly evident, especially since the second engineer reveals that the hellish conditions are partly caused by the precarious state of the *Patna* below decks.

The functions of this kind of imagery develop after *Lord Jim*. Apart from 'The End of the Tether' — where Whalley's presumption (stem-ming from pride, stemming from ego) is equated with the demonic by both Massy *(Y*, 231, 233) and Sterne *(Y*, 254–5) — and *The Shadow-Line* — where the narrator's high opinion of himself is again reflected by the assumption that opposition must be demonic and supernatural — the emphasis undergoes a change.

In *Nostromo* there are three main areas in which the demonic is to the fore, two of them geographical. The Golfo Placido on cloudy nights is said to be so dark that 'The eye of God Himself . . . could not find out what work a man's hand is doing in there; and you would be free to call the devil to your aid with impunity if even his malice were not defeated by such a blind darkness' *(N*, 7); the San Tomé gorge is referred to as a 'paradise of snakes' *(N*, 105) and Nostromo maintains a suspicion, towards the latter half of the book, that Doctor Monygham is a representative of the devil. Such references can be seen to operate on different levels, the most obvious of which is the literal superstitious belief held by most of the uneducated inhabitants of Costaguana and detailed in the previous chapter. On this level Nostromo's view of the doctor as tempter can be seen to indicate the power of a pervading heritage to fill the vacuum left by the loss of his sense of importance. Indeed, like the 'barefooted multitude' he too proves not immune to priestly indoctrination:

> "I mean that the king of devils himself has sent you out of this town of cowards and talkers to meet me tonight of all the nights of my life."
> Under the starry sky the Albergo d'Italia Una emerged, black and low breaking the dark level of the plain. Nostromo stopped altogether.
> "The priests say he is a tempter, do they not?" he added, through his clenched teeth.
> "My good man, you drivel. The devil has nothing to do with this."
> (*N*, 462)

Monygham's denial questions the superstition and invites a less traditional interpretation. One of the reasons for Nostromo's accusation is that the doctor had already mentioned the idea of taking the whole treasure before Nostromo and Decoud set sail (*N*, 259). Nostromo storms, 'Maledetta! You follow me speaking of the treasure. You have sworn my ruin. You were the last man who looked upon me before I went out with it. And Sidoni the engine-driver says you have an evil eye' (*N*, 463).

The authority for Nostromo's assumptions, it will be noted, has now descended from the priests to Sidoni the engine-driver; sources that would have been despised by the Capataz of earlier times. The comments are made because the thought of stealing the treasure has already been planted; the demonic thus indicates the means of awakening what will become a destructive obsession and heralds the eventual downfall of the character. Monygham is identified as demonic by Nostromo, not for anything he represents or opposes, but for the effect his words achieve.

Nostromo's decline takes place in the blackness of the Golfo Placido where, supposedly, God and devil cannot operate. This saying, initially, simply indicates the extent of the darkness and seems ironic in its exclusion of the devil from what is traditionally his natural element. On another level it can mean that man in such a situation is entirely responsible for his actions since, here at least, he has no supernatural agency to praise or blame; the kind of attitude Monygham seems to have adopted. It could be said, therefore, that Nostromo is externalising a temptation that is wholly within himself; originating in his bruised vanity, perhaps (which goes back to ego again). A third interpretation could be that the events of the novel prove the saying to be incorrect and that Nostromo's invoking of 'the curse of Heaven' to 'fall upon this blind gulf' has been all too effective (*N*, 269). It could also indicate a place where faith is to receive its severest tests, which would have special relevance for Decoud.

After its appearance in the opening chapter, the saying re-occurs twice more (in quick succession) towards the end of the novel at a time when the blackness seems peculiarly connected with Nostromo. His admission to Giselle of having obtained treasure 'Like a thief!' causes 'The densest blackness of the Placid Gulf . . . to fall upon his head' (*N*, 540), and her acceptance of this circumstance is followed by the renewed reminder of darkness:

> The Capataz de Cargadores tasted the supreme intoxication of his generosity. He flung the mastered treasure superbly at her feet in the impenetrable darkness of the gulf, in the darkness defying – as men said – the knowledge of God and the wit of the devil. (*N*, 541)

The saying is then repeated as Giselle looks into 'the black night' (*N*, 543) for Nostromo to return to her. Nostromo now seems to live in darkness, therefore, so that even when he has returned to Giselle, the light in her room goes out as he clasps her (*N*, 545). This clearly reflects his internal condition. His ego must submit itself to the performance of 'that work of a craven slave!' (*N*, 542) and, by invoking the previous ego-devil equation, this may explain why his darkness defies 'the wit of the devil'. Certainly, the four interpretations of the saying could all be applied to Nostromo's state at this time. Nostromo's association of Monygham with the demonic can be seen not only as temptation but also as warning; the darkness is the result of the temptation being followed and the warning being ignored.

This double-definition can also be applied to the demonic imagery that Charles Gould encounters when Don Pepe introduces the San Tomé Gorge as 'the very paradise of snakes, senora' (*N*, 105). Literally this means that the gorge would be an ideal place for a snake to dwell but the Edenic overtones are inescapable. The concept of this phrase denoting a fallen world (the usual interpretation) is, however, relative-ly meaningless unless it is meant to indicate that the paradise envisaged by Charles Gould is foredoomed. The snake in Eden was a tempter but paradise was lost only when man yielded to the temptation. The San Tomé gorge thus presents the promise of paradise with the threat of the Fall through destructive temptations. The phrase is remembered later by Emilia:

> "We have disturbed a good many snakes in that Paradise, haven't we?"
>
> "Yes, I remember," said Charles Gould. "It was Don Pepe who called the gorge the Paradise of snakes. No doubt we have disturbed a great many. But remember, my dear, that it is not now as it was when you made that sketch. . . . It is no longer a Paradise of snakes. We have brought mankind into it, and we cannot turn our backs upon them to go and begin a new life elsewhere." (*N*, 209)

The obvious implications of this exchange are that the temptations have been succumbed to and the warning ignored. By the end of the book Emilia can see exactly where the invasion of this paradise has led:

> She saw the San Tomé mountain hanging over the Campo, over the whole land, feared, hated, wealthy; more soulless than any tyrant, more pitiless and autocratic than the worst Government; ready to crush innumerable lives in the expansion of its greatness. He did not see it. He could not see it. (*N*, 521)

Thus, 'she saw clearly the San Tomé mine possessing, consuming, burning up the life of the last of the Costaguana Goulds; mastering the energetic spirit of the son as it had mastered the lamentable weakness of the father' (*N*, 522).

Gould is thus a slave of the silver mine in the same way as Nostromo is a slave of his treasure; the legend of the two spectral gringos on Azuera applies to both men. Gould's entry into the San Tomé gorge is equivalent to Nostromo's meeting with Monygham; both events evoke demonic references indicating a fatal step by each character that will lead him to disaster though, whilst Nostromo is aware of his true position, Gould is not aware of his. It is not for nothing that the silver escort proceeds through the waking Sulaco 'from end to end without a check in the speed as if chased by a devil' (*N*, 114) for the San Tomé mine can, it seems, employ the diabolic arts of insidious possession.

The demonic is used most pervasively in *Under Western Eyes*. Here the terminology is attached to systems. Haldin uses language, biblically associated with hell, to describe the work of the man he has killed when he talks of 'the sound of weeping and gnashing of teeth this man raised in the land' (*UWE*, 16), and Tekla's hatred for the Ministry of Finance is similarly expressed. Tekla comments, 'Upon my word, I would think that finances and all the rest of it are an invention of the devil; only that a belief in a supernatural source of evil is not necessary; men alone are quite capable of every wickedness' (*UWE*, 151).

The demonic here is that which causes oppression and ruins lives, though Tekla's use of the conditional is significant; she, at least, will not lift responsibility from man himself. Autocracy, which attracts these comments, follows the now familiar Conradian pattern of having deistic pretensions to sanction its activities. Mr de P— declares that 'God was the Autocrat of the Universe' (*UWE*, 8); Razumov's decision to aid the authorities is described as a religious conversion (*UWE*, 33–4); and the teacher of languages notes that 'Whenever two Russians come together, the shadow of autocracy is with them' (*UWE*, 107), this being a cruel parody of Christ's promise to be present 'when two or three are gathered together in my name' (Matt. 18:20). Autocracy appears to be present whether the gathering is in its name or not.

Revolution, however, makes similar claims. Haldin's mother regards his friends as 'disciples' and remembers that 'Even amongst the Apostles of Christ there was found a Judas' (*UWE*, 115); Madame de S— can anticipate revolutionary triumph in biblical terms (*UWE*, 223); and Peter Ivanovitch is likened to a missionary (*UWE*, 129) and 'a monk or a prophet' (*UWE*, 329), though it takes 'half a dozen young men' to come together 'in a shabby student's room' before one can be sure of his name being mentioned (*UWE*, 227).

But the realities of revolution have very quickly undermined such high-flying claims. To Haldin, Ziemianitch is a 'bright soul' but when Razumov enquires for him he finds that he is also regarded as a 'cursed driver of thieves' and as 'that driver of the devil' (*UWE*, 28). Ziemianitch is to be found in 'a long cavernous place like a neglected subterranean byre' (*UWE*, 29), where Razumov's guide explains:

> A proper Russian driver that. Saint or devil, night or day is all one to Ziemianitch when his heart is free from sorrow. "I don't ask who you are, but where you want to go," he says. He would drive Satan

himself to his own abode and come back chirruping to his horses.
(*UWE*, 29)

These conflicting views of Ziemianitch set to question Haldin's idealistic claims for the revolutionary movement for, if Ziemianitch will drive 'saint or devil,' in which of these categories does Haldin come? On leaving the eating-house, Razumov regards him as 'a subtle pest that would convert earth into hell' (*UWE*, 32), which is the kind of comment Haldin made about Mr de P—, but Razumov is chiefly thinking of the effects on his own life here (egoistical concern revealed by assumed demonic opposition again). Just as the cause of revolution will later persuade Kostia to break the commandment concerning theft (with an appropriate cry of 'to the devil with the ten commandments' [*UWE*, 313]), it has provoked Haldin, who 'wouldn't hurt a fly' (*UWE*, 22), to break the commandment concerning murder. This augurs badly for revolution which, in opposing obvious tyranny, has to deviate from the rules of commonly accepted morality. The higher the pretensions, it seems, the greater the potential for destructive results.

Ziemianitch hangs himself not long after Haldin's death but the devil continues to hover about his person as Sophia Antonovna complains about the illogical absurdity of the people:

"For instance — that Ziemianitch was notoriously irreligious, and yet, in the last weeks of his life, he suffered from the notion that he had been beaten by the devil."

"The devil," repeated Razumov, as though he had not heard aright.

"The actual devil. The devil in person . . . "

"But you, Sophia Antonovna, you don't believe in the actual devil?"

"Do you?" retorted the woman curtly. "Not but that there are plenty of men worse than devils to make a hell of this earth."

(*UWE*, 280–1)

The devil in this case is Razumov who had beaten the drunken sledge-driver in 'a weird scene' when possessed by 'A terrible fury — the blind rage of self-preservation' (*UWE*, 30); the most fundamental example of the ego coming to the fore. This association of the devil with Razumov is not new either. Earlier in the book he has restrained a 'diabolical impulse' to tell Haldin what he has done (*UWE*, 55),

ironically since such an impulse would have him telling the truth. Soon afterwards he avoids with difficulty 'a burst of Mephistophelian laughter' (*UWE*, 60) and, following the search of his room by the police, hears Kostia's verdict that 'A man doesn't get the police ransacking his rooms without there being some devilry hanging over his head' (*UWE*, 81). When he is with Peter Ivanovitch he has 'a satanic enjoyment of the scorn prompting him to play with the greatness of the great man' (*UWE*, 228), whilst, with Sophia Antonovna, he feels 'an infernal circle
bringing round that protest like a fatal necessity of his existence' and regards her news of Ziemianitch's death as 'a perfect diabolic surprise' (*UWE*, 280). He is ironically amused that all is now well for him 'Thanks to the devil' (*UWE*, 283):

> It was as if the devil himself were playing a game with all of them in turn. First with him, then with Ziemianitch, then with those revolutionists. The devil's own game this. ... He interrupted his earnest mental soliloquy with a jocular thought at his own expense. "Hallo! I am falling into mysticism too."   (*UWE*, 283–4)

What is happening at this stage is that the lie Razumov is living is becoming more and more secure and, since the perpetuation of falsehood is a traditional role of the devil, the evocation of the demonic is entirely appropriate here. It is similarly fitting for the bearer of the news concerning Ziemianitch, Sophia Antonovna, to have 'Mephistophelian eyebrows' (*UWE*, 245, 247) and a 'Mephistophelian frown' (*UWE*, 253), though the narrator is struck by 'the quaint Mephistophelian character of her inquiring glance because it was so curiously evil-less, so – I may say – un-devilish' (*UWE*, 327).[8] She is Mephistophelian because she encourages the continuance of the lie and 'un-devilish' because she does so unwittingly. This note of demonic temptation is continued by the narrator when considering the meetings between Razumov and Mikulin:

> To the morality of a Western reader an account of these meetings would wear perhaps the sinister character of old legendary tales where the Enemy of Mankind is represented holding subtly mendacious dialogues with some tempted soul. It is not my part to protest. Let me but remark that the Evil One, with his single passion of satanic pride for the only motive, is yet, on a larger modern view, allowed to be not quite so black as he used to be painted. With what

greater latitude, then, should we appraise the exact shade of mere
mortal man, with his many passions and his miserable ingenuity in
error, always dazzled by the base glitter of mixed motives, everlastingly betrayed by a short-sighted wisdom.   (*UWE*, 304–5)

This accords, in some respects, with the views of Tekla and Sophia
Antonovna that man can be evil enough on his own without supernatural assistance. Pride, of course, is a further manifestation of ego.

Even the teacher of languages is not free of demonic associations (in
Razumov's eyes, at least). In his letter to Natalia, Razumov writes:

He talked of you, of your lonely, helpless state, and every word of
that friend of yours was egging me on to the unpardonable sin of
stealing a soul. Could he have been the devil himself in the shape of
an old Englishman? Natalia Victorovna, I was possessed!
                                                              (*UWE*, 360)

As in *Nostromo* then, one of the functions of the demonic here is to act
as a link between a character and his destructive activities. Razumov
regards Haldin's remark that his sister has trusting eyes as meaning
that she is 'a predestined victim. . . . Ha! what a devilish suggestion'
(*UWE*, 349) and in this crucial scene with Natalia he continues with the
idea of being led by the devil:

You know, Natalia Victorovna, I have the greatest difficulty in
saving myself from the superstition of an active Providence. It's
irresistible. ... The alternative, of course, would be the personal
Devil of our simple ancestors. But, if so, he has overdone it altogether – the old Father of lies – our national patron – our domestic
god, whom we take with us when we go abroad. He has overdone it.
It seems that I am not simple enough.   (*UWE*, 350)

Sophia Antonovna thinks of a more practical source when she meets
the narrator after the drama is over:

Well, call it what you like; but tell me, how many of them would
deliver themselves up deliberately to perdition (as he himself says in
that book) rather than go on living, secretly debased in their own
eyes? . . . It was just when he believed himself safe and more –
infinitely more – when the possibility of being loved by that admir-

able girl first dawned upon him, that he discovered that his bitterest railings, the worst wickedness, the devil work of his hate and pride, could never cover up the ignominy of the existence before him.

(*UWE*, 380)

According to Sophia, therefore, the devil possessing Razumov is 'hate and pride' and such is Russia that even to escape the possession is to finish up in perdition. The tempter figures that Razumov encounters are thus externalisations of his own negative emotions; reflections, one could say, of his inner state and indications of the destructive path he is following.

In some ways the confession scene between Razumov and Natalia is a reversal of Marlow's interview with the Intended in 'Heart of Darkness'. Marlow had spoken in that book of his abhorrence of lies which had 'a taint of death, a flavour of mortality . . . which is exactly what I hate and detest in the world − which I want to forget. It makes me miserable and sick, like biting something rotten would do' (*Y*, 82). Having said this, of course, he ends his narrative with a description of his lie to the Intended so she can continue to live with her illusions of Mr Kurtz; he is forced into it by the power of her belief. Razumov, who has been living a lie throughout most of *Under Western Eyes*, is forced into truth by the power of Natalia Haldin's trusting honesty and the initial effect on her is akin to what Marlow must have feared would happen if he revealed the truth about Kurtz. Much of the demonic in *Under Western Eyes*, therefore, is connected with falsehood from the Father of Lies and we have already seen how Sophia Antonovna and the teacher of languages are unwittingly demonic in aiding the lie; perhaps the narrator rages 'like a disappointed devil' because the lie is no more (*UWE*, 361). It is safe to assert that Conrad would also have hated the concept of a lie since the very idea of falsehood is antithetical to the simple notion of Fidelity that he claimed to cherish so much. The comments of Tekla, Sophia Antonovna and the professor of languages thus serve as a warning to the reader that the demonic references should not be taken literally. Such references have associations with 'irrational' modes of behaviour according to some critics and this is a useful term to have in mind when considering the conduct of Conrad's characters when in the throes of their obsessions.[9] Irrationality, then, can be accepted as a condition of the demonic; faithlessness as its likely result.

Conrad's attitude to falsehood carries over into his letters and seems particularly to have affected his sense of artistic integrity. This sense appeared to be offended by the thought of writing for money; so much so that (as was noted in chapter three) he refers to this process on a number of occasions, as selling his soul to the devil. When the 'noble metals' came, the author was still able to maintain that 'because I have not enough satanism in my nature I can't enjoy it'.[10]

Even jokingly, such comments reveal some embarrassment at apparent instances of infidelity to the writer's creed that the image of a bargain with the devil is meant to reflect. The falseness that attracts the demonic imagery in *Under Western Eyes* is, thus, also evident (though with less intensity) within the author's letters.

In *Chance* and *Victory*, Conrad's focus changes from the social obsessions of their three predecessors to obsessions relating to self-conception and the demonic imagery is adapted accordingly to reveal life-negating attitudes on the part of Conrad's protagonists.

In *Chance*, the demonic is quickly invoked as young Powell describes with what desperation he attempted to obtain his first berth as second mate. He would, he reports, 'have gone boldly up to the devil himself on the mere hint that he had a second mate's job to give away' (*C*, 7); a sentiment that he repeats twice more in connection with his namesake Powell at the shipping office. This is a strange image really since boldness is not the traditional demeanour for approaching the devil. Young Powell explains that 'I never believed in the devil enough to be scared of him; but a man can make himself very unpleasant' (*C*, 10).

Since Powell (in the shipping office) is by no means demonic, young Powell's emphasis is curious, signifying an ominous desperation on his part which could lead to disaster. As it happens, it leads to the *Ferndale*, to which he is later assisted by a 'little devil' (*C*, 27, 28). Young Powell's phraseology here is perhaps meant as a warning, as a harbinger of what is to come, for the demonic presides on the vessel (not intentionally, but in effect), in the form of Anthony's excessive magnanimity which causes him to commit (in Marlow's words) 'a sin against life, the call of which is simple. Perhaps sacred' (*C*, 427). Part of the saloon has been 'consecrated to the exclusiveness of Captain Anthony's married life' (*C*, 410) but Anthony is not performing the rites (consummation of marriage) for which the saloon has been consecrated. Marlow comments, 'One may fling a glove in the face of nature and in the face of one's own moral endurance quite innocently, with a simplicity which wears the aspect of perfectly Satanic conceit' (*C*, 351). Conrad had written about 'fidelity to nature' and the tragedy of 'consciousness' to Cunninghame Graham some years before. Anthony is clearly conscious of nature, just as he is unfaithful to it.

The demonic operates at key points in the setting up of the situation on the *Ferndale*. The 'unholy prestige' of Flora's governess (*C*, 263) has convinced Flora that she is unlovable whilst the 'demon of bitterness' that has entered Little Fyne has persuaded Anthony that he is taking advantage of the girl and that she cannot love him. Marlow emphasises the spirit in which Fyne has conducted his argument by commenting that 'the possibilities of dull men are exciting because when they happen they suggest legendary cases of "possession" not exactly by the devil but, anyhow, by a strange spirit' (*C*, 251).

Such imagery has not been absent from de Barral's plight either; his ill-advised excursion into Thrift being accompanied by the press 'screeching in all possible tones, like a confounded company of parrots instructed by some devil with a taste for practical jokes' (*C*, 74). These inauspicious omens lead him to prison which is equated with the 'Nether Regions' by Marlow and with 'a real hell' by Anthony (*C*, 347). Once released and on board, de Barral is shunned by the crew of the *Ferndale* 'as if he had been the devil' (*C*, 351). Since it is his extreme egoism that demands Flora's exclusive attention, even to the extent of trying to poison Anthony, the comment has some point.

The demonic nature of the strange arrangement is emphasised by the complaints of Franklin, the mate:

> He begged Powell to understand that if Captain Anthony chose to strike a bargain with Old Nick tomorrow, and Old Nick were good to the captain, he (Franklin) would find it in his heart to love Old Nick for the captain's sake. That was so. On the other hand, if a saint, an angel with white wings came along and —
>
> He broke off short again as if his own vehemence had frightened him. (*C*, 301–2)

In a sense, of course, Anthony has made a bargain with 'Old Nick' since his excessive magnanimity stems from his 'Satanic conceit'.

The unnatural lack of normal marital relations, which defies nature and negates life, is thus equated with the demonic in *Chance*. Again egoism is at the root of the arrangement for Anthony's vanity is described as 'immense' and he has been 'touched to the quick' by Fyne (*C*, 332). It has led him, though, to deny life and this form of devilry is taken to its logical extreme in *Victory*.

Demonic identification is nowhere as explicit as with Mr Jones who represents a total negation of life. His abhorrence of women prevents any chance of procreation on his part whilst the fact that he is a cold-blooded murderer means that his negation is an active one. He will not help to create, only destroy. Even Gentleman Brown (whose arrival in Jim's Patusan Jones's invasion of Samburan so closely resembles) was no misogynist; Jones's total negativity is in a class of its own. He is directly equated with the devil by Heyst:

> Having been ejected, he said, from his proper social sphere because he had refused to conform to certain usual conventions, he was a rebel now, and was coming and going up and down the earth. As I really did not want to listen to all this nonsense, I told him that I had heard that sort of story about somebody else before. His grin is really ghastly. He confessed that I was very far from the sort of man he expected to meet. Then he said:
> "As to me, I am no blacker than the gentleman you are thinking of, and I have neither more nor less determination." (*V*, 317–18)

Here is demonic opposition once again which, on this occasion, reflects the life-negating doctrine which Heyst has adopted. Heyst's negation is passive (non-involvement) and benign but the scepticism that forms his attitude reaches its logical extreme in Jones's total nihilism. As Lena is dying, Heyst bends low over her, 'cursing his fastidious soul, which even at that moment kept the true cry of love from his lips in its infernal mistrust of all life' (*V*, 406). Heyst's attitude is also connected with the demonic, therefore, and in this respect there is point to the many devil references in the novel that are aimed at Heyst himself. Even Morrison wonders at one stage whether Heyst has been sent by the devil (*V*, 17) and both Schomberg's comment − 'He's turned Hermit from shame. That's what the devil does when he's found out' (*V*, 31) − and Heyst's own remark that action 'is devilish' (*V*, 54) can be seen as ironic: Schomberg's because, in a special sense, he is right (though he means only abuse), Heyst's because it is really lack of action that is devilish.

Schomberg himself, who negates life by his 'diabolical calumny' (*V*, 381) which can 'dry-rot the soul' (*V*, 362) has at times 'a sort of Satanic glee' (*V*, 93); the association of the demonic with falsehood is thus once more emphasised. When Jones arrives at the hotel this means that two kinds of life-negating forces meet and the demonic imagery intensifies when Schomberg mentions his wife:

"I wish you would carry her off with you to the devil! I wouldn't run after you."

The unexpected outburst affected Mr Jones strangely. He had a horrific recoil, chair and all, as if Schomberg had thrust a wriggling viper in his face.

"What's this infernal nonsense?" he muttered thickly . . . .

Schomberg, raising his eyes, at last met the gleams in the two dark caverns under Mr Jones's devilish eyebrows, directed upon him impenetrably. He shuddered as if horrors worse than murder had been lurking there, and said, nodding towards Ricardo:

"I dare say he wouldn't think twice about sticking me, if he had you at his back. . . . Ah, well, I've been already living in hell for weeks, so you don't make much difference."   (*V*, 114–15)

In a way Schomberg is, indeed, in hell but not as he implies. His lies and calumnies brand him as demonic; he is therefore living there as one of the devils. He sees himself as a suffering victim but he has created this situation entirely by himself by his egotistical and ludicrous assumption that he would be attractive to Lena. Part of his problem is the elevated manner in which he regards his table d'hôte, for he enters the dining-room 'as if into a temple, very grave, with the air of a benefactor of mankind' (*V*, 27) and his dislike of Heyst is largely based on the Swede's infrequent patronage. Thus for Schomberg, 'Whenever three people came together in his hotel, he took good care that Heyst should be with them' (*V*, 27), which, as a perversion of Christ's promise, can be said to have its roots in devilry; in this case combined with the familiar accompaniment of an excessive egoism. Heyst's rescue of Lena is naturally the final affront; the music room which has previously harboured 'an unholy fascination in systematic noise' (*V*, 68) is now described as 'desecrated' by the card tables of Mr Jones (*V*, 121). Negation attracts negation.

Martin Ricardo is another life-negating character whose instincts carry him towards rape (a perversion of the procreative function) and murder. He is also equated with the devil when he reveals that, in playing cards, he 'would play them for their souls' (*V*, 149) and, later, when Lena regards him as 'the viper' in her paradise (*V*, 399). It is an ironic inversion, therefore, that the guidance for Mr Jones and his henchmen to reach Heyst's island should be 'a pillar of smoke by day and a loom of fire at night' (*V*, 168) since this is similar to the way the Israelites were led out of Egypt (Exodus 13:21).

This sense of a life-negating attitude being devilish is carried through into *The Arrow of Gold*, though there is more emphasis here on the condition of a victim of this obsession rather than on the outlook itself. Jones immoderately shunned women; three of the characters of *The Arrow of Gold* immoderately pursue one particular woman — Rita de Lastaola — and the obsession makes them devilish and damned.

Rita, described as having 'the finer immobility, almost sacred, of a fateful figure seated at the very source of the passions that have moved men from the dawn of ages' (*AG*, 146), is almost regarded as a goddess figure by some of her admirers. M. George becomes a follower of this cult which he likens to 'some strange wild faiths that get hold of mankind with the cruel mystic grip of unattainable perfection, robbing them of both liberty and felicity on earth' (*AG*, 140). This veneration leads him to a night which is 'the abomination of desolation' (*AG*,154); an apocalyptic image which echoes an earlier one by J. M. K. Blunt that 'the end is not yet' (*AG*, 38). It is certainly bleak enough for George as he lies in 'that purgatory of hopeless longing and unanswerable questions to which I was condemned' (*AG*, 155).

M. George, then, endures purgatory but Ortega, one of Rita's other worshippers, suffers still more. He is, it seems, the logical extension of the cult of female attraction and the imagery that surrounds him is the imagery of hell. To M. George, Ortega gazes at him 'in a way in which the damned gaze out of their cauldrons of boiling pitch at some soul walking scot free in the place of torment' (*AG*, 271), for Ortega's soul is 'absent in some hell of its own.' Since George is willing to entertain thoughts of killing Ortega, it is clear that he too is dangerously close to the 'facile descent into the abyss' (*AG*, 276), and with the description of Ortega as 'an extraordinarily chilly devil' comes an appropriately warning apocalyptic image with the 'sickly gas flame' which 'was there on duty, undaunted, waiting for the end of the world to come and put it out' (*AG*, 277).

The ultimate fate of those who worship eternal woman is, thus, to become a 'damned soul' (*AG*, 310). Ortega finally attempts (but fails) to commit suicide (just as Conrad did it seems), whilst M. George is wounded in a duel with Blunt (just as Conrad claimed, it seems). For both Ortega and George the obsession with Rita has led almost to death. This obsession is also responsible, perhaps, for Blunt appearing 'positively satanic' (*AG*, 37) and knitting his brows 'very devilishly indeed' (*AG*, 38) as he relates Rita's story; it is certainly the cause of his duel with George.

It is, however, the sanctimonious and superstitious Therese who is most preoccupied with the devil, though it is George who first provokes her:

> "But you are very brave," I chaffed her, "for you didn't expect a ring, and after all it might have been the devil who pulled the bell."
> "It might have been. But a poor girl like me is not afraid of the devil. I have a pure heart. I have been to confession last evening."
> (*AG*, 137–8)

Therese has heard of a murder committed:

> "That's what carnal sin . . . leads to," she commented, severely and passed her tongue over her thin lips. "And then the devil furnishes the occasion."
> "I can't imagine the devil inciting me to murder you, Therese," I said, "and I didn't like that ready way you took me for an example, as it were." (*AG*, 138)

As has been seen, George is to contemplate murder later in the book.

Therese is convinced that Rita is evil (*AG*, 158) and advises George to make 'a practice of crossing yourself directly you open your eyes. . . . It keeps Satan off for the day' (*AG*, 159); intimating, perhaps, that George needs something to keep his obsession at bay. Later she reports, 'I said to her, "Rita, have you sold your soul to the Devil?" and she laughed like a fiend: "For happiness! Ha, ha, ha!" . . . She is possessed' (*AG*, 235). In the same outburst Rose (Rita's faithful servant) is accused of being 'leagued with the Devil.'

These again may be more than simply fanatical rantings, for the effects of Allègre's aesthetic but ultimately sterile world, (epitomised by the lifeless dummy which, like Rita, once gave service as the empress of Byzantium [*AG*, 21–2, 26]) and the ephemeral relationships Rita has observed thereafter have made her deeply suspicious of any kind of emotional attachment. Madame Leonore is correct when she pronounces that 'She is for no man' (*AG*, 135) and Rita's ringing of the bell just as she and George are sinking into an embrace emphasises her apprehensions of such a relationship (*AG*, 219–20). Rita is indeed possessed, therefore; possessed by the fear of succumbing to love and this fear can be seen to be life-negating since there will be no issue and certainly no happiness.

One can also say that M. George is deluding himself when he

remarks, 'It is only the Devil, they say, that loves logic. But I was not a devil. I was not even a victim of the Devil' (*AG*, 283). He is a victim of his own obsession and of Rita's rejection of life and love; both (figuratively) aspects of the devil that are highlighted by Ortega's claims that she is 'perdition' and 'more fit to be Satan's wife' (*AG*, 318). Rita carries her denial of life through to the end by leaving George once he is recovering from his duel with Blunt.

A more positive outlook is realised by Arlette in *The Rover*, of whom it is also said that 'She is for no man' (*Ro*, 225). She, at least, is able to escape the life-denying spell that has possessed her; indeed she can almost recognise the nature of the possession:

"And what if I have been possessed," she argued to herself, "as the abbé said, what is it to me as I am now? That evil spirit cast my true self out of my body and then cast away the body too. For years I have been living empty. There has been no meaning in anything."
(*Ro*, 159)

Basically, then, demonic imagery in Conrad's novels indicates a destructive outlook, characteristic, obsession or passion. It is used to reveal an excessive or unrestrained egoism by demonic identification or association (Wait, Podmore, Kurtz and Brown), by demonic possession (Willems) or by demonic opposition (Lingard, Jim and the narrator of *The Shadow-Line*); such usage frequently being combined with aspects of deification, either by the character or by others (Wait, Podmore, Willems, Lingard, Jim, Kurtz and the systems of autocracy and revolution). It can also denote an immoderate passion (Willems, Ortega and George), a cruel and selfish stupidity or mania (the pilgrims in 'Heart of Darkness') or a life-negating doctrine or obsession (in *Chance*, *Victory* and *The Arrow of Gold*). It acts as a link between savagery and civilisation and between reality and illusion in 'Heart of Darkness', and between a character and his obsession (in the form of catalyst or temptation) in *Nostromo* and *Under Western Eyes*. It can also act as a warning of future calamity (as it does for *Lord Jim*, *Nostromo* and *Chance*); as an epithet for the cause of oppression (*Under Western Eyes*); or as the externalisation of a character's destructive inner compulsions (Nostromo and Razumov). It is, finally, inseparable from falsehood (Razumov and Schomberg), infidelity (Willems) and irrationality (in most of the novels) and its effects are generally destructive or disruptive.

THE SOUL AND THE WILL

With such an extensive use of demonic imagery to accompany the destructive elements of his fiction, it is hardly surprising that the part of man that seems to suffer most as a result is his soul. This, too, is sometimes used in its literal theological sense (at least, characters such as Podmore would have that intention). The word is also used without deep meaning in such phrases as 'not a soul' where it simply indicates a human absence. The word had a number of meanings at the time Conrad was writing but generally retained the sense of being a spiritual or animating element.

Most of Conrad's readers, then, would have a vague idea of soul as some part of man, separate from mind and body, apparently transcending both. If they were of a literal turn of mind then Conrad's novels would seem to show man's soul being entrapped by the devil; if not, then some vital life force within man would appear to be at the mercy of his excessive egoism or his destructive obsessions. When Willems tells Lingard, 'If you want to drive my soul into damnation by trying to drive me to suicide you will not succeed,' he is using the term literally in this remembrance of Catholic doctrine (*OI*, 278). But his relationship with Aïssa is described as a loss of soul and clearly the word here means something a little different:

> Pressing against him she stood on tiptoe to look into his eyes, and her own seemed to grow bigger, glistening and tender, appealing and promising. With that look she drew the man's soul away from him through his immobile pupils, and from Willems' features the spark of reason vanished under her gaze and was replaced by an appearance of physical well-being, an ecstacy of the senses which had taken possession of his rigid body; an ecstacy that drove out regrets, hesitation and doubt, and proclaimed its terrible work by an appalling aspect of idiotic beatitude.   (*OI*, 140)

It is whilst he is in this position that Willems seems to see a vision of himself moving away (*OI*, 145) and is aware of the murderous approach of the blind Omar without being able to take any evasive action (*OI*, 149–50). Even the instinct for self-preservation, then (usually the most powerful of egoistical drives), is subservient to the immoderate sexual passion to which he has succumbed.

Bruce Johnson calls his chapter on Conrad's first two novels 'The Paralysis of Will' (referring to Schopenhauer for an understanding of the term),[11] and the will could indeed serve as a synonym for soul in this extract. The passion of Dain Maroola for Nina is described in almost identical fashion:

> She drew back her head and fastened her eyes on his in one of those long looks that are a woman's most terrible weapon; a look that is more stirring than the closest touch, and more dangerous than the thrust of a dagger, because it also whips the soul out of the body, but leaves the body alive and helpless, to be swayed here and there by the capricious tempests of passion and desire; a look that enwraps the whole body, and that penetrates into the innermost recesses of the being, bringing terrible defeat in the delirious uplifting of accomplished conquest. (*AF*, 171)

Little wonder that Dain should say to Nina soon after, 'I have delivered my soul into your hands' (*AF*, 178); she is his source of motivation just as Aïssa is for Willems. Almayer is in a similar plight since his daughter is 'that small and unconscious particle of humanity that seemed to him to contain all his soul' (*OI*, 320). His action of having sold himself to Lingard could be said to come under the same heading. The use of the word 'soul' reflects the totality of the man's passion or obsession; the completeness of his captivity. He is no longer an independent being; his whole view of life is seen by way of the woman he adores and it is his will that becomes subject to her domination since he can no longer conceive of any action or ambition that is not related to her. It is this circumstance that makes Ortega a 'damned soul' and M. George confess that 'The soul was already a captive before doubt, anguish, or dismay could touch its surrender and its exaltation' (*AG*, 124).

With different shades of application this definition of soul as will can be applied widely throughout the canon, but before noting the variations one must look carefully at the terms. Will usually denotes determination, desire or the power of conscious choice; clearly overcome in the foregoing instances with disastrous results (only Dain does not suffer from surrendering his soul to a woman). Bruce Johnson's invoking of Schopenhauer, however, brings a far more comprehensive concept of will to the fore, for Schopenhauer felt that 'all that directly constitutes our own weal and woe, desire and aversion, is clearly only affection of the will, is an excitation, a modification, of willing and non-willing, is just that which, if it takes outward effect, exhibits itself in an act of will proper.'[12] To Schopenhauer the will was the 'thing-in-itself';[13] its true operation being seen only in action since 'It is only in reflection that to will and to act are different; in reality they are one.'[14]

The form of the action depended on incentives, the chief of which was egoism, but Schopenhauer identified three fundamental causes for human deeds, claiming that 'all possible motives operate solely through their stimulation' and detailing them as follows:

(a) Egoism: this desires one's own weal (is boundless).
(b) Malice: this desires another's woe (goes to the limits of extreme cruelty).
(c) Compassion: this desires another's weal (goes to the length of nobleness and magnanimity).

>   Every human action must be attributable to one of these incentives, although two can also act in combination.[15]

The intellect seems to have been regarded as an 'instrument' of the will; a provider of information upon which action might be based but not capable itself of independent decisions. The will is thus likened to 'the strong blind man who carries on his shoulder the lame man who can see'.[16]

Johnson likens Conrad's 'ego' to Schopenhauer's 'will'[17] but in that case ego would not only be the source of man's prime incentive but also become the thing-in-itself, a transcendental reality, independent of time, space and causality. Neither 'will' nor 'ego' appears with any frequency in Conrad's works; in *Lord Jim*, for example, 'will' is noted only ten times other than as an auxiliary verb and 'ego' does not feature at all (though we have seen that Marlow mentions 'egoism' in respect of Brown). In contrast, 'soul' appears on 45 occasions and 'devil' on 49.[18]

Conrad (as was noted earlier) felt that egoism was 'the moving force of the world', which suggests his acceptance of it as man's prime and most potent source of motivation. The Conradian model would thus have 'soul' as 'will', urged initially (and inevitably) by egoism, tempered (ideally) by altruism and enlightened by the intellect. The portrait of Gentleman Brown implies that, under Conrad's scheme of things, malice is bound up with 'intense egoism' and is not separate (as it is in Schopenhauer). Compassion is included under altruism, whose source is external, but several characters (Anthony in particular) fall into difficulties because what they take to be altruism is actually subtle egoism.

When egoism and altruism have been enlightened and work in

conjunction with each other, this combination produces a healthy soul (or will) which is relatively detached and able to make balanced decisions. Such a balance becomes affected when some aspect of the ego achieves dominance (as it does with Jim) or when the source of enlightenment (the intellect) acts upon a false premise (as it does in the cases of Flora de Barral and Heyst). In these circumstances the actions directed by the soul (or will) become circumscribed or controlled by the assumption or false premise which has become an obsession, overwhelming the intellect and pervading every motivation produced by the ego.

Schopenhauer speaks only occasionally of the 'so-called soul'[19] and concentrates on the will which he regards as a 'vital force',[20] as 'the core of our true being',[21] as being sole possessor of 'a metaphysical reality by virtue whereof it is indestructible through death'[22] – all of which, in other eyes, would describe the soul. His separation of 'will' and 'intellect' is followed by Marlow who, on finding that Kurtz has left the cabin, feels 'as if something altogether monstrous, intolerable to thought and odious to the soul, had been thrust upon me' (*Y*, 141). Kurtz's conduct is 'odious to the soul' (or will) because Marlow is reluctant (or unwilling) to accept it, and the seaman attempts 'to break the spell – the heavy mute spell of the wilderness – that seemed to draw him to its pitiless breast by the awakening of forgotten and brutal instincts, by the memory of gratified and monstrous passions', reasoning that 'This alone . . . had beguiled his unlawful soul beyond the bounds of permitted aspirations' (*Y*, 144). Instincts, passions and aspirations are all recognisable urges; thus far the equation seems to fit. And, as Marlow carefully considers the state of Kurtz's soul, he once more clearly distinguishes it from the intellect:

> Soul! If anybody had ever struggled with a soul, I am the man. And I wasn't arguing with a lunatic either. Believe me or not, his intelligence was perfectly clear – concentrated, it is true, upon himself with horrible intensity, yet clear; and therein was my only chance. . . . But his soul was mad. Being alone in the wilderness, it had looked within itself, and, by heavens! I tell you, it had gone mad. I had – for my sins, I suppose – to go through the ordeal of looking into it myself. No eloquence could have been so withering to one's belief in mankind as his final burst of sincerity. He struggled with himself, too. I saw it – I heard it. I saw the inconceivable mystery of a soul that knew no restraint, no faith, and no fear, yet struggled blindly with itself. (*Y*, 144–5)

What is confusing Marlow at this point is that Kurtz is not just the benign (though egotistical) idealist he set out to be or the ruthless ivory hunter partaking in unspeakable native rites that he has become; he is both. The struggle within Kurtz is caused by two opposing aspects of will and the apparent insanity of this inner force stems from the irreconcilability of his conflicting desires. This is even more evident when Marlow adds:

> The shade of the original Kurtz frequented the hollow sham, whose fate it was to be buried presently in the mould of primitive earth. But both the diabolic love and the unearthly hate of the mysteries it had penetrated fought for the possession of that soul satiated with primitive emotions, avid of lying fame, of sham distinction, of all the appearances of success and power. (*Y*, 147–8)

It is, then, Kurtz's will, his ability to determine a course of action, that has been 'sealed' to the wilderness 'by the inconceivable ceremonies of some devilish initiation' (*Y*, 115). It follows that, if an aspiring angel can become a fiend when civilised restraints have been removed, this fate must be possible for all of us; this is what L. Feder calls 'the potential hell in the heart of every man.'[23]

Theologically Kurtz's internal battle reflects a sense of guilt, engendered by conscience and harrowing his tempted soul (man's inner reality). Figuratively it reveals a clash between intentions and desires derived from competing motivations. Kurtz's final cry, 'The horror! The horror!' (*Y*, 149), which Marlow considers as 'a judgement upon the adventures of his soul on this earth' (*Y*, 150), can thus be regarded as the idealistic side of Kurtz's will commenting on the overwhelming temptation (motivation) of the wilderness that has controlled his plans and actions among the natives; a recognition of man's primitive heritage co-existing with his civilised present.

Schopenhauer's idea of will does not fit here since, within his philosophy, man 'can *wish* two opposing actions, but will only one of them. Only the act reveals to his self-consciousness which of the two he wills'.[24] Conrad's 'soul', then, is closer to 'will' in the dictionary sense of power of choice – neither as all-embracing nor as directing as Schopenhauer's term. It is under this lesser definition that 'will' serves to define 'soul' in 'Heart of Darkness'. Kurtz 'had the power to charm or frighten rudimentary souls into an aggravated witch-dance in his honour . . . ' – which suggests the primitive, uncultivated nature of the natives (a very basic volition in other words) − 'he could also fill the small souls of the pilgrims with bitter misgivings . . . ' − indicating the narrow fixation for ivory and personal aggrandisement that forms their only motivation − 'and he had conquered one soul in the world that was neither rudimentary nor tainted with self-seeking' (*Y*, 119) − presumably the Intended, although it could also be the harlequin. The Intended has 'a soul as translucently pure as a cliff of crystal' (*Y*, 151–2), and its 'salvation' (*Y*, 156) is the cause of Marlow's lie, which enables her to retain her idealistic volition; her will is not exposed to the knowledge of primitive motivations. Thus, when Marlow talks of making 'a bargain for his soul with the devil' (*Y*, 117), this evocation of the Faustian legend need not simply be interpreted in its traditional fashion, but may also indicate the subjugation of one's will (the soul) for egoistical gain at the bidding of an unrestrained or excessive egoism (the devil).

   Soul as 'will' does prove capable of general application. When Jim's dreams 'carried his soul away with them and made it drunk with the divine philtre of an unbounded confidence in itself' (*LJ*, 20), this means that his romantic egoism is directing his will and laying down the path it should follow. When the instinct for survival momentarily (and disastrously) obtrudes on these desires, it is this frustrated will that writhes within him (*LJ*, 32), and causes Marlow to feel that 'he was only speaking before me, in a dispute with an invisible partner of his existence − another possessor of his soul' (*LJ*, 93). When the crew of the *Patna* push 'with all the might of their souls' (*LJ*, 104), this represents a total commitment on their part; mind, body and will. Similarly, when Nostromo returns to Sulaco after leaving Decoud and the treasure on the Great Isabel, he is fearful of being seen because 'With his own knowledge possessing his whole soul, it seemed impossible that anybody in Sulaco should fail to jump at the right surmise' (*N*, 424). Knowledge thus governs behaviour here and continues to do so throughout the remainder of the book. When he goes to ask Giorgio for the hand of Giselle, he cannot frame the words because 'neither dead nor alive . . . he belonged body and soul to the unlawfulness of his audacity' (*N*, 531). His freedom of choice (free-will) is thus confined and he allows himself to be affianced to Linda, which prompts Giorgio to decide that 'the soul of the dead is satisfied' (*N*, 532), it being Teresa's wish (or will) that Nostromo and Linda should marry. Finally the soul of Nostromo is said to die within him as he finds that he cannot even reveal the whereabouts of the treasure to Giselle (*N*, 542); he is truly its slave since it controls his will.

This reading can be applied to other characters, too. Hirsch's 'mercantile soul' (*N*, 203) reflects his motivating volition; Monygham's soul is 'withered and shrunk by the shame of moral disgrace' because his will to act is circumscribed by the knowledge that it succumbed under Father Beron's torture (*N*, 431); Decoud has 'the strangest sensation of his soul having just returned into his body' (*N*, 262) because the blackness of the Golfo Placido seems to have taken from him, momentarily, any power to make a decision.

Such a definition can also explain how, in *Chance*, the influence of the governess remains with Flora de Barral 'like a mark on her soul, a sort of mystic wound' (*C*, 118–19) since Flora's power of decision is circumscribed by the memories of the other's cruelty. It explains Franklin's 'ulcerated and pathetic soul' (*C*, 375) since his good wishes for the captain are being thwarted by the unusual situation that pertains on the *Ferndale*. In *Victory*, it shows how Ricardo and Jones are 'identical souls in different disguises' (*V*, 130) since, apart from the matter of females, their wills are at least similar; it accounts for the 'uneasy soul' of Heyst's father (*V*, 91), the power of calumny, which, according to Heyst, 'can even destroy one's faith in oneself — dry-rot the soul' (*V*, 362), and the reason why Heyst's 'fastidious soul' still keeps 'the true cry of love from his lips in its infernal mistrust of all life' (*V*, 406).

Clearly, though, this equation of soul with will works better in some places than in others. When Conrad speaks of the 'soulless autocracy' of Russia, separated by a 'black abyss' from 'the benighted, starved souls of its people' (*NLL*, 89), 'soulless' can hardly mean 'without will' since it is too much will on the part of the ruling powers that is being complained of. The implication is that autocracy here is devoid of normal human feelings (the more positive ones, that is) and is therefore heartless, devoid of pity, compassion or love and denying the individual wills of its people. To pin one's faith to a single definition and assume absolute application would be a presumptuous proceeding, therefore, and in no place more than in *Under Western Eyes*, where some 57 references to soul imply a more than usual importance to the use of the term. Haldin, for example, speaks at length about Russian souls:

Where did you get your soul from? There aren't many like you. Look here, brother! Men like me leave no posterity, but their souls are not lost. No man's soul is ever lost. It works for itself — or else

where would be the sense of self-sacrifice, of martyrdom, of conviction, of faith – the labours of the soul? What will become of my soul
when I die in the way I must die – soon – very soon perhaps? It
shall not perish. . . . My spirit shall go on warring in some Russian
body till all falsehood is swept out of the world. The modern
civilisation is false, but a new revelation shall come out of Russia. . . . I respect your political scepticism, Razumov, but don't
touch the soul. The Russian soul that lives in all of us. It has a future.
It has a mission. (*UWE*, 22)

This passage contains many words which have religious connotations
('sacrifice', 'martyrdom', 'faith', 'revelation'); 'soul' fits naturally with
such rhetoric. 'Will' could still be applicable, though here it seems to
be collective and hereditary, inspired by a perpetual and idealistic
motivation passed on through successive generations, rather than individual and unique. When, later, Sophia Antonovna speaks of 'an
unstable state of soul' which accompanies the conversion to revolution
(*UWE*, 261), this is clearly 'will' once more.

'Soul' is rather harder to define when Razumov considers the word
in connection with the visions he has of Haldin. 'Souls do not take a
shape of clothing,' he comments at one stage (*UWE*, 84) and later he
decides 'It was not his soul, it was his mere phantom he had left behind
on this earth' (*UWE*, 94). But he is to change his mind when confronted by Madame de S— who claims 'I can see your very soul'
(*UWE*, 224), though she is probably deluding herself into thinking she
understands a revolutionary motivated will. The remark goads
Razumov into speaking of 'Some sort of phantom in my image,'
supposing that 'a soul when it is seen is just that. A vain thing. There
are phantoms of the living as well as of the dead.'

Razumov appears to be thinking along almost theological lines here
and, indeed, the constant use of the word reinforces the religious
language that accompanies revolution. But when he writes of stealing
Natalia's soul from her (*UWE*, 359) this would essentially mean dominating her existence or will. The solitude of Razumov's soul, however,
tempts the teacher of languages to try a definition:

This was Mr Razumov's feeling, the soul, of course, being his own,
and the word being used not in the theological sense, but standing,
as far as I can understand it, for that part of Mr Razumov which was
not his body, and more specially in danger from the fires of this

earth. And it must be admitted that in Mr Razumov's case the
bitterness of solitude from which he suffered was not an altogether
morbid phenomenon.   (*UWE*, 291–2)

As a definition this is not helpful since it is better at explaining what
'soul' is not (soul 'in the theological sense') rather than what it is (which
remains vague and, perhaps, indicates some perplexity on the part of
the narrator). It does reveal that torment for Razumov was on this
plane (fires obviously denoting tortures of some kind). What is suggested here is some life force, some inner controlling reality, the core
of his existence from which his free-will emanates. When Conrad
speaks of 'the soul of a great truth'[25] he is clearly referring to some
heart, to the essence, the epitome, the totality of something. But the
dangers of attempting to over-define are just as great as accepting a less
specific term; once one has started to probe the core of existence one
could define ad infinitum. That Conrad had no clear belief in a soul as
such is shown by a letter he wrote to Cunninghame Graham in 1920:

> As to the soul You and I cher ami, are too honest to talk of what we
> know nothing about. Still, after all these years, I think I may
> venture to say to you this: that if there is such a thing, then yours
> Don Roberto is a very fine one, both in what it receives from the
> world and in what it gives to it.[26]

This should, at least, preclude assumptions of literal usage on the
part of the author except when reflecting the beliefs of his characters.
Indeed, the whole process of defining terms can come dangerously
close to obscuring their metaphorical possibilities and ignoring the fact
that Conrad used the religious words for a purpose. Devil and soul are
simply two features of a religious lexis that forms part of a metaphorical backcloth to Conrad's major themes. In isolation their roles have
been carefully scrutinised and found to be secular. To rely solely on
literal theological interpretations is thus to lessen their value; almost to
ignore them. It remains to be seen how, in their secular roles, they
form part of a pattern set up by the religious lexis as a whole.

8

The Purposes of Conrad's Religious Imagery

It was noted earlier that, in Conrad's novels, literal religion offers little spiritual sustenance to his characters, and, accordingly, very few of them can give a definite answer to any question of faith. Thus, when Razumov asks Haldin about his belief in God (*UWE*, 23) and later enquires of Sophia Antonovna, firstly whether she is 'a materialist' (*UWE*, 251) and then (in contrast) whether she believes in 'the actual devil' (*UWE*, 281), the answer he receives in each case is equivocal. When questioned about hell and eternal punishment by her father, Flora de Barral can only make a vague and inarticulate reply (*C*, 394); asked about his belief by Heyst, Morrison's response, despite his admission of prayers, is similarly indirect (*V*, 14); and M. George completely evades the accusations of 'scoffing and irreverence,' brought by the fanatical Villarel (*AG*, 251). For the most part, therefore, the certainties of belief or disbelief are not held by the inhabitants of Conrad's fiction; even the sceptical Martin Decoud will not admit the charges of being 'godless − a materialist' and a 'victim of this faithless age' (*N*, 198). In the few cases where faith is proclaimed (such as Whalley), the claim is rigorously tested and the nature of the belief shown to be illusory. Thus, with this source of comfort apparently inadequate or unavailing, many of Conrad's characters are forced to look elsewhere for their spiritual fulfilment, and the figurative use of religious language indicates these new objects of devotion. The chief engineer in *Nostromo* speaks truly when he refers to 'the spiritual value which everyone discovers in his own form of activity' (*N*, 318), and Martin Decoud is no less perceptive when he says of the materialists in Charles Gould's salon, 'Those gentlemen talk about their gods' (*N*, 199).

With devil and soul already noted, the aspects that remain can be categorised as biblical allusions, classical allusions and religious terms of a general nature. Since they inter-lock as part of an overall pattern, it is not really satisfactory to divide them up, but Conrad's biblical allusions, in particular, have attracted critical attention (mostly in isolation) and (keeping in mind the overall pattern), it is necessary, briefly, to consider them on their own.

BIBLICAL ALLUSIONS

Firstly, special attention must be paid to Dennis Walsh's assertion that 'The biblical story of creation is central to a deep understanding of 'Typhoon'.[1] Walsh's concentration on Genesis is unduly selective since there are strong reminders in the story, not only of the beginning but also of the end of the Bible. Of MacWhirr, it is said, 'Had he been informed by an indisputable authority that the end of the world was to be finally accomplished by a catastrophic disturbance of the atmosphere, he would have assimilated the information under the simple idea of dirty weather, and no other' (*T*, 20). The setting sun 'had a diminished diameter and an expiring brown, rayless glow, as if millions of centuries elapsing since the morning had brought it near its end' (*T*, 28). These ominous warnings (both biblical and scientific) are repeated with Jukes's impression of MacWhirr's voice during the typhoon; a 'frail and indomitable sound that can be made to carry an infinity of thought, resolution, and purpose, that shall be pronouncing confident words on the last day, when heavens fall, and justice is done' (*T*, 44).

There is, therefore, a combination of pre-creation chaos and apocalypse here — neither of which is unexpected in the circumstances. Jukes's reference to the Siamese flag as incorporating 'a ridiculous Noah's Ark elephant' (*T*, 9) may also be prophetic of the typhonic deluge to come.

There are other allusions, too. Walsh quotes the reference to Jukes as being 'as ready as any half-dozen young mates that may be caught by casting a net upon the waters' (*T*, 39) — presumably an allusion to the early disciples — but says nothing more about it. Other gospel echoes include the reference to men like the second mate, who leave their berths 'with an air of shaking the ship's dust off their feet' (*T*, 29). This is clearly ironic (if it is deliberate), since the admonition to 'shake the dust off your feet' is given by Christ to the disciples as the procedure to be adopted when departing from a heedless house or city (Matt. 10:14). Its use here reveals the self-righteous egocentricity of the second mate and his kind.

This last point raises a common problem about biblical allusions, namely: how deliberate are they? The Bible is one of the main sources of European heritage and, as such, many of its verses have become little more than clichés (shaking the dust off one's feet being a good example). There may, moreover, be a warning early in the book to the effect that it is misleading to assume biblical import for an apparently biblical allusion. This, after all, is the mistake of the curate who causes Mrs Rout so much mirth by his flustered reaction to 'Solomon says' (*T*, 16). Inevitably, a typhoon will evoke images of chaos, apocalypse and hell; the dangers of over-application are obvious.

To ignore them, however, could be just as incorrect, for they are a part of the whole. The effect created by the combined destructive imagery that has been noted, is that of a deliberate methodical assault. When the real power of the typhoon hits the ship, it comes 'like the sudden smashing of a vial of wrath' (*T*, 40); an image of divine censure, in other words, that has come about because MacWhirr has proclaimed himself unable to follow his book's advice on avoiding storms 'if every word in there was gospel truth' (*T*, 33). In thus refusing to circumvent 'the winds of heaven' (*T*, 35). MacWhirr is making 'his confession of faith' and Jukes, looking on, is 'like a man invited to behold a miracle' (*T*, 34). But it is a false faith that MacWhirr confesses for, just as, in biblical terms, to turn away from the Word of God (in this case the gospels) is to invite the wrath of God, so, to turn away from the word of storm strategy is to invite the wrath of the elements. In this kind of frame, an earlier incident can be considered: Mac-Whirr's censure of the second engineer. The captain refers to him as 'profane' and decides that 'If this goes on, I'll have to get rid of him the first chance.' Jukes, however, feels that 'It's the heat' and that the weather 'would make a saint swear' (*T*, 25). Jukes's concern is that the engineer would be 'a jolly good second' and in this case it is the mate who is correct as a later scene shows:

> "Blowing off all the time," went on yelling the second. With a sound as of a hundred scoured saucepans, the orifice of a ventilator spat upon his shoulder a sudden gush of salt water, and he volleyed a stream of curses upon all things on earth including his own soul, ripping and raving, and all the time attending to his business. (*T*, 71)

The last line is the important one here for it shows that the second engineer does not lose his head. As far as the *Nan-Shan* is concerned, he is a saint since he unflaggingly fulfils his duty − Conrad's constant criterion for a good seaman. The real act of profanity comes from

MacWhirr in his deliberate flouting of recommended procedures which causes him to place his ship, its crew and passengers in deadly peril.

Jukes's ironical connection between MacWhirr and a quarrelsome angel (*T*, 25) is indicative of the inconstant way in which he regards his commander. During the height of the typhoon, he leans heavily on MacWhirr; when he speaks to the captain through the speaking-tube from the engine room it seems to him that 'a small voice shoved aside the shouting hurricane quietly' (*T*, 72). C. Wegelin says of this incident, 'In its quiet smallness, the voice in which MacWhirr directs Jukes may remind us of the "still and small voice" in which the Lord directs Elijah; its setting may recall the voice in which He answers Job "out of the whirlwind".'[2] This comparison illustrates Jukes's reliance on his captain at this stage, as Wegelin points out, but is misleading since (unlike Jehovah) MacWhirr is not in control of the elements that surround him. This is emphasised, in fact, by the apocalyptic image that was noted earlier where confident words are sounded on the last day.[3] Such confidence is clearly unfounded, and MacWhirr's declaration – 'I wouldn't like to lose her' (*T*, 86, 90) – and his admission to his wife that he 'did actually think that his ship could not possibly live another hour in such a sea' (*T*, 94), reveal that he has undergone some kind of initiation, albeit a limited one. Jukes's experience also seems to have lacked any profound lasting effect, since the letter he writes at the end of the story reveals no hints of a chastened mate, newly aware of life's profundities and suitably matured as a result.

Basically, then, in addition to reinforcing the obvious conflicts between light and darkness, order and chaos and man and nature, the biblical allusions of 'Typhoon' (taken with other religious terminology), underline, once more, Conrad's familiar lesson of the essential devotion of a sailor to his ship and to his companions. MacWhirr tells Jukes that a saint who swears is 'No more saint than yourself, I expect' (*T*, 25), but, since the mate still does his duty, though complaining and, in the early stages of the storm, 'corrupted by the storm that breeds a craving for peace' (*T*, 53), Jukes, indeed, proves to be just as much a saint as the second engineer. MacWhirr hangs about Jukes's neck 'as heavy as a millstone' at the time when Jukes's heart is rebelling 'against the tyranny of training and command' (*T*, 53). This is again, perhaps, a reminder of the necessity of following the creed since the image is used by Christ to stress the importance of children. The Bible states that, 'whoso shall offend one of these little ones which believe in me, it were better for him that a millstone were hanged around his neck, and *that* he were drowned in the depth of the sea' (Matt. 18:6). Drowning in the depth of the sea will be exactly Jukes's fate if he does not fulfil his duties.

It is necessary to keep a sense of perspective, therefore, when considering the impact of allusions. Broadly speaking, it is an understanding of the importance of men fulfilling their duties that is central to the meaning of 'Typhoon' and the biblical references support this. Conrad's sense of vocation is uppermost here and his comment to Garnett about *The Nigger of the 'Narcissus'* – 'I must enshrine my old chums in a decent edifice'[4] – could equally well be applied to some of the characters of 'Typhoon'. Jukes's momentary corrupting by the storm is shared by the crew, of whom the boatswain relates, 'They seemed to take it ill that a lamp was not instantly created for them out of nothing. They would whine after a light to get drowned by – anyhow!' (*T*, 54). This yearning for light may well be a reminder of the first act of creation in Genesis, but it also illustrates faithless hearts since to sit and wait for a miracle is never a valid form of conduct on Conrad's ships. The point is made more explicitly in 'The Secret Sharer' when Captain Archbold relates how his ship survived a terrible storm:

"That reefed foresail saved you," I threw in.

"Under God – it did," he exclaimed fervently. "It was by a special mercy, I firmly believe, that it stood some of those hurricane squalls."

"It was the setting of the sail which—" I began.

"God's own hand in it," he interrupted me, "Nothing less could have done it."   (*TLS*, 118)

But the crucial order, it is shown, came not from the captain but from Leggatt. Divine intervention in the *Sephora*'s case is clearly incalculable but the solid actions of the crew have just as clearly had an effect and it is the area of duty on board ship that is the province of the captain, not an arrogation of providential power.

On the *Nan-Shan*, unlike the crew with their unwillingness to stir, Solomon Rout is described as 'fighting this fight in a pair of carpet slippers' (*T*, 69) which implies that he is a true follower of his creed since the phrase is an echo of St Paul's admonition to 'Fight the good fight of faith' (1 Tim. 6:12). But, just as the biblical solemnity of his Christian name is undercut by the curate's mistake, so the drama of the biblical phrase is undercut by the detail of the 'carpet slippers' which brings an incongruous note of mundaneness into the action. Like most of Conrad's good seamen Solomon Rout's heroism is a matter-of-fact affair, affording no time for gestures or slogans; he simply gets on with the job. The New Testament references to disciples and their conduct are, therefore, as important as those of creation and apocalypse since they bolster the spirit of resistance and underline the essential devotion to the ship. They act as constituents of the pattern, in other words, but do not constitute the pattern itself.

An unusual approach to biblical allusions is taken by Dwight H. Purdy in a study of *Under Western Eyes*. Purdy suggests that here 'the professor's allusions resemble mixed metaphors: tenor and vehicle, scriptural and fictional contexts collide. This wreckage reduces to absurdity typological interpretations of history, interpretations of life got by gazing into the dark glass of scripture'.[5] Purdy points out that 'when the professor is outside his direct experience, scriptural texts flourish',[6] noting that such allusions are most abundant in parts I and III (for which the narrator relies on Razumov's notebook) and thinnest in parts II and IV (in which the professor participates).[7] The old teacher of languages thus 'tries to clothe the politics and passions of Russian *mouvements* with the decent black broadcloth of the English Bible',[8] and achieves some misleading effects as a result:

> If Haldin seems a bizarre imitation of Christ, if Sophia Antonovna seems the Paul of Russian revolt, if Tekla is the Samaritan who, in a most unLukan vein, adores Razumov because he can "kill the monsters" (236), it is because Haldin's Gethsemane, Sophia's good fight, and Tekla's golden rule are products of an English rhetoric hopelessly at odds with Russian revolt and Russian mysticism.[9]

This is a more profound interpretation than that of the simple allegorist. For a start Purdy considers the fictional source of the allusions and sees them as reflecting aspects of the narrator, endorsing in the process a widespread view that the professor is not reliable as a narrator and cannot fully understand the story he is telling. But Purdy seems to go too far when he comments that 'However these "inconceivable" Russians may converse, we can be sure that they do not recite the English Bible',[10] since, if Conrad wanted his allusions to be noted by an English audience, he would have to allude to an English Bible. There is, after all, no reason why Russians should not refer to a Russian Bible which, translated, becomes an English one.

Explaining why scriptural texts do not flourish at the beginning of

Part IV (also based on Razumov's diary), Purdy comments that 'the narrator never uses scripture to characterize the autocrats; they are made to refer to Providence and God, but not directly to scripture, perhaps because the professor's stable English mind can comprehend autocracy far more readily than revolt'.[11] But this statement comes close to revealing the danger of taking biblical allusions in isolation. For the myth of Holy Russia hangs heavily over *Under Western Eyes* and counts both autocrats and revolutionaries among its adherents as, indeed, the professor recognises when citing 'cynicism' as 'the mark' of both.[12] If 'strange pretensions of sanctity' form part of this 'spirit' (*UWE*, 67), it is little wonder that scriptural allusions should be part of the pattern. 'Haldin's Gethsemane, Sophia's good fight, and Tekla's golden rule' are thus a natural part of Russian mysticism as Conrad understands it; not at all 'hopelessly at odds' with it. If biblical allusions do reflect the professor's inadequate understanding, they do it by contrast; the contrast between the way he understands them and makes use of them and the way the Russians do. When Kostia comments 'It's done', after stealing his father's money and continues, 'The old boy'll think the end of the world has come' (*UWE*, 313), this allusion may well have come to us via Razumov's diary and the professor of languages, but one must still assume that the source of the comment is the speaker, Kostia. Since he continues by sighing 'I've made my little sacrifice', the allusion here serves to add to the 'pretensions of sanctity' that revolution (like autocracy) arrogates to itself. The narrator's understanding of the events he relates may be defective but we must, surely, be allowed to rely on the accuracy of his transcription. When Haldin tells Razumov that 'the guests for the feast of freedom must be sought for in byways and hedges' (*UWE*, 56), this evoking of a biblical parable (Luke 14:23) helps to set up the speaker's attitude to revolution; an attitude held by his fellow revolutionaries and sympathisers (such as Kostia). It is entirely appropriate, therefore, for Haldin's mother to be reminded of Judas when fearing her son's betrayal (*UWE*, 115); the connection is obvious and is not dependent on the professor. Purdy is probably closer to the crux of the matter in an earlier essay when (again discussing the professor) he comments: 'The nature of Conrad's attack on both revolutionaries and autocrats suggests that the Christian values which once provided a solution have been so perverted that they no longer serve.'[13]

One of the problems encountered in studying Conrad's use of the Bible is that references to Christianity's Holy Book were far more common in his day than they are now. That same biblical phrase, 'byways and hedges', for example, is also adapted by Galsworthy in *The Man of Property* when describing how Winifred Dartie is let down by Augustus Flippard.[14] Such allusions appear from time to time in Conrad's correspondence. Thus Conrad is 'content to remain gratefully unexplained' to one correspondent 'as long as your charity prevents you casting stones';[15] he laments that 'my style is not more popular' and that 'I don't write less slow' since 'Of such that do is the Kingdom of the Earth';[16] and he comments (about reviews), 'D'you think I will get my share of loaves and fishes'[17] − all manifest references to the scriptures. This is a random selection, of course, hardly sufficient for a general pattern to be discerned; nevertheless the ironic tone that pervades is interesting for irony is a useful term to have in mind when studying Conrad's use of the Bible. Purdy makes this point when dealing with the allusions to Belshazzar's Feast (the 'writing on the wall'), indicating that this ominous portent is often misread by Conrad's characters as a favourable augury, and he cites Captain Whalley and Charles Gould as examples of this. Whalley presumes upon his continued uninterrupted health on the Sofala 'as though he had seen his Creator's favourable decree written in mysterious characters on the wall' (*Y*, 291−2), whilst Gould imagines a letter to Holroyd about backing a revolution with the San Tomé mine, 'as if written in letters of fire upon the wall' (*N*, 379). The latter example is noted as being especially pertinent since King Belshazzar 'praised the gods of silver' (Dan. 5:23). But Purdy also regards Sophia Antonovna as using the allusion in her cry, 'Crush the Infamy! A fine watchword! I would placard it on the walls of prisons and palaces, carve it on hard rocks, hang it out in letters of fire on that empty sky for a sign of hope and terror − a portent of the end' (*UWE*, 263), and feels that she reads her evoked omen aright, understanding 'that the letters of fire signify terror for the oppressors, hope for the oppressed'.[18] This interpretation seems to owe much to historical hindsight, however, since the novel itself gives no signs that Sophia's slogan is prophetic; indeed the insurrection which the revolutionaries are so carefully plotting, proves a failure (*UWE*, 330).

Elsewhere, the use of scriptural allusions must, for the time being, be swiftly summarised. Apocalyptic imagery is the most pervasive and has already been noted in 'Typhoon'. Apocalyptic skies accompany Lingard's arraignment of Willems in *An Outcast of the Islands*, are in attendance at Jim's death at the hands of Doramin (*LJ*, 413) and prefigure the final calamity in *Victory* (*V*, 355). A deluge follows Lingard's judgement (*OI*, 283−4), succeeds Razumov's confession (*UWE*, 357),

precedes Peyrol's setting out on his final voyage (*Ro*, 248), and receives detailed discussion from Heyst and Lena before Jones arrives
(*V*, 191). The 'abomination of desolation' — one of the signs of the
time of the end (Matt. 24:15) — is evoked by Lena (*V*, 190) and by M.
George (*AG*, 154). But in each of these cases, the imagery pre-figures
simply destruction or near-destruction, not a miraculous millenium.
Except in the case of Peyrol, what is judged is the obsession of the
character which has been attracting devotion and faith and is frequently indicated by the use of biblical language.

Much the same kind of comment can be made of other favourite
allusions. We have already seen how Christ's promise to be present
'when two or three are gathered together in my name' is echoed by the
shadow of autocracy (*UWE*, 107), by Peter Ivanovitch (*UWE*, 227)
and by Schomberg's evoking of Heyst at every opportunity at his table
d'hôte (*V*, 27). To these instances can be added that of Napoleon (*Sus*,
93, 261). Another repeated image is that of 'a pillar of smoke by day
and a loom of fire at night,' which, already noted in *Victory* (*V*, 168),
can also be observed rising from Tengga's camp in *The Rescue* (*Re*,
367). Such allusions need to be studied in the context of the religious
lexis as a whole which must now be considered.

EGOISM, PASSION AND PERSONAL ILLUSION

Conrad's first novel begins with a statement of Almayer's illusions.
Almayer likes to gaze at the river 'about the time of sunset; perhaps
because at that time the sinking sun would spread a glowing golden
tinge on the waters of the Pantai, and Almayer's thoughts were often
busy with gold' (*AF*, 3). The dreams of wealth and power that absorb
him, however, are, in reality, as illusory as the gold tinge on the water
(the reflection of the sun), and, significantly (and prophetically),
'There was no tinge on it this evening, for it had been swollen by the
rains, and rolled an angry and muddy flood under his inattentive eyes'
(*AF*, 4); an indication of the imminent end of his visions amidst the
harshness of reality, to which (it will be noted) he is 'inattentive'. His
Christian background, which should protect him from such unrealistic
speculations, is not in evidence, for Almayer applies the terms of
religion to his visions in which 'crowning all, in the far future gleamed
like a fairy palace the big mansion in Amsterdam, that earthly paradise
of his dreams' (*AF*, 10). This inter-mingling of religious imagery with
that of myth or fairy tale helps to underline not only the extent of

Almayer's obsession (or folly), but also the falsity of its premise, and one recalls Ian Watt's point that folly may indicate a mania. Almayer cannot abide the realities of Sambir; his imagination must soar into the west 'where the paradise of Europe was awaiting the future Eastern millionaire' (*AF*, 63). When he realises that Nina will leave him for the warrior prince, Dain Maroola, it is like the foundering of a faith (*AF*, 192). Thereafter, the 'commercial anchorite'[19] can turn only to the opium of Jim Eng, his dreams of paradise having dwindled to his own new house, called by his Chinese lodger 'House of heavenly delight' (*AF*, 205); his final ambition being to achieve the illusion of forgetfulness, which he seems to obtain prior to his death (*AF*, 208).

Almayer is not alone is applying religious terms to non-religious objects. Nina evokes such attentions from Dain, a Brahmin (Hindu) and, in Mrs Almayer's eyes, 'a son of Heaven' (*AF*, 51).

For the practical Abdulla, Nina would be the first of his nephew, Reshid's four wives, and Almayer's refusal is inferred and accepted (*AF*, 46). The effect of Nina on Dain is rather different, for 'Now he wanted but immortality, he thought, to be the equal of gods, and the creature that could open so the gates of paradise must be his – soon would be his for ever!' (*AF*, 72–3). The effects, as noted earlier, are felt in his soul, which he claims to have delivered into Nina's hands (*AF*, 178). Paradise, which for Almayer and Abdulla lie in the future (though, by Almayer's standards, Abdulla already has an earthly paradise), is thus immediately obtainable for Dain.

Nina's reaction to this adoration is also described in religious terms, as she thinks 'of moulding a god from the clay at her feet. A god for others to worship' (*AF*, 172). Their relationship is a happy one and they have had a child by the time the story ends.

Paul Kirschner describes the religious feeling in *Almayer's Folly* as signifying 'consolation, hope of reward or the projection of a personal idea of superiority,'[20] which is a useful contribution to a summary. Almayer's obsession, exemplified by the use of religious terms, constitutes his folly just as Dain's obsession with Nina (similarly described) becomes (in Nina's eyes) his weakness. In Sambir, the crafty Abdulla triumphs. In this life he does not seek the unattainable.

Figurative religious language in the early novels relates to excessive egoism, personal illusions or sexual passion, and the ways in which these preoccupations involve Willems, Lingard and Almayer in *An Outcast of the Islands* have been indicated earlier. They also apply to two of the later novels – *The Arrow of Gold* and *The Rescue* – though, since each book had its conception in the 1890s, this is not really surprising. There has already been cause to mention Conrad's problems with the sprawling maze of *The Rescue* manuscript. The considerably shorter fragment of *The Sisters* seems to have been reworked into *The Arrow of Gold*, since both works share some of the same characters (the sisters, Rita and Therese, and their uncle, the fiery Basque priest). In the fragment, the predicament of Stephen, a young artist who (like Conrad) comes to France from the Ukraine, epitomises the spiritual problem which Conrad's characters face. For, when the youth leaves his devoutly-believing father, his search is described explicitly as a quest for 'an unveiled religion of art' (*Sis*, 34), and, accordingly, attracts religious terms. Stephen is 'a lonely and inarticulate Mage, without a star and without companions' (*Sis*, 33), who senses a hypocritical attitude among his fellow artists towards 'the august world of the infinite, the Eternal' (*Sis*, 36); who has 'camped in the land of Bohemia; in that strange holy land of art abandoned by its High Priests' (*Sis*, 62); and who even applies Catholic theology to his quest when he refuses to return home after the death of his parents because he feels that this would be 'worse than suicide, which is the unpardonable crime' (*Sis*, 53).

Stephen and Rita have not met by the end of the fragment and one cannot tell whether their relationship would have been akin to that of M. George and Rita in *The Arrow of Gold*. Certainly, it seems that Stephen's quest would have been unsuccessful since, as early as the opening page, it is revealed that 'his search for a creed' had uncovered only 'an infinity of formulas' (*Sis*, 33).

In the later work, the religious language mainly gathers around the passion of George (and others) for Rita. Mills says of her, 'I am not meddling with theology but it seems to me that in the Elysian fields she'll have her place in a very special company' (*AG*, 23), and feels 'that she looked as though Allègre had caught her in the precincts of some temple . . . in the mountains' (*AG*, 33). This effect is heightened by a background of classical imagery which likens Henry Allègre to Jove (*AG*, 34) and Ortega to 'a wretched little Prometheus with a sparrow pecking at his miserable little liver' (*AG*, 111). Once he has met her, George can talk of 'the sovereign charm in that woman's face wherein there seemed to beat the pulse of divinity rather than blood' (*AG*, 88). To George, she sits 'as if carved six thousand years ago in order to fix for ever that something secret and obscure which is in all women,' with 'the finer immobility, almost sacred, of a fateful figure seated at the very source of the passions that have moved men from the dawn of ages' (*AG*, 145–6).

M. George, it will be noted, adheres to the traditional biblical age of the world (6000 years) in describing the timeless quality Rita seems to possess. When he describes, some time afterwards, the state this puts him into, he once more falls back on the terminology of religion to do so, citing her body as the object of his 'adorations' and 'profanations', denying his 'spiritual abasement before a mere image', and claiming that he had 'as clear a flame as ever burned on earth from the most remote ages before that eternal thing which is in you, which is your heirloom. And is it my fault that what I had to give was real flame, and not a mystic's incense' (*AG*, 299).

As we have seen earlier, however, the images of apocalypse, purgatory and hell figure most pervasively in the pursuit of this obsession. Thus, although Rita is usually described (by George and others) in classical terms,the effects she produces are alluded to in gloomily theological ones, and only physical wounds succeed in releasing her admirers from their mutual predicament.

Such effects have been caused by the 'cult of aesthetic impressions' (*AG*, 186) which, combined with a rampant intellectualism, has harnessed Rita's thinking. She comments to George, 'I am sensible to aesthetic impressions. I have been educated to believe there is a soul in them' (*AG*, 211). Earlier, Mills has considered her as 'a young virgin intelligence, steeped for nearly five years in the talk of Allègre's studio, where every hard truth had been cracked and every belief had been worried into shreds. They were like a lot of intellectual dogs, you know'. These remarks prompt Blunt's assessment that Rita is 'the intellectual personality altogether adrift, a soul without a home' (*AG*, 56). Rita, herself, is later to admit that earlier pervasive influence with regret:

> I have too much reverence in me to invoke the name of God of whom clever men have robbed me a long time ago. How could I help it? For the talk was clever and ... and I had a mind. And I am also, as Therese says, naturally sinful. Yes, my dear, I may be naturally wicked but I am not evil and I could die for you. (*AG*, 300)

Typical of the life-negating force that pervades, this comment promises only death, but not life.

To George, Rita is a goddess; to Mrs Blunt, she is an image belonging to that part of life 'where art and letters reign undisputed like a sort of religion of beauty' (*AG*, 181); to Allègre, there is 'something in her of the women of all time' (*AG*, 181); to Therese, she is possessed; to no-one, not even herself, is she just a normal woman, and it is the chance of love (a normal woman's right) that she has 'sacrificed' by the end of the book (*AG*, 350). The faith she has lost is not just in religion but in life itself.

Essentially, in *The Rescue*, Conrad repeats the major themes of *An Outcast of the Islands*, the main difference being that whilst Willems' passion for Aïssa causes him to betray Lingard's secret intentionally, the betrayal effected by Lingard's passion for Mrs Travers is unintentional, though just as comprehensive. In each story, religious imagery reveals the excessive extent of the protagonist's egoism and of the passion that envelops him.

Lingard's 'absurd faith in himself,' which was evident in the earlier novel, thus receives more detailed attention in *The Rescue*; his self-regard being built up by a whole host of religious images from several different sources. He is seen to have the power to divert Muslims from their true belief, for his crew (including two Hadjis) endow him with the knowledge of 'magic words' (*Re*, 47) and 'charms' (*Re*, 48). Belarab, the Muslim leader, despite being 'a professed servant of God famed for many charities and a scrupulous performance of pious practices' (*Re*, 281), still believes 'absolutely both in Lingard's power and in his boldness' (*Re*, 434), and this apparent duality is also seen in the attitude of the faithful Jaffir:

> "Yes. Our refuge is with Allah," assented Jaffir, who had acquired the habit of pious turns of speech in the frequentation of professedly religious men, of whom there were many in Belarab's stockade. As a matter of fact, he reposed all his trust in Lingard who had with him the prestige of a providential man sent at the hour of need by heaven itself.   (*Re*, 334)

Lingard, himself, exchanges the sentiments of Islamic fatalism with Daman when taking charge of the Arab's prisoners, yet what he really believes is that 'power, too, is in the hands of a great leader' (*Re*, 295). His rescue of Prince Hassim and his followers is accompanied by hints of supernatural assistance by the inhabitants of Wajo (*Re*, 86–7) whilst Lingard views that land as 'unscathed and motionless under hooked darts of flame, like some legendary country of immortals, withstanding the wrath and fire of Heaven' (*Re*, 80). In Lingard's eyes, even his ship (the *Lightning*) becomes inflated by religious terms as she floats 'at rest in a wavering halo, between an invisible sky and an invisible sea, like a miraculous craft, suspended in the air' (*Re*, 205).

His confidence that he can restore Hassim to his throne is overwhelming as he lives 'in the long intoxication of slowly preparing success' (*Re*,
106).

This picture of Lingard's egoism is completed by echoes of Christ
that become attached to him. When he visits Edith at night, he has 'the
appearance of standing upon the sea' (*Re*, 153), and he enjoins her,
later, to 'Follow me' (*Re*, 207). If these allusions seem forced, a far
more specific one comes towards the end of the book:

> "God knows," he answered. "What would have happened if the
> world had not been made in seven days? I have known you for just
> about that time. It began by me coming to you at night — like a thief
> in the night. Where the devil did I hear that? And that man you are
> married to thinks I am no better than a thief."   (*Re*, 398)

He would have heard the phrase, of course, in biblical prophecies
concerning the Second Coming (II Peter 3:10). Such references are
complemented by the descriptions of Jörgenson to whom Lingard has
given a new lease of life by involving him in the enterprise, for
Jörgenson is likened to 'a man raised from the dead' (*Re*, 116) with
'resurrected eyes' (*Re*, 370). Since Jörgenson's past is much akin to
Lingard's present, the Rajah Laut should take more heed of the
warning of the uncertainties of life that his very presence conveys.
D'Alcacer also sounds an ominous note when he refers to Lingard as 'a
rough man naïvely engaged in a contest with heaven's injustice' (*Re*,
346); a description that implies supernatural opposition rather than
supernatural approval.

Once this self-appointed saviour pose has been annihilated by the
final disaster, in which the neglected Jörgenson's 'black scepticism of
the grave' has overwhelmed 'the fascinating trust in the power of life'
(*Re*, 116) and brought death and destruction as the final fruits of his
resurrection, Lingard's fall is correspondingly immense. He feels 'a
stranger to all men and abandoned by the All-Knowing God' (*Re*,
444); a term that he applies to Jaffir also, though it is not clear whether
the god who abandoned Jaffir is the Almighty or Lingard.

There is in Lingard 'crime, sacrifice, tenderness, devotion, and the
madness of a fixed idea' (*Re*, 215) but it is the dislodging of this idea by
the presence of Edith that proves to be his undoing. Like Dain
Maroola, Lingard receives a glimpse of paradise through a woman, but
in Lingard's case it reduces him to 'the state of a man who, having cast
his eyes through the open gates of Paradise, is rendered insensible by

that moment's vision to all the forms and matters of the earth; and in the extremity of his emotion ceases even to look upon himself but as the subject of a sublime experience which exalts or unfits, sanctifies or damns – he didn't know which' (*Re*, 415). This state and this image are repeated twice more (*Re*, 433, 436) and, once the fatality has occurred, the cause of his downfall is confirmed:

> Once more Wasub raised his eyes to Lingard's face.
> "Paradise is the lot of all True Believers," he whispered, firm in his simple faith.
> The man who had been undone by a glimpse of Paradise ex-changed a profound look with the old Malay.   (*Re*, 449)

What the religious language of these novels reveals, therefore, is the true object of a character's devotion, and of the four characters whose point of adoration is a woman, only Dain benefits. Throughout the canon, the figurative religious lexis functions in this way, though the objects it becomes attached to develop in accordance with Conrad's major themes.

THE VOCATION OF THE SAILOR

Conrad's exalted attitude towards the life of a sailor and its fictional representation in *The Nigger of the 'Narcissus'*, have been noted pre-viously; it remains here to illustrate the consistency with which this view of a seaman's duty as an exacting creed is maintained in other works.

This creed withstood assault in *The Nigger of the 'Narcissus'*, but the attack there was external, rather than from within. The threat that is posed in *Lord Jim* is more insidious and disturbing to the master mariners who encounter it. For Jim's act of jumping from the *Patna* undermines the whole basis of the faith.

Allistoun had no difficulty in recognising Donkin and Wait for what they really were, and the misplaced fanaticism of Podmore only pre-sented him with a familiar and summarily dealt with problem. Three of the members of the crew who desert the pilgrim-filled, apparently sinking *Patna* also cause no concern; their absence from the inquiry is in keeping with their image. But Jim does attend the inquiry and it is his appearance that seems so clearly to mark him down as 'one of us' that so disturbs sailors like Marlow. This factor alone is enough to shake a belief. It causes one of the assessors, Brierly, to drown himself, 'as though on that exact spot in the midst of waters he had suddenly perceived the gates of the other world flung open wide for his reception' (*LJ*, 59); and suicide, theologically, is an act of spiritual despair. Brierly, in other words, has lost his faith; a faith which seems to depend on appearance denoting reality. Marlow has thought previously (of Brierly) that 'The sting of life could do no more to his complacent soul than the scratch of a pin to the smooth face of a rock' (*LJ*, 58), but appearances have proved deceptive here, too.

Jim's presence also disturbs the other assessor, a 'pious sailing-ship skipper' who 'appeared excited and made uneasy movements, as if restraining with difficulty an impulse to stand up and exhort us earnestly to prayer and repentance' (*LJ*, 158). This would be the action of a priest undertaken for the benefit of those in danger of straying from the sacred fold. Here the fold is seamen; their creed, the solidarity that Jim's action has belied.

Marlow shows his adherence to the creed by using a religious comparison to describe the way he would feel if Jim took to drink; this eventuality being 'more trying to a man who believes in the solidarity of our lives than the sight of an impenitent deathbed to a priest' (*LJ*, 224). Jim has, indeed, been treating the elder man as if he were a priest, as Marlow himself makes clear:

> Didn't I tell you he confessed himself before me as though I had the power to bind and to loose? He burrowed deep, deep, in the hope of my absolution, which would have been of no good to him. This was one of those cases which no solemn deception can palliate, which no man can help; where his very Maker seems to abandon a sinner to his own devices. (*LJ*, 97)

Whether 'solemn deception' can be taken as a criticism of the Catholic confessional is, perhaps, by the way here; what is clear is that the creed of the sea does not adopt such remedies. In any case, Marlow claims that he is 'not particularly fit to be a receptacle of confessions' as he laments the 'devious, unexpected, truly diabolical ways' in which all manner of men come to choose him 'for their infernal confidences; as though, forsooth, I didn't have enough confidential information about myself to harrow my own soul till the end of my appointed time' (*LJ* 34).

The 'ways' are 'diabolical' and the confidences 'infernal', presumably, because they serve to undermine Marlow's faith in his creed

Together with his own doubts, he has those of others to contend with as well. Little wonder that Jim's story and his sudden question, 'What do *you* believe?' should seem to Marlow to have startled him 'out of a dream of wandering through empty spaces whose immensity had harassed my soul and exhausted my body' (*LJ*, 132). His desperate efforts to maintain the faith of solidarity are exemplified by his interview with the chief engineer, where he freely admits to 'looking for a miracle', hoping 'to obtain from that battered and shady individual some exorcism against the very ghost of doubt' (*LJ*, 51). Instead, a 'wolfish howl' searches 'the very recesses' of his soul (*LJ*, 52), and his faith remains shaken.

Jim's desertion of the *Patna*, therefore, has had a profound effect on at least three people: the pious assessor (unless his apparent desire to preach is a manifestation of Marlow's own disquiet), Brierly and Marlow himself. It attacks their ideas of solidarity, exalted to a belief by the religious terminology; a faith that Jim, unwittingly, undermines. For such a belief attempts to ignore certain realities, one being that in an emergency the instinct for self-preservation can seize 'one of us' just as it affects the likes of the master of the *Patna*. The external narrator comments that 'in our own hearts we trust for our salvation in the men that surround us', and Jim regards the obese master of his ship as 'the incarnation of everything vile and base that lurks in the world we love' (*LJ*, 21). But Jim, in 'contemplating his own superiority' (*LJ*, 23), is, in this respect, similar to Podmore. His egoism is different but is just as unsuitable to the creed of the sea, and not only proves disastrous for him but also creates severe doubts in the minds of those who are upholders of that creed.

In 'Heart of Darkness', Marlow is referred to as being 'the only man of us who still "followed the sea"' (*Y*, 48), and the same phrase, with its vocational and religious connotations, is repeated in *Chance* (*C*, 4). It is here, in fact, that one of the most direct comparisons between religion and the vocation of seamen is made (by the external narrator):

> But I have observed that profane men living in ships, like the holy men gathered together in monasteries, develop traits of profound resemblance. This must be because the service of the sea and the service of a temple are both detached from the vanities and errors of a world which follows no severe rule.   (*C*, 32–3)

Of the varying objects that attract religious language, this seaman's vocation alone elicits the author's approval, though a glib complacency on the part of any skipper is severely punished. It is this that the narrator of *The Shadow-Line* must learn.

Conrad's Author's Note to *The Shadow-Line* disclaimed any intentions of evoking the supernatural in the story (*SL*, ix—x), and it may be pertinent to begin with those elements which might suggest such an interpretation. Very early in the story, there are hints of supernatural power that no western mind would accept in the picture of the owner of the ship which the narrator is about to leave. The owner is 'an Arab . . . and a Syed at that' who possesses 'a great occult power amongst his own people' (*SL*, 4). Just as one can look on this from the outside, as it were, and dismiss out of hand any actual mysterious powers, one can also regard in the same light the climactic scene on the voyage where Mr Burns's laugh releases the, till then, dormant winds. It is the narrator who evokes the supernatural to describe the process, deciding that, 'By the exorcising virtue of Mr Burns's awful laugh, the malicious spectre had been laid, the evil spell broken, the curse removed. We were now in the hands of a kind and energetic Providence' (*SL*, 125).

To some degree this parallels the situation on the *Narcissus*, where the winds seem to await the despatch of James Wait's dead body to the waves before springing into action, apparently in accordance with the prophecies of old Singleton. The position in *The Shadow-Line* is just as equivocal as it is in the earlier story, but ties in very well with the attitude of the narrator to his charge. For the religious and supernatural references begin when he throws up his berth on the Arab's ship even though he confesses that 'I could not have been happier if I had had the life and the men made to order by a benevolent enchanter' (*SL*, 5). When he signs off, the official hands him his papers 'with a sorrowful expression, as if they had been my passport for Hades' (*SL*, 7) and the narrator reacts 'in the hardened manner of an impenitent criminal' (*SL*, 8). These are ominous portents for what is to come.

The narrator's innocence and sense of importance are exhibited when he realises that a command is waiting for him. The very way he regards Captain Ellis, who gives this post, is a tacit recognition of the superiority he begins to feel, even though this is conveyed as Ellis's own high opinion of himself:

> Captain Ellis looked upon himself as a sort of divine (pagan) emanation, the deputy-Neptune for the circumambient seas. If he did not actually rule the waves, he pretended to rule the fate of the mortals whose lives were cast upon the waves.

This uplifting illusion made him inquisitorial and peremptory.
(*SL*, 29–30)

Ellis's self-esteem is relevant because it rubs off on the narrator whose own feeling of importance is naturally increased by the high station of the official appointing him. The obsequious behaviour of the chief clerk soon after is regarded by the narrator as an example of how 'The favour of the great throws an aureole round the fortunate object of its selection' (*SL*, 34) and as 'only another miraculous manifestation of that day of miracles' (*SL*, 35). He feels 'as if I had been specially destined for that ship I did not know, by some power higher than the prosaic agencies of the commercial world' (*SL*, 40) and thinks of the vessel as being 'spellbound . . . like an enchanted princess.' When he boards her in Bangkok harbour he has the sense of being 'brought there to rule by an agency as remote from the people and as inscrutable almost to them as the Grace of God' (*SL*, 62).

This combination of religion and magic, which elevates the new captain's view of his command to the realms of a mystical mission, gives an impression of one who needs to be brought down to reality. Although he encounters problems, he continues to make use of these terms. Thus, with sickness aboard, he opens his medicine chest 'full of faith as a man opens a miraculous shrine' (*SL*, 79), and expresses his faith in the powers of quinine, which 'like a magic powder working against mysterious malefices,' would 'secure the first passage of my first command against the evil powers of calms and pestilence' (*SL*, 88).

One will note from this that, not surprisingly, anything that tends to oppose the steady progress of this command is 'evil'; the word being also associated with the late captain (*SL*, 62), the fever from the land (*SL*, 79), the virtual becalming at sea (*SL*, 83) and the island of Koh-ring (*SL*, 86). A sudden adverse wind is regarded as having the motives of 'purposeful malevolence' (*SL*, 87), 'infernal powers' are evoked to explain the loss of the quinine (*SL*, 93) and the ship seems to be in the grip of a 'fever-devil' (*SL*, 103). Meantime, the crew continues to suffer 'the ordeal of the fiery furnace' (*SL*, 88), which, as an allusion to the biblical story of Shadrach, Meshach and Abd-nego (Dan. 3), implies their loyalty to a true creed.

The captain's faith is thus severely tested. His command becomes 'A stubborn pilgrimage of sheer restlessness', and the view from the bridge seems like 'the formidable work of the Seven Days, into which mankind seems to have blundered unbidden. Or else decoyed' (*SL*, 97). Moreover, he likens himself to 'a mad carpenter making a box. Were he ever so convinced that he was King of Jerusalem, the box he would make would be a sane box' (*SL*, 101). This appears to parody the earlier feelings of mystic mission within the narrator since Christ's background was that of a carpenter.

In this more humble mood, the captain becomes more aware of the fortitude of his crew. When they haul up the mainsail, it seems that 'if ever a sail was hauled up by sheer spiritual strength it must have been that sail' and their captain can feel 'only the sickness of my soul. I waited for some time fighting against the weight of my sins, against my sense of unworthiness' (*SL*, 109).

Here is a complete volte-face from his earlier attitude; he has gone from heavenly messenger to unworthy sinner and, as is made clear later, neither feeling is valid. For what the narrator has learnt by the end of the voyage is that 'one must not make too much of anything in life, good or bad' (*SL*, 131); his attitude to the job of Master has drastically changed. The language of religion and magic has thus served to highlight his egocentricity; from his sense of mystic mission and demonic opposition to his opposing sense of unworthiness. The breaking of the spell by Burns's laugh succeeds in dissipating the narrator's preoccupation with his feelings; the apparent advent of the supernatural has bestowed upon him a more practical attitude towards his craft. It serves as the culmination of such references, both favourable and unfavourable; acting, in short, as a logical denouement.

The lesson learnt by the narrator of *The Shadow-Line* has already been experienced by Marlow and Young Powell by the time of their discussion in *Chance*, where Powell refers to 'the peace of the sea':

> "A very good name," said Marlow looking at him approvingly. "A sailor finds a deep feeling of security in the exercise of his calling. The exacting life of the sea has this advantage over the life of the earth, that its claims are simple and cannot be evaded."
> "Gospel truth," assented Mr Powell. "No! they cannot be evaded." (*C*, 31–2)

Powell's biblical approval of Marlow's statement is ironic in a way, since a helpless reliance on Providence (as exhibited by Archbold in 'The Secret Sharer') is one way of evading these claims. The difference between land and sea values, asserted by Marlow, is important to the shorter story and supported by the use of religious terminology, particularly the biblical allusions to the Cain and Abel story. Such allusions would clearly form part of the world of Captain Archbold, of Leggatt's father, 'a parson in Norfolk' (*TLS*, 101, 103), and (in all probability) that of 'old "Bless my soul — you don't say so"' (*TLS*, 103), the narrator's first mate, who has to be shaken into action in the final crisis in a milder version of the fatal scene on the *Sephora*. That violence is sometimes a necessary part of life at sea is shown in *The Nigger of the 'Narcissus'* (*NN*, 40–1). Where devotion to duty is so vital to the existence of all, the proselytising of Podmore or a resigned hope of supernatural intervention by Archbold can only be dangerous aberrations. Leggatt is Cain by the values of the land but the circumstances of his action at sea would be beyond the understanding of a land-based jury (*TLS*, 103), and the biblical allusion is deliberately inappropriate in this case when set against the essential creed of the sea. The disobedience of Leggatt's victim has threatened the lives of his shipmates — 'an Abel of that sort' (*TLS*, 107) is clearly some way from the good-hearted and innocent brother of the Bible story.

In his fictional writings also, therefore, Conrad set forth the vocation of seamen as a form of positive belief, though not without detailing the possible pitfalls of the creed. An undue innocence on the part of the crew of the *Narcissus*, which makes them vulnerable to the egotistical enigma of the dying James Wait, turns them away, temporarily, from their prescribed devotion to the ship, and only the firmness of their captain prevents disastrous results. The vulnerability of a creed that relies on a sailor's appearance and the trust that appearance must command is revealed in *Lord Jim* and shakes the faith of some of its senior practitioners. The innocent egoism of the narrator of *The Shadow-Line* requires the fever-racked horrors of his first voyage to chasten him to a more practical outlook. Any belief, Conrad suggests (even the positively presented creed of the sea), has to be held with knowledge; an innocent trust is like a blind faith — vulnerable and precarious.

SOCIAL OBSESSIONS

After the early novels, Conrad's religious imagery can be seen to be reflecting man's social preoccupations. These are sometimes caused by a sense of idealism which becomes confronted by an unruly reality and, as a starting point to this study, it is pertinent to consider 'Youth' and the young Marlow's reverence for names. Such an outlook is shown to be invalid by the events of his voyage but it is only the older reminiscing Marlow that can recognise this; the youthful romanticism of the younger seaman survives the tale. The very sound of the name *Judea* has a more heroic (and biblical) ring to it than the lingering *Palestine* (just as 'Kurtz' is more abrupt and dramatic than 'Klein'), and her gallant motto – 'Do or Die' (*Y*, 5) – has an immediate appeal for the young Marlow.

But the ship begins by leaking so badly that she has to be returned to port and finishes by sinking after her cargo of coal has exploded. Marlow, however, regards her reverentially, commenting that, 'I would just as soon have abused the old village church at home for not being a cathedral' (*Y*, 18) – a comparison that continues the idea of following the sea being akin to following a religion – and regards her sinking as 'A magnificent death . . . come like a grace' despite the reality that is symbolised immediately after. For 'The unconsumed stern was the last to sink; but the paint had gone, had cracked, had peeled off, and there were no letters, there was no word, no stubborn device that was like her soul, to flash at the rising sun her creed and her name' (*Y*, 35).

To the waters that receive her, therefore, the *Judea* has become an anonymous hulk, indicating the insubstantiality of names and the futility of laying any importance upon them. The name 'Abraham' evokes memories of the steadfast Old Testament Prophet, but, early in the voyage, it is held by the steward, 'that poor devil of a mulatto' (*Y*, 14). Marlow longs to get to Bangkok, 'Magic name, blessed name' (*Y*, 15), and, after the ship has sunk, feels the same way about Java as he steers his 'first command' (a ship's longboat [*Y*, 36]).

The use of the word 'blessed' for Bangkok and Java indicates the extent of Marlow's reverence for names and this continues into port, where he feels 'the first sigh of the East on my face. That I can never forget. It was impalpable and enslaving, like a charm, like a whispered promise of mysterious delight' (*Y*, 37). He is then sworn at and cursed as if he has 'sinned against the harmony of the universe' (*Y*, 39), and this barrage of abuse comes from a steamer called the *Celestial*; a name that, in additional to its obvious meaning, was also used as a slang term for a Chinaman in Conrad's time (*T*, 7, 79). This, then, marks Marlow's introduction to the 'blessed name' of Java and the mysterious East and, if one can admit both meanings of 'Celestial', he can be said to have been abused from the heavenly realm (the 'blessed' and 'mysterious') and from a Chinaman (the 'East'). Certainly the incident acts as another example of the irrelevant nature of names, and insults from the *Celestial* make the point more clearly than they would coming from the *Sissie* (the ship in Conrad's voyage). The religious language of 'Youth', therefore, reflects an attitude, a state of mind that, since it continues to ignore the unromantic realities it encounters, is particularly vulnerable to illusions; a fertile breeding ground for the acceptance of any powerful social obsession to flourish.

These obsessions, especially those of progress and science, receive attention from Conrad in his essays and letters, together with ironical religious accretions. Such connections were not new, though. Matthew Arnold, in the 1860s, had written that 'The scientific intellect' could 'willingly let the religious instincts and the language of religion gather around it',[21] and J. R. Seeley, writing in the same decade, proved him correct, deciding that 'We live under the blessed light of science, a light yet far from its meridian and dispersing every day some noxious superstition, some cowardice of the human spirit.'[22] John Ruskin applied the terms ironically to progress, naming the presiding deity of a Bradford Stock Exchange the 'Goddess of Getting-on'.[23] Conrad's tone is close to that of Ruskin and the attitude he criticises is that of Seeley since it is the esteem in which science is held rather than science itself that evokes his antipathy. His religious irony at science's expense is at its most scathing when applied to his old vocation, the sea, especially when considering the ill-fated *Titanic* and the pretensions of technicians:

> It is amusing, if anything connected with this stupid catastrophe can be amusing, to see the secretly crestfallen attitude of technicians. They are the high priests of the modern cult of perfected material and of mechanical appliances, and would fain forbid the profane from inquiring into its mysteries. We are the masters of progress, they say, and you should remain respectfully silent.   (*NLL*, 230)

Though stressing that he had 'neither the competence nor the wish to take a theological view of this great misfortune, sending so many souls to their last account,' he also comments that 'if ever a loss at sea fell under the definition . . . of Act of God, this one does, in its magnitude, suddenness and severity; and in the chastening influence it should have on the self-confidence of mankind' (*NLL*, 213). Conrad makes similar remarks when dealing with the loss of another liner (*NLL*, 250–1). He was thus severely critical of the arrogance with which mankind seemed to be treating his scientific discoveries and his indignation at the suggestion that poetry should be enlisted to extol science is evident in 'The Ascending Effort'. The emphasis on material progress also attracted his ire and is criticised ironically in 'The Happy Wanderer'.

Here Conrad regards the author of the book he is reviewing as a 'convert from the creed of strenuous life,' having ground 'virtuously at the sacred handle,' and considers that Mr Roosevelt 'would promptly excommunicate him with a big stick' (*NLL*, 62). This is because 'The convert, the man capable of grace (I am speaking here in a secular sense) is not discreet' and thus becomes related to Don Quixote, 'the secular patron-saint of all mortals converted to noble visions' (*NLL*, 61–2). Conrad considers that the author 'is in sympathy with suffering mankind and has a grasp on real human affairs. I mean the great and pitiful affairs concerned with bread, love, and the obscure, unexpress-ed needs which drive great crowds to prayer in the holy places of the earth' (*NLL*, 64). He wishes this wayfarer well:

> Let the rich and powerful of this globe preach their sound gospel of palpable progress. The part of the ideal you embrace is the better one, if only in its illusions. No great passion can be barren. May a world of gracious and poignant images attend the lofty solitude of your renunciation.   (*NLL*, 64–5)

Conrad obviously shares the concerns of this author and by ironical-ly applying the language of the spiritual to the material clearly exposes which of the concerns of progress is uppermost. This application (though not its playful chaffing mood) carries through into his fiction.

In many ways Conrad's ironic use of religious terms brings him close to being a satirist, though one of a particularly bitter kind. Thus in 'Heart of Darkness' Marlow sardonically condemns the cause of prog-ress in which he is engaged simply by adopting the very language that idealists in Europe have applied to it. Foremost among these is Mar-low's aunt:

> It appeared, however, I was also one of the Workers, with a capital – you know. Something like an emissary of light, something like a lower apostle. There had been a lot of such rot let loose in print and talk just about that time and the excellent woman, living right in the rush of all that humbug, got carried off her feet. She talked about "weaning those ignorant millions from their horrid ways," till, upon

my word, she made me quite uncomfortable. I ventured to hint that the Company was run for profit.

"You forget, dear Charlie, that the labourer is worthy of his hire," she said brightly.   (*Y*, 59)

Such fervour, with its obvious biblical reference (Luke 10:7), is undercut by Marlow's earlier allusion when he likens the city in which she lives to a 'whited sepulchre' (*Y*, 55) — a biblical simile for a hypocrite — and side by side with the aunt's enthusiasm come such words as 'rot' and 'humbug', which may come from Marlow's hindsight since, at the time, he admits to being charmed by a snake. Amidst these religious references, such an attraction does not seem propitious.

Faced with the realities of Africa, Marlow deliberately continues such religious language in circumstances where it is grossly inappropriate, to expose the insubstantiality of his aunt's ideas. Thus, the accountant who, amidst death and suffering, is concerned only with the impeccable state of his appearance and his figures, becomes described as a 'miracle' (*Y*, 67), whilst at the Central Station, the white men are noted as wandering aimlessly 'with their absurd long staves in their hands, like a lot of faithless pilgrims bewitched inside a rotten fence. The word "ivory" rang in the air, was whispered, was sighed. You would think they were praying to it' (*Y*, 76). Thereafter, the agents are unfailingly referred to as 'pilgrims' (on no less than twenty-nine occasions, in fact) to ensure that those early religious sentiments should not be forgotten.

As was noted earlier, the same ironical tone is used for the brickmaker, short of 'straw maybe' and awaiting 'An act of special creation perhaps' (*Y*, 77) — like an Israelite suffering Pharaoh's tyranny in Egypt — and for the Eldorado expedition which enters with echoes of Christ's entry into Jerusalem but is likened to the plagues of Egypt. The irony becomes still more manifest when, after his experiences with Kurtz, Marlow meets the Intended (back in Europe), becomes aware of her 'unextinguishable light of belief and love' (*Y*, 158), bows his head 'before the faith that was in her' (*Y*, 159) and hears her use the word 'sacrificed' to describe Kurtz's death (*Y*, 160); all to a background that resembles a mausoleum (*Y*, 156).

Marlow is not ridiculing the Intended (as he has the pilgrims); it is her fervent belief, in the context of his horrific memories, that causes the contrast. The overall effect, therefore, is that of an ironical religious framework for the tale, to which can be added the allusions to

Buddha, the excessive use of demonic imagery and the references to the soul. It may have been to maintain this tone − even the harlequin is regarded as Kurtz's 'disciple' (*Y*, 132) − that Conrad deliberately omitted the two religious influences that were present on the Congo when he made his voyage − the Christianity of the missionaries and the Islām of the Arabs. Clearly, in Conrad's eyes, these were irrelevant to what was really going on there.

A similar picture is painted in 'An Outpost of Progress', where the cross − symbol of Christianity and here (significantly) 'much out of the perpendicular' (*TU*, 87) − serves only to mark the grave of the previous white man at the post and to act as a place for Kayerts to hang himself from after his fatal collision with Carlier. Here, too, the new agents are introduced to the religious sentiments connected with progress by a European newspaper, exhibiting some of the 'rot let loose in print' that Marlow mentioned by speaking 'of the sacredness of the civilizing work' and extolling 'the merits of those who went about bringing light, and faith and commerce to the dark places of the earth' (*TU*, 94). Appropriately enough, the storehouse of the station is called the fetish, 'perhaps because of the spirit of civilization it contained' (*TU*, 93). In this earlier tale, the Europeans are skilfully manipulated by Makola (also known as Henry Price) who 'cherished in his innermost heart the worship of evil spirits' (*TU*, 86), and, during the time between Europeans at the station 'dwelt alone with his family, his account books and the Evil Spirit that rules the lands under the equator. He got on very well with his god. Perhaps he had propitiated him by a promise of more white men to play with by and by' (*TU*, 87). Makola's Afro-European connections (suggested by his two names) are thus heightened by the 'account books', and the diminished station of white men (to that of playthings) makes it clear that Makola is really in charge here.

Thus there are two religious elements present − the extolling of the civilising work to the position of a religious duty and the suggestion of devil worship of some kind − and the second of these is shown to be the reality of the first. For, as the story progresses, the unfortunate station men, who are unhappy, regretting 'the festive incantations, the sorceries, the human sacrifices of their own land' (*TU*, 100), are sold off to slave traders by Makola in exchange for ivory. Carlier and Kayerts, who also regret their old lives (*TU*, 92) and may thus be equated with their luckless servants, are concerned but eventually accept the *fait accompli*, for, as the narrator explains, 'Nobody knows what suffering or sacrifice mean − except, perhaps, the victims of the mysterious purpose of these illusions' (*TU*, 105−6). As a result, the previously friendly village chief, Gobila, offers 'extra human sacrifices to all the Evil Spirits that had taken possession of his white friends' (*TU*, 107). This emphasis on human sacrifice is appropriate since the cause of progress, in accepting ivory for human beings, is also indulging in the practice. Trade, a euphemism for the ruthless acquisition of ivory, can thus be seen as the Evil Spirit that hangs over the land and Kayerts and Carlier are as much its victims as the natives.

In both stories, therefore, the concern with the ideal of progress (by some) and with its sordid reality (by others) is described in religious terms, which indicate (ironically in 'Heart of Darkness', more directly in 'An Outpost of Progress') the extent to which these preoccupations have been taken and the false premises from which their followers begin. Marlow quickly recognises the naïvety of idealists such as his aunt but he also feels a sense of unreality among the materialistic ivory-hunters. Paradoxically, the reality of progress is itself unreal and it is as well to remember that the 'pilgrims' are initially introduced as 'faithless' (*Y*, 76). Little wonder that the imagery used to accompany this state of affairs should be demonic (theologically, the end of all false beliefs), and that its final effects on Kurtz should be described in terms of his soul.

As characters, the pilgrims are generally seen as an amorphous group, spellbound together, rarely exhibiting any flashes of individuality. Conrad affirmed solidarity (especially on board ship) but, whilst this involved each individual committing himself to his duty, it did not mean de-personalisation. Indeed, the crew of the *Narcissus* only lose their individuality to become 'a dark mass' when they are on the point of mutiny (*NN*, 122). The dangers inherent in people not being able to think for themselves are clearly perceived by Conrad and his advice to Edward Noble − 'Everyone must walk in the light of his own heart's gospel'[24] − will be readily recalled. Neither superstitious religious beliefs nor materialistic concerns could contain the spiritual values Conrad thought important and in 'The Return' he illustrates this by treating the desire for conformity itself as a kind of false faith that a single incident could dissolve. The story, he claimed, 'is as false as a sermon by an Archbishop. Exactly. Another man goes out than the man who came in. T'other fellow is dead. You have missed the symbolism of the new gospel (that's what the Return is) altogether'.[25] This apparent flippancy conceals an underlying seriousness, as the story shows.

Alvan Hervey is the epitome of social conformity; a circumstance which is parodied by the mirrors in his room which make it appear that each of his actions is being performed by several other men at the same time (*TU*, 124). When this comfortable but soulless existence is threatened by his wife's desertion and subsequent return, Hervey begins to treat this conformity as a religion:

> And more than ever the walls of his house seemed to enclose the sacredness of ideals to which he was about to offer a magnificent sacrifice. He was the high priest of that temple, the severe guardian of formulas, of rites, of the pure ceremonial concealing the black doubts of life. And he was not alone. Other men, too — the best of them — kept watch and ward by the hearthstones that were the altars of that profitable persuasion. He understood confusedly that he was part of an immense and beneficent power, which had a reward ready for every discretion. He dwelt within the invincible wisdom of silence; he was protected by an indestructible faith that would withstand all the assaults — the loud execrations of apostates, and the secret weariness of its confessors!   (*TU*, 156)

His wife, having acted outside the accepted social conventions, becomes 'that sinner' to whom he speaks down 'from a height' in his extolling of 'the received beliefs' as 'the best, the noblest, the only possible' (*TU*, 157). But the initial shattering of his illusions has already been likened to the expulsion from Eden:

> He stood alone, naked and afraid, like the first man on the first day of evil. There are in life events, contacts, glimpses, that seem brutally to bring all the past to a close. There is a shock and a crash, as of a gate flung to behind one by the perfidious hand of fate. Go and seek another paradise, fool or sage. There is a moment of dumb dismay, and the wanderings must begin again; the painful explaining away of facts, the feverish raking up of illusions, the cultivation of a fresh crop of lies in the sweat of one's brow, to sustain life, to make it supportable, to make it fair, so as to hand intact to another generation of blind wanderers the charming legend of a heartless country, of a promised land, all flowers and blessings.   (*TU*, 134)

Such imagery reflects the extent of Hervey's conformist ideals and of his sudden inability to fulfil them, making him an individual for the first time, no longer uniform in life-style with his look-alike peers. The illusion of social conformity as a viable belief has broken down. Hervey's creed, part of which looks on any excess of feeling as 'unhealthy — morally unprofitable; a taint on practical manhood' (*TU*, 172), has left no room for spirituality and is seen by his wife as 'abominable materialism' (*TU*, 176).

Unable to know the truth about his wife — a circumstance that suitably evokes thoughts of the Day of Judgement in his mind, since the end of his present faith and current way of life is certainly nigh (*TU*, 174) — Hervey becomes converted to a belief in the enigma of faith and love (presumably the 'new gospel' Conrad spoke of). He cannot find the formula, however, for 'The enigma is only made by sacrifice, and the gift of heaven is in the hands of every man. But they had lived in a world that abhors enigmas, and cares for no gifts but such as can be obtained in the street' (*TU*, 176). He needs 'faith in a human heart, love of a human being! That touch of grace, whose help once in life is the privilege of the most undeserving, flung open for him the portals of beyond' (*TU*, 177). He speaks to his wife 'with the naïve austerity of a convert awed by the touch of a new creed' (*TU*, 177–8); the stillness around him seems like 'the lying solemnity of a temple devoted to the rites of a debasing persuasion' (*TU*, 184), and he is forced to decide whether he will follow his new faith, since it involves 'an awful sacrifice to cast all one's life into the flame of a new belief'. Thus Hervey, who had earlier harboured feelings of being one of the 'elect' (*TU*, 171), abandons his life of social conformity and leaves.

One obvious feature of the religious imagery in 'The Return' is that it is more explicit and more sustained than usual, revealing not only the grotesque extent to which regard for the mores of society may be taken but also the importance of Hervey's final decision which defies them. Once his wife's actions have planted the fateful questions within his hitherto uninspiring mind and forced him to recognise his individuality, Hervey is able to reject the materialistic base from which his life has been led. Conrad described his former state as exemplifying 'the gospel of the beastly bourgeois',[26] and this is so much in accord with the author's attitude to material progress shown in his essays, letters and other fiction that it is strange to see some critics regarding the story as being inconsistent with his other writings. R. A. Gekoski feels that 'it is the story of a religious conversion of an unmistakably Christian kind' and that 'The affirmation of love and faith with which the story ends rings utterly false.'[27] But he is judging this message against the touchstone of the letters to Cunninghame Graham later in the year and, as was seen earlier, those letters reflect a mood rather than a philosophy.

The affirmation is, in fact, entirely consistent with Conrad's outlook; it fits well with the 'few simple ideas' (such as fidelity) that he extols elsewhere (*PR*, xix). Such ideas might not be readily attainable (as, indeed, Hervey discovers) but that does not diminish their worth.

Materialism is the base for Hervey's conformity and is a continual target for Conrad, particularly in *Nostromo*, where the corrosive power of material interests is symbolised by the San Tomé silver mine. Silver is an appropriate symbol for materialism, for, although Nostromo regards it as an 'incorruptible metal' (*N*, 300), Conrad seems to use it frequently as a symbol of betrayal (for which there is the biblical precedent of Judas's payment for betraying Christ).

The fates of Nostromo and Charles Gould as victims of the silver and the shortcomings of institutionalised religion in Costaguana have received attention elsewhere. *Nostromo*, in fact, is as explicit as any of Conrad's novels in describing the modern spiritual dilemma as he saw it. With religion either easily malleable to the whims of tyrants such as Guzman Bento or subtly manipulated by material interests whilst, in its turn, seeking to re-establish its own power base under less rigorous regimes, it is little wonder that the chief-engineer should decide that 'things seem to be worth nothing by what they are in themselves' and believe 'that the only solid thing about them is the spiritual value which everyone discovers in his own form of activity' (*N*, 318). Here, then, is one alternative spiritual outlet but its validity is quickly questioned by Doctor Monygham with the words 'Self-flattery. Food for that vanity which makes the world go round.'

They are talking specifically about Holroyd here. To the engineer-in-chief 'The introduction of a pure form of Christianity into this continent is a dream for a youthful enthusiast' and although 'Holroyd is not a missionary . . . the San Tomé mine holds just that for him' (*N*, 317). To Emilia Gould, however, 'it seemed . . . that he looked upon his own God as a sort of influential partner, who gets his share of profits in the endowment of churches. That's a sort of idolatry'. She thus discerns that Holroyd's real belief is 'The religion of silver and iron' (*N*, 71); the forerunner of 'the most awful materialism' (*N*, 83).

This proves to be true of others too; material interests claim the obeisance of almost everyone in the book at one time or another. Sir John, it will be recalled, promises Emilia a greater future than that of the ecclesiastical past, indicating, perhaps, the succession of beliefs. General Barrios, about to leave to fight Montero, announces that, once victorious, 'we shall convert our swords into ploughshares and grow rich' (*N*, 148). The biblical peace scheduled to arrive at the time of the end is thus totally connected with materialism by the general, described as 'our saviour Barrios' by the sceptical Decoud (*N*, 188). Gould's visitors are discussing future profits and the coming of a railway when Decoud claims that they 'talk about their gods' (*N*, 199), whilst the silver of which Nostromo is to take charge is described as being for 'the very salvation of the San Tomé mine' (*N*, 219). Charles Gould, who in the early stages of the novel has the look of 'a sort of heretic pilgrim' (*N*, 47), proclaims that 'I pin my faith to material interests' (*N*, 84), and his later determination to destroy the mine rather than lose it reveals how this faith has replaced his belief in a deity; a fact that is made clear by his comments on Holroyd's response to this move:

> " . . . he said something about holding on like grim death and putting our trust in God. I should imagine he must have been rather startled. But then" − pursued the Administrador of the San Tomé mine − "but then, he is very far away, you know, and, as they say in this country, God is very high above."
>
> The engineer's appreciative laugh died away down the stairs, where the Madonna with the Child on her arm seemed to look after his shaking broad back from her shallow niche.   (*N*, 206)

Gould's remark recalls the stories of the Golfo Placido (too dark for either God or devil) but the view of the Madonna and Child (following the use of his official title) suggests that his faith is misplaced. It has already been shown to have limitations for, though material interests can 'awaken also in human hearts an unbounded devotion to the task' and a force 'almost as strong as a faith' (*N*, 41), they 'can't move mountains,' a feat that faith is commonly reputed to perform.[28] Gould, indeed, should heed the view of Antonia Avellanos that, in reality, his 'inexhaustible treasure' lies in his character, not in his wealth (*N*, 361). As he becomes more and more a slave of the mine, his wife is left lonely and forsaken. The Madonna on the stairs is an ironic commentary on Emilia's lot − a virgin and yet a mother to gaze on a married woman who will never be a mother.

Nostromo's more overt enslavement by the treasure has already been seen, but not everyone is a devotee of the material interests, although no one can remain unaffected by them. Giorgio dislikes priests but still believes in God (*N*, 29), though his divinity appears to be Liberty and its prophet is Garibaldi; a belief whose religious connections are made explicit by the way he is known as the "'Gari-

baldino" (as Mohammedans are called after their prophet)' (*N*, 16).
Events, however, have 'instilled into him a gloomy doubt of ever being
able to understand the ways of Divine justice' (*N*, 29). His despising of
materialism (or money, at least), is described as 'a puritanism of
conduct, born of stern enthusiasm like the the puritanism of religion',
but the gloom persists 'because the cause seemed lost' (*N*, 31).

If Giorgio holds a stubborn and apparently fruitless belief, one
which materialism will do nothing to further, Martin Decoud can
believe only in the evidence of his own sensations and engages in an
interesting exchange with Father Corbelán as the crisis approaches.
He agrees that 'I certainly do not believe in miracles' and hears himself
analysed by the priest as a 'sort of Frenchman – godless – a materialist' and as 'a victim of this faithless age' (*N*, 198).

Whatever his own preoccupations, Corbelán's assessment here is
perceptive and, in the event, prophetic. Decoud's attitude stands him
in poor stead when he is faced with the loneliness of life on the Great
Isabel, where a belief in miracles would, in fact, be more practical than
the despair to which he becomes a victim. For, though he claims that
'I'm not so much of an unbeliever as not to have faith in my own ideas,
in my own remedies, in my own desires' (*N*, 213), all these dissolve in
the darkness of the Golfo Placido where, in a 'foretaste of eternal
peace,' only his thoughts appear to survive (*N*, 262). Alone on the
Great Isabel, he dies 'from solitude and want of faith in himself and
others' (*N*, 496). His solitude has become 'a state of soul in which the
affectations of irony and scepticism have no place' (*N*, 497). Thus, to
lose all belief is the worst fate of all.

Perhaps the one redeeming feature about life in Sulaco is Emilia
Gould. With the emphasis that Catholicism gives to the Virgin, it is no
accident that the statue of the Madonna and Child should stand in her
hallway in constant association with her. She it is whose character
attracts the devotion and causes the redemption of Dr Monygham; she
it is, 'cloaked and monastically hooded,' to whom Nostromo feels
compelled to make the final confession of his guilt and the existence of
the treasure – a confidence she is not willing to receive (*N*, 558). She it
is who is likened to a 'good fairy' (*N*, 520) and an 'angel' (*N*, 399)
during the course of the book. Emilia may not have found happiness in
Sulaco but she has proved an inspiration to those around her.

To a background of religious terms, the social obsession of material
interests exercises its baleful influence over all those who come within
its grasp. The corruptness of the religious systems is clearly shown,

but the inadequacy of non-religious materialism shows itself in an even worse light. In the face of this overpowering preoccupation, it is difficult to determine a satisfactory attitude to take. Giorgio's beliefs in Liberty prove unrealistic; Decoud's scepticism pessimistic and suicidal. Only, it seems, the actions of such as Emilia can prove anything of an inspiration. In a way the doctor's soul is saved by her example, but unspiritual materialism, which attracts, in its various facets, the spiritual values of its various functionaries, is capable of no such benefits, only an insidious and unrelenting process of enslavement.

In *The Secret Agent*, Mr Vladimir decides that an outrage must be committed against 'the fetish of the hour' which is 'neither royalty nor religion. Therefore the palace and the church should be left alone' (*SA*, 30–1). According to Vladimir, 'The sacrosanct fetish of today is science' (*SA*, 31); an ideal target since 'The attack must have all the shocking senselessness of gratuitous blasphemy' (*SA*, 33). The churches must be left alone since 'No matter how revolutionary and anarchist in inception, there would be fools enough to give such an outrage the character of a religious manifestation' (*SA*, 31–2).

Thus science, whose discoveries had caused many Victorians to lose their beliefs, has become the successor to religion in Vladimir's eyes. But, as a replacement for religion, science does little of benefit in the novel. It is a manifestation of science − a bomb − which causes the disintegration of the harmless Stevie and, less directly, that of the whole Verloc household.

The allies of science in the book and its most devoted admirers come from the ranks of the anarchists. One of these, Ossipon, appears as a fervent apostle of the fetish; his 'Apollo-like' hair adding an ironic classical touch to his standing in the scientific ranks (*SA*, 309). His saint is Lombroso and he regards as 'blasphemy' a suggestion by a fellow anarchist that 'Lombroso is an ass' (*SA*, 47). Thus introduced, his scientific devotions do not re-appear until the final chapters when Winnie Verloc runs into him on her way to throwing herself in the Thames after stabbing her husband. To Winnie, Ossipon is 'like a radiant messenger of life' (*SA*, 274) and she proceeds to cast this apostle of science in the role of saviour (*SA*, 292). Ossipon, however, becomes terrified on discovering that she has just killed Mr Verloc and abandons his plans to seduce her. The consciously scientific nature of his thought processes are given religious overtones again as he invokes Lombroso 'as an Italian peasant recommends himself to his favourite saint' and gazes 'Scientifically' (*SA*, 297). But this conduct only results in his desertion of her (having first obtained her money), and Winnie is left to drown herself in the Channel. The scientific saviour thus returns her to the death from which he had unwittingly saved her.

Winnie has placed her trust misguidedly, therefore, and the religious references underline this. Earlier, they have been used with similar effect when describing the relationship betweeen the ill-fated Stevie and the morose Verloc, once Winnie's mother has 'sacrificed' Winnie for Stevie's welfare and consigned herself to the almshouse (*SA*, 161). The cab which conveys her thence is appropriately drawn by 'the steed of apocalyptic misery' (*SA*, 165), since this act is, unwittingly, to lead to the destruction of the Verloc household. Both women have instilled into Stevie the lesson of Mr Verloc's goodness upon which his security depends, not knowing that the place of Mr Verloc's 'pilgrimage' is the embassy (*SA*, 37), which regards his marriage as 'apostasy' (*SA*, 36). Winnie knows but ignores her husband's anarchistic connections, even though she complains to him that their talk causes Stevie to go 'out of his mind with something he overheard about eating people's flesh and drinking blood' (*SA*, 59), which sounds like a parody of the Christian sacrament and suggests that anarchism, too, is a perverted successor to religion.

Thus Verloc's goodness becomes 'established, erected, consecrated' (*SA*, 175), so that, when he returns from the Continent, Stevie gapes at him 'with reference and awe' and bears off his bag 'with triumphant devotion' (*SA*, 182). Verloc's hat is taken off 'reverently into the kitchen' (*SA*, 184) and Verloc is informed that the boy 'just worships you' (*SA*, 186). Winnie has persuaded Stevie to become Verloc's 'admiring disciple' so that her husband can become aware of his 'submission and worship' (*SA*, 235). Thus 'the doctrine of his supreme wisdom and goodness, inculcated by two anxious women' leads to Stevie's death; misplaced devotion again ending in disaster.

There have been two cases thus far of trust in individuals leading to destruction (Stevie's worship of Verloc and Winnie's acceptance of Ossipon as saviour), and science (through a bomb and an apostle) has been ruthless to both an unwitting attacker and a despairing supplicant. It has, as one of its chief practitioners, the ultimate anarchist, the Professor, whose quest in life is to perfect a detonator so that the bombs he makes can be instantly lethal.

The Professor is an example of fanaticism in science being derived from fanaticism in religion, represented by the egoistic fervour of his preaching father; the suggestion being that, in Conrad's eyes, both forms are destructive. Much of the father's personality has become vested in the son whose outlook is expressed in religious terms, as if to justify Vladimir's earlier claims:

> In the son, individualist by temperament, once the science of colleges had replaced thoroughly the faith of conventicles, this moral attitude translated itself into a frenzied puritanism of ambition. He nursed it as something secularly holy. To see it thwarted opened his eyes to the true nature of the world, whose morality was artificial, corrupt and blasphemous.   (*SA*, 80–1)

To add to this image of a scientific puritan of a rigid anarchistic sect, the Professor's home is described as a 'hermitage' (*SA*, 82). He can thus be seen to have inherited certain faults of religionists (bigotry and fanaticism) and applied them to science and anarchism, though, as was shown with Podmore, the root of such an inheritance is excessive egoism. Science has succeeded in producing no saviours, only destroyers, and the ironical sense of religion present in the Professor's character only emphasises the grotesque extent of his perversity and (by implication) that of the rigidly scientific world he represents.

The Professor, in the final chapter, has just come from a visit to Michaelis, the 'ticket-of-leave apostle' (*SA*, 107) who is presented throughout in religious terms. Being forced to leave Marienbad is 'a martyrdom' (*SA*, 42), whilst the idea he pursues grows 'like a faith revealed in visions' which masters him 'irresistibly and complete like an act of grace' (*SA*, 44–5). He is described as 'angelic' (*SA*, 303), as a 'mere believer' with 'the temperament of a saint' (*SA*, 109), and is likened to 'those saintly men whose personality is lost in the contemplation of their faith' (*SA*, 107). The 'invincible and humanitarian creed, which he confessed rather than preached' (*SA*, 107) is expounded by the Professor at the end when he explains, 'He has divided his biography into three parts, entitled – "Faith, Hope, Charity." He is elaborating now the idea of a world planned out like an immense and nice hospital, with gardens and flowers, in which the strong are to devote themselves to the nursing of the weak' (*SA*, 303). This sounds like a simplistic version of Christianity, and the simplicity of Michaelis, which, in some ways, aligns him with the half-witted Stevie and allows him to proclaim his view but not to argue it, is perhaps a further ironic comment by Conrad on the state of religion in his day. Yet there is no doubt that Michaelis's ideas are healthier than those of his chief critic, the Professor. The world of *The Secret Agent* has frequently been likened to a kind of hell and it may be no coincidence that the man most anxious to have Michaelis back behind bars should be Chief-Inspector Heat, a man who is 'conscious of having an authorised mission on this earth and the moral support of his kind' (*SA*, 96), one 'whose reputation was established as if on a rock' (*SA*, 133), being thus compared with the Church.

Once more, then, religious imagery denotes false and disastrous beliefs. It indicates the misplaced devotion of Winnie and Stevie, reveals science as the successor to religion in the life of the Professor and in Vladimir's assertions, and insinuates, through Michaelis, that a simplistic Christian-like outlook is out of joint in a world in which science is dominant and an 'infernal Heat' (*SA*, 113) with an 'authorized mission' can stand in opposition. Science proves destructive (through the Professor) and treacherous (through Ossipon) – as the social obsession of the day it has few redeeming features.

Mixed in with the materialism of *Nostromo* and the science of *The Secret Agent* are the political considerations of various Costaguanan governments and of the anarchists. In *Under Western Eyes*, the religious references denote social obsessions that are almost entirely political. Both autocracy and revolution surround themselves with religious language; those 'strange pretensions of sanctity' that were noticeable during the earlier discussion of the demonic. Only a few more comments need to be added here.

As one might expect, the religious terms connected to autocracy and revolution tend to be very similar. Autocracy (in the persons of Mr De P— and the chaplain) decrees acts against it as 'sin' (*UWE*, 8, 93), for which it exhorts the traditional theological remedies of repentance, atonement and confession. But it is in 'a spirit of repentance' that Peter Ivanovitch begins to conspire against the state (*UWE*, 120), whilst Razumov is tempted to confess, not only to the autocratic Mikulin (*UWE*, 297), but also to the revolutionary Haldin (*UWE*, 40). Just as Razumov feels 'the touch of grace upon his forehead' as he turns towards autocracy (*UWE*, 34), so Sophia Antonovna thinks that the conclusive stage of becoming a revolutionary is 'the final appeasement of the convert in the perfect fierceness of conviction' (*UWE*, 269). The venerable chaplain of the fortress equates 'the Divine laws' with 'the sacred Majesty of the Ruler' during his ministrations to Haldin (*UWE*, 93), but Kostia affirms 'the sacred will of the people' (*UWE*, 314), Sophia Antonovna speaks of the 'sacred task of crushing the infamy' (*UWE*, 270), and Peter Ivanovitch's 'sacred trust' is the gospel of feminism which he claims to uphold (*UWE*, 121). Autocracy, naturally, claims exclusive belief so that General T— can regard its opponents as 'people that deny God Himself — perfect unbelievers' (*UWE*, 51) and, on hearing that Haldin 'believed in God,' Councillor Mikulin can remark 'with a shade of scorn that blasphemers also had that sort of belief' (*UWE*, 91). To the revolutionaries, on the other hand, autocracy is demonic, being regarded by Peter Ivanovitch as 'the devil' who 'is not combated by prayers and fasting' (*UWE*, 127). Little wonder that Razumov should decide that the lot of one who remains unconverted to either of these rival creeds is 'perdition' (*UWE*, 367). Little wonder, too, that Razumov's deafness (the reward for his confession) should be at the hands of Nikita, the 'fiend' who 'killed . . . in both camps' (*UWE*, 381).

Both sides, then, use the terminology of religion in similar ways but neither shows much inclination to follow religious teaching. Peter Ivanovitch (whilst dismissing prayer and fasting as a valid course of action) comments that 'Sin is different in our day, and the way of salvation for pure souls is different too. It is no longer to be found in monasteries but in the world' (*UWE*, 128), to which Natalia responds, 'I don't mean to retire into a monastery. Who would look for salvation there?' They may both claim to be speaking 'figuratively,' but the exchange is ironic in two separate ways. Its rejection of the traditional *raison d'être* of certain religious orders implies, once more, the inadequacy of institutionalised religion and its irrelevance to human life; secondly, its assertion that salvation is to be found in the world is belied by the events of the novel, especially as far as Razumov is concerned. Peter Ivanovitch's autobiography sets out the passage of his conversion to feminism, 'the conviction of woman's spiritual superiority — his new faith confessed since in several volumes' (*UWE*, 121), and the professor of languages comments ironically on the way aspects of his journey (an escape from the mines in which he had been sentenced to labour) lend themselves 'to mystic treatment and symbolic interpretation' (*UWE*, 125). Much of this kind of view is obviously deliberately engendered by Peter Ivanovitch himself who revels in his role as 'the noble arch-priest of Revolution' (*UWE*, 210), and it is in this role that he can pontificate on salvation to Natalia. The religious aspects utilised by revolution become selective, therefore; salvation remains but prayer and fasting are dropped. Like autocracy, revolution makes use only of those religious aspects that seem convenient.

Tekla reveals the shortcomings of both Peter Ivanovitch's creeds. Her treatment at his hands shows that his pursuance of 'the cult of the woman' is a very selective one whilst a comment by Natalia towards the end of the book — 'She is a good Samaritan by an irresistible vocation.

The revolutionists didn't understand her' (*UWE*, 374) – is a damning indictment of revolutionary attitudes.

In manuscript, Peter Ivanovitch's pretensions are still more explicit. There, he links himself with Christ, commenting, 'I have dwelt forty days in the wilderness and I know what the Prince of Darkness is like' (f. 463).[29] He also compares himself with the prophets of Israel (f. 469) and speaks of the need for a new gospel (f. 482). He is said to have spent a night with Madame de S— 'in tears and on his knees seeing visions and waiting for a final feminist revelation' (f. 500). The titles of his works are announced as 'The Resurrection of Yegor', 'The Pride of Darkness' and 'Parables of Decay' (f. 591), which sound both biblical and Tolstoyan.[30] The final view, as presented by the novel, is less blatant, yet retains this deliberately evoked sense of the prophetic figure, come from the wilderness to preach.

Also of interest are some of the early sections of the manuscript, where the narrator reports that, in his diary, Razumov 'apostrophizes the Deity with considerable violence and bitterness,' but feels that the outburst cannot be regarded as 'blasphemous' because 'Mr Razumov held no religious faith or belief of any kind.' The Professor continues by lamenting that his own life seems to have been 'forgotten by the God of wonders and perhaps for that very reason disdained by the devil'. No one can deny, however, that Razumov's life 'is touched by the gloom of the bottomless pit' (f. 9–11).[31]

This picture of Razumov – addressing a God in which he does not believe – seems an exercise in futility, though there may be some point if it is the deities of autocracy and revolution that stir his wrath. The sense of the narrator as being 'forgotten by God' and 'disdained by the devil' is also less pronounced in the book which is, thus, less specific with each of these three characters. In the final version Razumov's lack of belief is not so bluntly stated; as noted earlier, Conrad's characters tend to be evasive when questioned about faith. There are even times when Razumov is tempted to regard himself as an agent of Providence, the mystical view that Prince K— and Councillor Mikulin incline to (*UWE*, 301). Ironically, belief here would lead to destruction – destruction of a spiritual kind (or of his peace of mind). Only by forgoing that belief can Razumov find spiritual peace or peace of mind, though at the cost of physical mutilation, which brings out, as it were, the spiritual mutilation that was present previously.

To pour one's religious ardour into the political polarities existing in *Under Western Eyes*, whose roots lie in the deification of the state and the myth of Holy Russia (attacked by Conrad in 'Autocracy and War'), proves as futile and destructive as to apply it to materialism, science or progress. These social obsessions, the fate of those who adhere to them and even (in Razumov's case) of those who cannot adhere to them, proclaim society's spiritual crisis and the ill-directed nature of its apparent solutions. Madame de S— wished to 'spiritualize the discontent' (*UWE*, 221), but the spirituality produced by each of these social concerns is vitiating, not uplifting.

SELF-CONCEPTUAL OBSESSIONS

The object of an obsession is not always external but internal — with one's own self-conception. Jim's view of himself as thwarted hero is an example of this. The 'course of light holiday reading' that prompts his decision to go to sea (*LJ*, 5) becomes a controlling factor in his outlook on life. His dreams 'were the best parts of life, its secret truth, its hidden reality. They had a gorgeous virility, the charm of vagueness, they passed before him with a heroic tread; they carried his soul away with them and made it drunk with the divine philtre of an unbounded confidence in itself' (*LJ*, 20).

After the *Patna* incident has caused 'some mysterious, inexplicable, impalpable striving of his wounded spirit' (*LJ*, 182), Jim's acute consciousness of lost honour dominates his existence. Such an attitude even seems to possess its own kind of priest in the figure of the French Lieutenant who stayed thirty hours on the *Patna* to see her safely into port. He appears to be an expert on the subject of honour and Marlow equates him explicitly with a religious figure:

> . . . he reminded you of one of those snuffy, quiet village priests, into whose ears are poured the sins, the sufferings, the remorse of peasant generations, on whose faces the placid and simple expression is like a veil thrown over the mystery of pain and distress. He ought to have had a threadbare black *soutane* buttoned smoothly up to his ample chin, instead of a frock-coat with shoulder-straps and brass buttons.   (*LJ*, 139)

But just as the creed of the sea (which Jim has betrayed) has been seen to offer no absolution, so the creed of honour (to which Jim has been unfaithful) is similarly unhelpful. Jim's later status as a saviour figure in Patusan is an outward manifestation of the exalted conception he holds of himself; a conception to which he finally proves a martyr.

Similarly it is an idea of self that dictates the actions of Anthony and Flora in *Chance*. Anthony's excessive magnanimity has been seen before; what makes it so life-negating is Flora's own feeling that she is unlovable and Marlow describes the whole development of this attitude in religious terms. When the news of de Barral's bankruptcy is about to break, he announces that 'her unconscious was to be broken into with profane violence, with desecrating circumstances like a temple violated by a mad, vengeful impiety' (*C*, 99), and he repeats the image in more detail later:

> A young girl, you know, is something like a temple. You pass by and wonder what mysterious rites are going on in there, what prayers, what visions? The privileged man, the lover, the husband, who are given the key of the sanctuary do not always know how to use it. For myself, without claim, without merit, simply by chance I had been allowed to look through the half-opened door and I had seen the saddest possible desecration, the withered brightness of youth, a spirit neither made cringing nor yet dulled but as if bewildered in quivering hopelessness by gratuitous cruelty.   (*C*, 311–12)

This cruelty (by the governess) remains with the girl 'like a mark on her soul, a sort of mystic wound, to be contemplated, to be meditated over' (*C*, 118–19), and this effect is augmented by the attitude of Flora's relatives who seem intent on instilling a sense of unworthiness within her. In Marlow's words, she has had 'an ugly pilgrimage' (*C*, 210); one that continues on board the *Ferndale* once the strange tripartite arrangement between Flora, Anthony and de Barral has been engaged. Marlow explains: 'It was as if the forehead of Flora de Barral were marked. Was the girl born to be a victim; to be always disliked and crushed as if she were too fine for this world? Or too luckless – since that also is often counted as sin' (*C*, 309).

In Flora too, therefore, there is an inadequate attitude (albeit one that has been inculcated in the first instance and nurtured by mischance thereafter). Her struggles take place to a backcloth of immensity and indifference. When she goes missing from the Fynes Marlow describes his sensations as he steps outside and finds 'one of those dewy, clear, starry nights, oppressing our spirit, crushing our pride, by the brilliant evidence of the awful loneliness, of the hopeless obscure insignificance of our globe lost in the splendid revelation of a glittering, soulless universe' (*C*, 50). Previously the external narrator has under-

cut an attempt to reconcile the traditional Christian view of the age of
the universe with ideas of evolution:

> The late Carleon Anthony, the poet, sang in his time, of the domes-
> tic and social amenities of our age with a most felicitous versifica-
> tion, his object being, in his own words, "to glorify the result of six
> thousand years' evolution towards the refinement of thought, man-
> ners, and feelings." Why he fixed the term at six thousand years I
> don't know.   (*C*, 38)

Flora herself, when being conducted through the docks by Anthony,
thinks 'that it was not good to be bothered with what all these things
meant in the scheme of things (if indeed anything had a meaning)' (*C*,
337).

This sense of the infinite may well serve the role of indicating still
further the futility of an obsessive attitude, be it the consciousness of
possessing a virtue (Anthony) or of being a victim (Flora). It also re-
emphasises the fact that Flora is to receive little help from religion.
While these obsessions remain, Anthony's panacea of life at sea is
likely to be no more successful than the attractions of Mrs Fyne's
feminism, which, while attracting its 'disciples' (*C*, 42, 49), holds
nothing for Flora.

Flora is saved by chance; chance, however, that is introduced by an
image from the Bible (Matt. 13:11–16) as Powell comments, 'He who
has eyes, you know, nothing can stop him from seeing things as long as
there are things to see in front of him' (*C*, 412). The biblical sense of
'see' is that of understanding and it is a general understanding amongst
the major characters, brought about by the revelation of what Powell
sees, that his comment heralds.

Flora's final happiness is to be in the hands of Powell, whose enthusiasm for her – an 'almost sacrilegious hint' by Marlow – 'allowed a
gleam to light up his eyes like the reflection of some inward fire tended
in the sanctuary of his heart by a devotion as pure as that of any vestal'
(*C*, 441). The religious terms here describe a natural emotion and
recall the earlier images of a desecrated temple. It seems that rededica-
tion is now taking place.

At first sight, a withdrawal from the world of action – the path taken
by Axel Heyst – might suggest an attitude of detachment, combined
with a healthy layer of the scepticism that Conrad had recommended
to Galsworthy. Such a withdrawal, however, indicates, paradoxically,

that one has become attached to detachment. Scepticism must be balanced, therefore; too much produces a Decoud, too little, a Jim.

Much has been made of Heyst's surname but far less attention has been paid to the name 'Axel' which probably derives from the play of that name by Philippe Villiers de l'Isle-Adam. In that play, Axel makes the ultimate withdrawal from life (suicide) with the comment, 'Live? Our servants will do that for us.'[32] Heyst has one servant, Wang, who, by settling down with a native wife, can be said to be fulfilling the role of living, whilst Heyst is restrained by his scepticism and also ends by killing himself. But, as Katherine Hayes Gatch suggests, whilst the author of *Axel* seems to condone the attitude of his protagonist, Conrad condemns it.[33]

Heyst is introduced as a man around whom epithets naturally gather, such as 'enchanted' and 'Hard Facts'; the latter after his statement that 'There's nothing worth knowing but facts. Hard facts! Facts alone' (*V*, 6−7). This remark, ironically, makes him sound like the Commander in *Axel* (Axel's adversary), when he says 'Grab hold of life, just as it is, with no illusions and no weaknesses.'[34]

The names sometimes contradict each other since Heyst is also called an 'utopist' (*V*, 8), and his physical resemblance to Charles XII is noted as being misleading (*V*, 9); these are factors which should counsel caution when attempting to equate him with Christ because he rescues a Magdalen or with Adam in an Edenic Samburan. Put together, though, these nomenclatures do form a pattern. Heyst is indeed under a spell − the spell of his father's admonition to observe but not participate in the affairs of mankind. He has no faith (hence the insistence of facts), yet inherits his father's sense of idealism to which humanity can never attain. He is also referred to as the 'Enemy' (*V*, 25), and proves to be this, both to himself and to life and love.

The religious imagery of *Victory* is usually direct and biblical, emphasising the essential negativity of Heyst's stance. The final advice he receives from his father, for example ('Look on − make no sound'), is accompanied by images of apocalypse and futility, being given by a man 'who had spent his life in blowing blasts upon a terrible trumpet which had filled heaven and earth with ruins, while mankind went on its way unheeding' (*V*, 175).

The effects of this valediction on Heyst are described in spiritual terms when Davidson, a friendly sea captain, takes an interest. Davidson's concern is with 'the danger of spiritual starvation; but this was a spirit which had renounced all outside nourishment, and was sustaining itself proudly on its contempt of the usual coarse aliments which life offers to the common appetites of men' (*V*, 177). Heyst's conviction that to participate in mankind's affairs is a mistake, causes him to ridicule or ignore the positive religious utterances that accompany his two acts of rescue. The over-charitable Morrison, having admitted to praying for help on the very morning when Heyst meets him (*V*, 14), regards his helper as an agent of Providence, 'sent by God in answer to my prayer' (*V*, 17). Similarly, when Heyst rescues Lena, he discovers that she is called 'Alma' and 'Magdalen' (*V*, 88). Andreach claims that 'Alma' means life or soul;[35] it certainly has a sense of bounteousness, appropriate to one in danger of 'spiritual starvation'. The biblical connotations of 'Magdalen' are obvious, giving a very clear sign that Heyst has done the right thing. Lena, indeed, begins to have faith 'in the man of her destiny, and perhaps in the Heaven which had sent him so wonderfully to cross her path' (*V*, 292). Even Ricardo echoes such feelings when he says, 'I would have just as soon expected to meet an angel from heaven' after Heyst has saved the trio in the boat from dying of thirst (*V*, 238).

But the religious imagery that Heyst evokes from these acts is entirely negative. Whilst musing on Samburan after Morrison's death and the failure of the Tropical Belt Coal Company, he decides that 'There must be a lot of the original Adam in me, after all'; an assertion that is ominously underlined when it is confirmed that 'There was in the son a lot of that first ancestor who as soon as he could uplift his muddy frame from the celestial mould, started inspecting and naming the animals of that paradise which he was so soon to lose' (*V*, 173–4). This reference also emphasises the fact that Heyst cannot set himself apart from mankind; he is inextricably part of the human race.

The sense of having rebelled against a creed is made evident when Heyst's father's furniture arrives, for Heyst 'must have felt like a remorseful apostate before these relics. He handled them tenderly; and it was perhaps their presence there which attached him to the island when he woke up to the failure of his apostasy' (*V*, 177).

Heyst's negative doctrine of non-involvement, therefore, causes him to misread the signs, for whilst these have equated his actions with those of an agent of God and even with those of Christ, he sees them as indicating his state as fallen Adam and as evidence of apostasy from his father's creed. The ill-fated Morrison, he regards as 'so representative of all the past victims of the Great Joke,' and the view of him as an agent of God he sees as comical:

What captivated my fancy was that I, Axel Heyst, the most detached of creatures in this earthly captivity, the veriest tramp on this
earth, an indifferent stroller going through the world's bustle — that
I should have been there to step into the situation of an agent of
Providence. *I*, a man of universal scorn and unbelief.   (*V*, 198–9)

It was noted earlier that Heyst's prevailing mood is akin to that of
Conrad while he was writing his excessively morbid letters to Cunninghame Graham in the late 1890s and that *Victory* represents a fictional
refutation of that mood. It was noted also that the demonic is used to
reflect the logical culmination of such an outlook in the person of the
misogynic killer, Mr Jones; another very obvious example of negation
attracting negative religious imagery. Once Jones is in sight of the
island, images of the Apocalypse and the Flood begin to pervade,
though this again is a persistent reminder of Heyst's own negation. To
Lena, the view of the sea is 'the abomination of desolation' whilst
Heyst is reminded of 'the story of the deluge. . . . The vision of a world
destroyed' (*V*, 190–1). Lena seems aware of Heyst's duality as she
feels herself 'swinging between the abysses of earth and heaven in
the hollow of his arm' (*V*, 209) but Heyst continues his obsession with
detachment (and its negative connotation) by maintaining, 'As if it
could matter to me what anybody had ever said or believed from the
beginning of the world till the crack of doom' (*V*, 210). Having earlier
equated himself with the first Adam, he is soon to refer to himself as a
'man of the last hour' (*V*, 359).

Nevertheless, it is Lena who is moved to interpret the 'ill-omened
chaos of the sky' (*V*, 355), because she, too, is possessed by a negative
outlook at this stage (the sense of sin) causing her to regard the advent
of Jones and the others as 'retribution from an angry Heaven' and
herself as 'the tempter' (*V*, 354). Her love for Heyst enables her to
overcome this attitude, but it is fitting that she should regard her
success in removing Ricardo's knife in Edenic terms as 'the venom of
the viper in her paradise, extracted, safe in her possession — and the
viper's head all but lying under her heel' (*V*, 399), since this reflects her
new positive mood.

The story ends in tragedy because of Heyst's pessimistic inertness
which prevents him tackling Jones. Davidson's arrival as Lena is dying
shows that a more optimistic view of life would have led to a happier
result and his assessment of Heyst's suicide — 'fire purifies everything'
(*V*, 411) — is a positive interpretation of the act (a purgatorial rite) in
contrast to the previous negativity. The 'Alma' part of Lena is thus the

means of giving spiritual sustenance to Heyst, whilst the 'Magdalen' part of her indicates her power to love and participate in the world.

Religious references in *Victory*, therefore, act as indicators of attitude. Heyst ignores the positive signs that accompany his acts of rescue and can think of himself only as fallen Adam or failed apostate; a view that is complemented by Lena's own self-conception as sinful woman, descended from Eve. It is important to note, incidentally, that the Edenic allusions are in the minds of the characters themselves, indicating not allegory but outlook, reflected later by images of deluge and apocalypse and by the demonic references that accompany Jones and Ricardo. Heyst's sterile scepticism is ultimately destructive because, lacking the vitality of life, it must end in extinction, in nothing (appropriately, the last word in the book).

Summing up, then, one can say that the figurative religious lexis exposes the secular nature of man's latter-day devotions. Sometimes (as in 'The Return' and *Under Western Eyes*) these images are deliberately utilised by characters to give additional justification to a particular mode of behaviour or a cause. In instances such as that of M. George, they reveal the awareness of an obsession, too powerful to be escaped. Sometimes they are produced with intentional irony, to show the obsessions of others, by such characters as Marlow in 'Heart of Darkness' and Decoud, who follows Father Corbelán's denunciation of General Barrios — 'Senores, the God of your General is a bottle!' (*N*, 194) — with the comment, 'But is it perhaps that you have not discovered yet what is the God of my worship?' (*N*, 197).

Such metaphorical use of religious language thus reveals the way a character is paying undue attention to one particular object; be that his ego, a woman, a personal illusion, a vocation, a social preoccupation or a certain self-conception that engulfs him. Whatever that object may be (whatever god he may worship), it dominates his vision, forcing all else to be regarded in relation to it, and the distortion is rarely a healthy one.

9

Conclusion

Conrad's use of a religious lexis in his writings indicates the spiritual nature of society's malaise. The inadequacies of established beliefs had left a gap in man's existence which he endeavoured to fill with his own concerns. This had happened in Conrad's own life with the sense of vocation he brought to his two professions once that early Catholic faith of his childhood had faded. It had happened earlier and less positively when his father had been influenced by Mickiewicz's mystical writings, which perceived a Messianic role for Poland in the world. Apollo Korzeniowski, therefore, had much in common with the fictional characters of his son; his ardent protestations of faith notwithstanding, Poland proved to be the true object of his adoration. The importance of Polish Messianism in this context is that its expectations were secular ones. Despite all the mystical teachings that encircled it, the outcome of the Third Day was not fondly foreseen as a spiritual event but as a physical victory over the Russians which would see them expelled from Poland's sacred soil. Such material expectations were completely disappointed.

Conrad's perceptive eyes noted, in later years, that it was not just the Poles who applied religious sentiments to areas other than those of their actual religion (Christianity). The 'madness of a fixed idea,' which so grips Lingard, pervades the characters of all Conrad's novels and is almost always destructive. It is 'the idea' that causes Cantelucci and others to have such respect for Napoleon, for example, prompting Doctor Martel to comment, 'Devil only knows what that idea is, but I suspect it's vague enough to include every illusion that ever fooled mankind' (*Sus*, 182).

It is devotion to the 'idea' that brings about the downfall of many of Conrad's characters and Martel is clearly right to connect it with illusions. Almayer has faith only in his dreams; when they are shattered, so is he. But those without a belief, however ill-founded, fare no better and, indeed, loss of faith is never presented in a positive light. Rita de Lastaola seems bitter about the 'clever men' who 'robbed' her of God (and, in the event, of love as well), and Decoud proves to be, truly, 'The victim of this faithless age.' Axel Heyst regrets 'that he had

168

no Heaven to which he could recommend this fair, palpitating handful of ashes and dust [Lena]' (*V*, 354–5), whilst the slave girl, Taminah, who adores Dain Maroola to no avail, is forced to feed 'her dumb ignorant soul on her despair' (*AF*, 116) because she 'could find no words to pray for relief, she knew of no heaven to send her prayer to' (*AF*, 118–19).

The balance, presumably, lies in moderation. When Conrad tells Galsworthy in one letter that he needs 'more scepticism at the very foundation of your work',[1] and then writes in an essay, four years later, that the artist in fiction must cherish 'an undying hope' (*NLL*, 8), these statements are not necessarily contradictory. The implication is that one needs a measure of both. Scepticism is necessary (it keeps at bay superstition), but too much is destructive, as Decoud and Heyst show. Conrad's novels, in this respect, expose immoderation, and the figurative religious lexis is particularly useful in revealing this. Only the vocation of the seaman is seen to merit, indeed, demand a total commitment, and that, too, is shown to contain its illusions, which, when proved unreliable, create unease among its adherents.

There are, in this figurative sense, several deities clamouring for worship from the individual soul in need of spiritual nourishment. But religious fervour (or absorption) carried into science and anarchy produces the destructive Professor; brought to materialism, it raises up the insidious, soul-sapping San Tomé mine; conveyed into the politics of Russia it creates two systems, equally oppressive to non-believers – none of which offers any hope. On a personal level, it proves equally destructive when applied to the regard for an individual (Almayer for Nina, Stevie for Verloc), for oneself (Willems) or for one's capabilities (Lingard), to dreams of wealth (Almayer) or to sexual passion (Willems, M. George, Ortega and Lingard).

There is a qualification in this last instance. Heyst is condemned because his philosophy prevents him from loving Lena, and Anthony is similarly mistaken in placing his sense of excessive magnanimity before his love for Flora. In these cases, negative religious imagery operates to emphasise the point. The glimpse of paradise, which undoes Lingard, does not have the same result for Dain Maroola and Nina and the later liaison of Arlette and Réal – 'a miracle' to Réal (*Ro*, 216), a 'terrestrial revelation' to Arlette (*Ro*, 160) – is also destined to be successful.

The backgrounds of these affairs differ, however. The passions of Willems and Lingard are illicit, for example (Willems and Edith being married), which would involve an act of infidelity on the part of the marriage partner. Rita cannot escape the sterilising efects of Allègre's aestheticism and thereby blights the existences of Blunt, George and Ortega. For Nina, Flora and Arlette, however, love (as opposed to sheer sexual passion), proves a form of release. Dain's adoration of Nina enables her to escape from the oppressiveness of Almayer's dreamworld; Powell's revelations allow Flora to overcome her conviction of being unlovable, firstly with Anthony (no longer tied by his magnanimity) and then with Powell himself; whilst the relationship between Arlette and Réal frees both from the negating memories of revolution which, in common with previous social obsessions, is likened to a religion with its 'republican god' (*Ro*, 76), its 'sacred revolutionary principles' (*Ro*, 209), its evoking of sacrifice and a 'sacred fire' (*Ro*, 81) and its comparison (by Peyrol) with 'the tale of an intelligent islander on the other side of the world talking of bloody rites and amazing hopes of some religion unknown to the rest of mankind' (*Ro*, 94).

Here, then, is one form of solution – the same, indeed, as that sought for by Alvan Hervey in 'The Return' – namely, 'Faith in a human heart, love of a human being' (*TU*, 177). This is the lesson that Heyst comes to learn when it is too late. Conrad's tone to Garnett is not a serious one when he talks of the 'new gospel', but it is still one of the few simple notions that succeeds in quieting troubled souls. In *The Rover*, the revolution is likened to 'the terrors of a Judgement Day in which the world had been given over to the devils' (*Ro*, 145), whilst the prelude to Peyrol's sacrifice which will allow the two lovers to come together is an apocalyptic storm, 'the beginning of a destroying and universal deluge – the end of all things' (*Ro*, 248). But it is an end to negativity for Réal and Arlette and a beginning of life; life that triumphs over the negating advice of the Catholic Abbé (literal religion) and over the destructive influence of the revolution (figurative religion). Elsewhere, though, figurative religious terminology usually portends only disaster, frequently made apparent by the use of demonic imagery (denoting, usually, an excessive egoism or a life-negating philosophy) and the related destructive effects on the soul (generally standing for man's will or power of choice), whose operations become controlled or circumscribed by whatever obsession commands the character's devotion.

It is against this secular religious background that any archetypal patterns should be considered and, in this sense, Claire Rosenfeld's conclusion that such patterns reflect the sickness of modern life by implicitly contrasting it with the stability of the past, has much to recommend it, even though some of her examples seem dubious.[2] Spirituality is lacking in the modern world and the secular use of religious terminology in the novels makes this plain. The failings of Christianity are mirrored by Islām in the early works and made grotesquely manifest in more direct ways later on, whilst Buddhism promises only annihilation — all exemplifying Conrad's mistrust of formulas. Yet the need for some form of belief is still there as Peyrol seems to suggest when he muses, 'I have heard of and seen more gods than you could ever dream of in a long night's sleep, in every corner of the earth, in the very heart of forests, which is an inconceivable thing. Figures, stones, sticks. There must be something in the idea' (*Ro*, 76).

Conrad tries to accommodate this need in his idea of a creation whose aim is spectacular, giving room for 'every religion except for the inverted creed of impiety, the mask and cloak of arid despair; for every joy and every sorrow, for every fair dream, for every charitable hope' (*PR*, 93). But, whilst he had diagnosed the disease, he had not found a cure and distrusted those (such as Tolstoy) who thought they had. Though frequently deceived by their illusions, most of his characters (and perhaps Conrad himself) are in a situation that can best be summed up by the words that introduce Stephen in the fragment of *The Sisters*:

. . . yet it must be said he was only a lonely and inarticulate mage, without a star and without companions. He set off on his search for a creed — and found only an infinity of formulas. No angel's voice spoke from above to him. Instead, he heard, right and left, the vociferations of idle fanatics extolling this path or that with earthly and hoarse voices that rang out, untrustworthy, in empty darkness.

(*Sis*, 33)

Notes

INTRODUCTION

1. *The Forsyte Saga* (London: Heinemann, 1924) pp. 255–6.
2. 'Conrad Criticism and *The Nigger of the "Narcissus"* ', *Nineteenth Century Fiction*, 12 (1958) 272–5.
3. Rev. of Claire Rosenfeld, *Paradise of Snakes: an Archetypal Analysis of Conrad's Political Novels*, *Modern Language Review*, LXV (1970) 407.
4. *Mythology in the Modern Novel* (Princeton University Press, 1971) p. 51.
5. *Anatomy of Criticism* (Princeton University Press, 1957) p. 158.
6. Ibid., p. 365.
7. Tanner, p. 407.
8. See, for example, Robert J. Andreach, *The Slain and Resurrected God* (New York University Press, 1970) p. 36; Bernard Meyer, *Joseph Conrad: a Psychoanalytic Biography* (Princeton University Press, 1970) p. 352.
9. See, for example, Adam Gillon, *Conrad and Shakespeare and other Essays* (New York: Astra Books, 1976) pp. 177–9; Leo Gurko, *Joseph Conrad: Giant in Exile* (New York: Macmillan, 1962) p. 133; Meyer, p. 353.
10. *Pseudonyms of Christ in the Modern Novel* (University of Pittsburgh Press, 1963) p. 3.
11. Ibid., pp. 29–30.
12. *Conrad's Models of Mind* (University of Minnesota, 1971) pp. 91–3.
13. W. L. Godshalk, 'Kurtz as Diabolical Christ', *Discourse*, 12, no. 1 (Winter 1969) 100–7; Stanley Renner, 'Kurtz, Christ and the Darkness of "Heart of Darkness"', *Renascence*, 28, no. 2 (Winter 1976) 95–104.
14. Renner, pp. 95–6. The two examples that follow are also from this source.
15. 'To Karol Zagorski', 22 May 1890, Letter 9, *Conrad's Polish Background*, ed. Zdzisław Najder, trans. Halina Carroll (London: Oxford University Press, 1964) p. 211.
16. Some examples are given in Ruth Slade, *King Leopold's Congo* (London: Oxford University Press, 1962) p. 68 and Norman Sherry, *Conrad's Western World* (London: Cambridge University Press, 1971) pp. 120–1.
17. Godshalk, p. 101.
18. 'Freud, Conrad and the Future of an Illusion', *Literature and Psychology* V (Nov. 1955) p. 79.
19. '"Heart of Darkness": a Bodhisattva Scenario', *Conradiana*, 2, no. 2 (Winter 1969–70) 46.

20. *Man's Changing Mask: Models and Methods of Characterisation in Fiction* (University of Minnesota Press, 1971) p. 272. When the English Department of the University of Canterbury in New Zealand offered a paper at master's level on Conrad's novels, it was interesting to note that at least half the students pronounced the name 'Haste'. The Swedish pronunciation would seem to be 'Hayoost'.
21. Ibid., p. 268.
22. Ibid., p. 275.
23. Ibid., p. 275.
24. Andreach, p. 96.
25. Sam Bluefest, 'Samburan: Conrad's Mirror Image of Eden', *Conradiana*, 1, no. 3 (1969) 90.
26. See, for example, Paul L. Wiley, *Conrad's Measure of Man* (1954; rpt. New York: Gordian Press, 1970) p. 209; Dennis M. Walsh, 'Conrad's "Typhoon" and the Book of Genesis', *Studies in Short Fiction*, 11 (1974) 99–101.
27. 'Eastern Logic Under My Western Eyes: Conrad, Schopenhauer and the Orient', *Conradiana*, 10 (1978) 244–5.
28. *Conrad's Eastern World* (London: Cambridge University Press, 1966) p. 17.
29. 'Ironic Symbolism in Conrad's "Youth"', *Studies in Short Fiction*, 11 (Spring 1974) 120.
30. Ibid., p. 123.
31. Sherry, *Conrad's Eastern World*, p. 297. In the circumstances it is surprising that nothing has been made of the fact that the fire goes out on the *Judea* on a Friday and the ship blows up on the Sunday (*Y*, 22); an obvious temptation for critics seeking biblical parallels, especially since on the historical *Palestine* the fire would have gone out on a Monday and the ship blown up on a Wednesday (12 and 14 March 1883 – Sherry, p. 298).
32. 'Conrad Criticism', p. 273.
33. Andreach, p. 44.
34. Ibid., p. 82.
35. Ibid., p. 115.
36. Ibid., p. 116.
37. Claire Rosenfeld, *Paradise of Snakes* (University of Chicago Press, 1967) p. 50.

1: RELIGION IN POLAND, 1820–70

1. Conrad wrote: 'Don't forget that with us religion and patriotism are closely akin'; 'Conrad to Marguerite Poradowska', 8 Sept. 1894, Letter 72, *Letters of Joseph Conrad to Marguerite Poradowska 1890–1920*, trans. and eds. John A. Gee and Paul J. Sturm (1940; rpt. Port Washington, N.Y.: Kenniyat Press, 1973) p. 78.
2. *The Cambridge History of Poland from Augustus II to Pilsudski (1697–1935)*, ed. W. F. Reddaway *et al.* (Cambridge University Press, 1941) p. 282.

(University of London, The Athlone Press, 1963) p. 51.

4.   Quoted in Leslie, p. 51.
5.   Leslie, p. 50.
6.   *Cambridge*, p. 380.
7.   Leslie, p. 66.
8.   Ibid., p. 107.
9.   Ibid., p. 123.
10. Ibid., p. 124.
11. Ibid., p. 94.
12. Manfred Kridl, *A Survey of Polish Literature and Culture*, trans. O. Scherer-Virski (New York: Columbia University Press, 1956) p. 243. The link with the attitude of Father Corbelán in *Nostromo* is obvious.
13. Fredriech Heyer, *The Catholic Church from 1648 to 1870* (London: A. & C. Black, 1969) p. 234.
14. Ibid., p. 235.
15. E. E. Y. Hales, *Revolution and Papacy 1769–1846* (London: Eyre & Spottiswoode, 1960) p. 279.
16. *Cambridge*, p. 321.
17. Ibid., p. 325.
18. E. K. Hay, *The Political Novels of Joseph Conrad* (Chicago University Press, 1963), p. 36.
19. Zdzisław Najder quotes the following comments from Conrad given in an interview in 1914: 'My father read me *Pan Tadeusz* and asked me to read it aloud too. More than once. I preferred *Konrad Wallenrod* and *Grazyna*. Later I preferred Słowacki. Do you know why Słowacki? Il est l'âme de toute la Pologne, lui' (*Conrad's Polish Background*, p. 9).
20. Quoted in *Cambridge*, p. 323.1
21. Garibaldi, it seems, became 'the hero of the Warsaw youth and town poor'; S. Arnold and M. Zychowski, *Outline History of Poland* (Warsaw: Polonia Publishing House, n. d.) p. 127.
22. *The Cambridge History of Poland* cites Apollo Korzeniowski (Conrad's father) as being the moving spirit behind this society (*Cambridge*, p. 369) but this is disputed by E. K. Hay (p. 42).
23. O. Halecki, *A History of Poland* (1942; rpt. London: Dent, 1955) p. 240.

2:   RELIGION IN CONRAD'S LIFE, 1857–95

1.   Quoted in Najder, *Conrad's Polish Background*, p. 8.
2.   Ibid., p. 5.
3.   Quoted in Jocelyn Baines, *Joseph Conrad: a Critical Biography* (London: Weidenfeld & Nicolson, 1959) p. 10.
4.   Quoted in Andrzej Busza, *Conrad's Polish Literary Background and Some Illustrations of the Influence of Polish Literature on His Work*, Antemurale 10 (Rome: Institutum Historicum Polonicum, 1966) p. 164.
5.   Quoted in Baines, p. 16.
6.   Ibid., pp. 19–20.
7.   Ibid., p. 23.

8. 'To Stefan Buszczynski', 13 June 1868, *Conrad Under Familial Eyes*, ed. Zdzisław Najder, trans. Haline Carroll-Najder (Cambridge University Press, 1983) p. 117.
9. 'To Kazimierz Kaszewski', 24 June 1868, *Conrad Under Familial Eyes*, p. 118.
10. 'To Edward Garnett', 20 Jan. 1900, *Letters from Conrad 1895–1924*, ed. Edward Garnett, (London: The Nonesuch Press, 1928) p. 168.
11. Quoted in Baines, p. 24.
12. 'Bobrowski to Conrad', 8/20 Sept. 1869, Letter 1, *Conrad's Polish Background*, p. 35. Najder explains that Bobrowski often gave both Julian and Gregorian dates in his letters.
13. *The Polish Shades and Ghosts of Joseph Conrad* (New York: Astra Books, 1976) p. 40.
14. 'To Edward Garnett', 22 Dec. 1902, *Letters from Conrad*, p. 188.
15. Busza, p. 133n.
16. *The Polish Heritage of Joseph Conrad* (New York: Haskell House, 1965) p. 110.
17. *The Sea Years of Joseph Conrad* (New York: Doubleday, 1965) p. 89.
18. 'Bobrowski to Conrad', 16/28 May 1878, Letter 7, *Conrad's Polish Background*, p. 52.
19. 'Bobrowski to Conrad', 24 Mar./5 Apr. 1886, Letter 32, *Conrad's Polish Background*, p. 100.
20. Quoted in R. Poggioli, 'The Autumn of Ideas', *Massachusetts Review*, 2 (1960–1) 663.
21. 'To Marguerite Poradowska', 15 Sept. 1891, Letter 30, *Letters to Poradowska*, p. 36.
22. 'To Marguerite Poradowska', 5 Mar. 1892, Letter 35, ibid., p. 42.
23. 'To Marguerite Poradowska', 16 Oct. 1891, Letter 32, ibid., pp. 38–9.
24. 'Conrad in Love', *Polish Perspectives*, 15, no. 11 (Nov. 1972), 30.
25. 'To Marguerite Poradowska', 4 Oct. 1892, Letter 39, *Letters to Poradowska*, p. 47.
26. 'To Miss Watson', 27 June 1897, G. Jean-Aubry, *Joseph Conrad: Life and Letters*, 2 vols (London: Heinemann, 1927) I, 205. Hereafter abbreviated as '*LL*'.
27. 'To R. B. Cunninghame Graham', 8 Feb. 1899, Letter 31, *Joseph Conrad's Letters to Cunninghame Graham*, ed. C. T. Watts (Cambridge University Press, 1969) p. 117.
28. 'To Marguerite Poradowska', 8 July 1891, Letter 25, *Letters to Poradowska*, pp. 30–1.
29. 'To Marguerite Poradowska', 5 Mar. 1892, Letter 35, ibid., p. 41.

3: CONRAD'S LATER RELIGION

1. *Joseph Conrad and His Circle* (London: Jarrolds, 1935) p. 151.
2. *Joseph Conrad: Times Remembered* (Cambridge University Press, 1981) p. 152.
3. *Joseph Conrad and His Circle*, pp. 228–9.
4. 'Conrad to Gordon Gardiner', 8 Oct. 1923, quoted in Hay, p. 192n. The

letter is in the Houghton Library at Harvard.

5. Ibid., p. 193n.
6. Meyer, p. 351. In a misleading footnote on the same page Meyer takes Jessie Conrad's comments about a French guide and applies them, instead, to Conrad. (See also Burgess, 'Conrad's Catholicism', p. 111.)
7. *Some Victorian and Georgian Catholics* (1932; New York: Books for Libraries Press, 1969) p. 142.
8. Ibid., p. 166.
9. 'Conrad's Catholicism Questioned', *America*, 19 Apr. 1924, p. 14.
10. For other Catholic comments see, for example, A. Hilliard Atteridge, 'Conrad the Catholic', *The Catholic Mind*, 22 Feb. 1925, pp. 78–80; Phillips Temple, 'The Fatalism of Joseph Conrad', *America*, 28 Nov. 1942, pp. 213–14; Michael Williams, 'Literature XIII – Joseph Conrad', *America*, 15 Nov. 1915, pp. 113–14.
11. Working on this assumption, it seems, has caused at least two critics to misread a passage of *The Nigger of the 'Narcissus'*, claiming an atheistic narrative stance in consequence. The passage in question reads: 'till the weary succession of nights and days tainted by the obstinate clamour of sages, demanding bliss and an empty heaven, is redeemed at last by the vast silence of pain and labour, by the dumb fear and the dumb courage of men obscure, forgetful and enduring' (*NN*, 90). Albert J. Guerard's interpretation of this is 'The dignity of man lies in his vast silence and endurance; a dignity tainted by those who clamor for the reward of another life' (*Conrad the Novelist* [Cambridge, Mass.: Harvard Univ. Press, 1958], p. 104) whilst H. M. Daleski comments, 'Indeed the passage insists it would be the height of folly to seek for manifestations of the divine in nature since "heaven" is "empty", and the "sages" who have obstinately demanded "bliss" despite the fact of that emptiness have only succeeded in "tainting" life, which is "redeemed" not by their "clamour" but by the "vast silence" of dogged suffering and work' (*Joseph Conrad: The Way of Dispossession* [London: Faber, 1977], p. 30). But the punctuation of the passage makes it clear that it is, in fact, the sages who are demanding 'an empty heaven' in addition to 'bliss' and the tainting effect of this shows that such a position is condemned by the narrator.
12. '"Peace that Passeth Understanding": the Professor's English Bible in *Under Western Eyes*', *Conradiana*, 13 (1981) 91.
13. 'Conrad's Catholicism', *Conradiana*, 15 (1983) 125.
14. Ibid., p. 113.
15. 'To Marguerite Poradowska', 4 Sept. 1892, Letter 37, *Letters to Poradowska*, pp. 45–6.
16. 'Bobrowski to Conrad', 28 Oct./9 Nov. 1891, Letter 62, *Conrad's Polish Background*, p. 154.
17. *The Dual Heritage of Joseph Conrad* (The Hague: Mouton, 1967) p. 76.
18. 2 Nov. 1895, *LL*, I, 184.
19. 26 Aug. 1901, *Joseph Conrad: Letters to William Blackwood and David S. Meldrum*, ed. William Blackburn (Durham, N C: Duke University Press, 1958) p. 133.

20. 14–15 Jan. 1898, Letter 7, *Conrad to Cunninghame Graham*, p. 65.
21. 23 Mar. 1896, *Letters from Conrad*, p. 23. One could note, perhaps, that
     in the next year Conrad was writing to Miss Watson (about E. L.
     Sanderson) that 'You must sacrifice the best of your impulses to do the
     most good . . . ' (27 June 1897, *LL*, I, 206). Clearly any absolutist stand
     Conrad made needed to be qualified.
22. 5 Aug. 1896, *Letters from Conrad*, p. 42.
23. Ibid., p. 43.
24. 14 August 1896, ibid., p. 47. Where ellipsis points appear in the original
     material (as here), this is indicated by three unspaced periods.
25. 10 Jan. 1897, ibid., p. 67.
26. 7 Feb. 1897, ibid., p. 73.
27. 'To E. L. Sanderson', May 1897, *LL*, I, 205.
28. 'To Edward Garnett', 11 June 1897, *Letters from Conrad*, pp. 84–5.
29. 5 Aug. 1897, Letter 1, *Conrad to Cunninghame Graham*, p. 45.
30. 11 Oct. 1897, *Letters from Conrad*, p. 100.
31. 5 Dec. 1897, ibid., pp. 107–8.
32. Letter 5, *Conrad to Cunninghame Graham*, pp. 56–7.
33. Letter 7, ibid., pp. 63–5. This particular despair was strangely contra-
     dictory in a way since, if one accepts the theories of evolution, human
     beings have changed radically in form over a few million years (a mere
     pittance as far as time goes). It is illogical, therefore, to assume that we
     shall remain in our current shapes for more than an aeon or two, and
     what we shall be like (and be able to achieve) some billion years hence is
     anybody's guess.
34. 6 Dec. 1897, Letter 3, *Conrad to Cunninghame Graham*, p. 49.
35. Between 11 June 1896, when part one of the manuscript of *The Rescuer*
     was sent off to London, and 19 Dec. 1898, when part four was begun,
     Conrad wrote less than 300 pages of the novel (about 150 in the final
     version). Of the 200 pages written for part four, almost half were
     eventually scrapped. The last 78 pages of manuscript, in fact, became
     only 1½ pages of book. (*The Rescuer* manuscript is item 4787 of the
     Ashley-Wise Collection in the British Museum, London.)
36. 29 Mar. 1898, *Letters from Conrad*, pp. 126–7.
37. June 1898, ibid., p. 132.
38. 26 Aug. 1898, Letter 24, *Conrad to Cunninghame Graham*, p. 101.
39. Ibid., p. 102.
40. 17 May 1910, *LL*, II, 108.
41. 'To Marguerite Poradowska', 23–5 Mar. 1890, Letter 5, *Conrad to
     Poradowska*, pp. 8–9.
42. 'To Angielo Zagorska', 18 Dec. 1898, *LL*, I, 262.
43. 'To Arthur Symons', 29 Aug. 1908, *LL*, II, 83–4.
44. 'To Edward Garnett', 28 Aug. 1908, *Letters from Conrad*, p. 225.
45. 'To Arthur Symons', Monday, Aug. 1908, *LL*, II, 72–3.
46. 'To E. V. Lucas', 6 Oct. 1908, *LL*, II, 89.
47. 10 May 1921, *LL*, II, 257.
48. Galsworthy wrote (in terms similar to Conrad's), 'In this age I think we
     all have to find ourselves – no glib formulas will help us, and those

people who believe in flogging the dead horse of outworn religions are dead wood in our tree' (M. E. Reynolds, *Memories of John Galsworthy* [London: Robert Hale, 1936], p. 81).

49. 'To Edward Garnett', 3 Sept. 1904, *Letters from Conrad*, p. 194.
50. 22 Dec. 1902, ibid., pp. 188–9.
51. 23 Feb. 1914, ibid., p. 265.
52. Wednesday 1908, *LL*, II, 77.
53. Hay, pp. 192–3.
54. Ibid., p. 192n.
55. *Conrad: The Later Moralist* (Amsterdam: Rodopi N. V., 1974) p. 29.
56. 'To Ford Madox Hueffer', Tuesday 1903, *LL*, I, 313. Certainly the following passage from *Beyond Good and Evil* is interesting when applied to *Lord Jim*. Nietzsche is talking about the man who attempts independence:

> He ventures into a labyrinth, he multiplies by a thousand the dangers which life as such already brings with it, not the smallest of which is that no one can behold how and where he goes astray, is cut off from others, and is torn to pieces limb from limb by some cave-minotaur of conscience. If such a one is destroyed, it takes place so far from the understanding of men that they neither feel it nor sympathize – and he can no longer go back! He can no longer go back even to the pity of men! (trans. R. J. Hollindale [Harmondsworth: Penguin, 1973], p. 42).

57. Enid Starkie, *From Gautier to Eliot* (London: Hutchinson, 1960) p. 28.
58. 'To Edward Garnett', 23 Feb. 1914, *Letters from Conrad*, p. 265.
59. 24 Sept. 1919, ibid., pp. 289–90.
60. 'To John Galsworthy', 1 Nov. 1910, *LL*, II, 121–2.
61. 23 Mar. 1896, *Letters from Conrad*, p. 23.
62. 6 Dec. 1897, Letter 3, *Conrad to Cunninghame Graham*, p. 50.
63. 19 Dec. 1899, Letter 35, ibid., p. 128.
64. 3 Jan. 1917, Letter 71, ibid., p. 185.
65. 7 Jan. 1898, Letter 6, ibid., p. 59.
66. 22 Dec. 1921, *Letters from Conrad*, pp. 310–11.
67. 28 Aug. 1908, ibid., pp. 226–7.
68. 4 Jan. 1900, Letter 36, *Conrad to Cunninghame Graham*, p. 129.
69. 'Inveni Portum – Joseph Conrad' in *Redeemed and Other Sketches* (London: Heinemann, 1927); rpt. *Selected Modern English Essays*, 2nd series, comp. Humphrey Sumner Milford (London: Oxford University Press, 1932) p. 55.
70. Quoted in Hay, p. 193n.
71. Ibid., p. 193n.
72. J. H. Buckley, *The Triumph of Time*, (Cambridge, Mass.: Harvard University Press, 1966) p. 13.

4: THE MIRROR OF ISLĀM

1. Charles Burton Buckley, *An Anecdotal History of Old Times in Singapore 1819–67* (1902; Kuala Lumpur: University of Malaya Press, 1965) p. 565; quoted in Sherry, *Conrad's Eastern World*, p. 206.

2. Buckley also makes favourable mention of a Syed Omar and a Syed Allie (Buckley, pp. 563–4).
3. Sherry, *Conrad's Eastern World*, pp. 206–7.
4. The name is spelt 'Abdulla' in the novels and 'Abdullah' in *A Personal Record* (*PR*, 82) and 'Because of the Dollars' (*WT*, 177). In the absence of a standard form of transliteration of Arabic names in the nineteenth century, many variations in spelling will be noted. Syed, for example, can also be spelt Saiyyid, Siyyid (the currently accepted spelling), Sayyid, Seiyid, Seyyid or Saiyid. Original spelling has been retained in all quotations and, to avoid confusion, Conrad's version of Syed is retained for the text.
5. 1 May 1898, Letter 15, *Conrad to Cunninghame Graham*, p. 84.
6. Slade, *King Leopold's Congo*, p. 98.
7. Sherry, *Conrad's Western World*, p. 68.
8. *A Year Among the Persians* (1893; London: A. and C. Black, 1970).
9. *Mogreb-El-Acksa* (London: Heinemann, 1898).
10. J. W. H. Stobbart, *Islam and Its Founder* (London: Society for Promoting Christian Knowledge, 1878) p. 90n.
11. Ibid., pp. 96–7.
12. Ibid., p. 106.
13. Sir William Muir, *The Life of Mohammad* (1861; Edinburgh: John Grant, 1912) pp. 510ff.
14. Ibid., p. 522.
15. John P. Brown, *The Darvishes or Oriental Spiritualism* (1868; London: Frank Cass, 1968) p. v.
16. Ibid., p. 76.
17. W. H. Wilkins, preface to Sir Richard Burton, *The Jew, The Gypsy and El Islam* (London: Hutchinson, 1898) p. xiv.
18. Elizabeth Longford, *A Pilgrimage of Passion: the Life of Wilfrid Scawen Blunt* (London: Weidenfeld & Nicolson, 1979). Blunt was investigating Islām in Jeddah when the ship of that name, carrying hundreds of Muslim pilgrims, was abandoned by her British crew; this incident forming the basis for the first part of *Lord Jim* (Sherry, *Conrad's Eastern World*, pp. 41–64). Blunt wrote about this 'ugly' story in his articles for the *Fortnightly Review* and Longford cites Graham Greene's letter to the *Times Literary Supplement* (6 Dec. 1974) which suggests that this account has been generally overlooked by Conrad's biographers (Longford, p. 168). Coincidentally, Blunt was also disillusioned with the conduct of his countrymen whilst in the Indian city of Patna in Jan. 1884. He was being farewelled by some Muslim friends at the railway station when the Chief Medical Officer of the Punjab ordered them away. A row ensued between the two Europeans and Blunt took legal action to enforce an apology (Longford, pp. 203–4). Whether Conrad knew of this incident as well is not known but he mentions Blunt as an acquaintance of Cunninghame Graham in a letter dated 30 July 1898 (*Conrad to Cunninghame Graham*, p. 94).
19. Burton, *El Islam*, p. 332.
20. Qur'ān 2:257; 10:99–100.
21. *Mogreb-El-Acksa*, p. 18n.

22. Ibid., pp. 103–4.
23. Ibid., p. 24.
24. Ibid., p. 123.
25. Ibid., p. 43.
26. 3 vols (London: Longmans, 1855–56). All subsequent references to Burton (mostly within the text) are to this edition of this work.
27. Quoted in *Conrad to Cunninghame Graham*, p. 112. I had overlooked this reference when this part of the chapter first appeared in print in *Conradiana*, 13 (1981) 166, and am grateful to Hans van Marle for bringing it to light in his 'Conrad and Richard Burton on Islam', *Conradiana*, 17 (1985) 137.
28. *The Malay Archipelago*, 2 vols (London: Macmillan, 1869) II, 278.
29. Ibid., pp. 103–4.
30. Ibid., p. 11.
31. A. S. Bickmore, *Travels in the East Indian Archipelago* (London: John Murray, 1868) pp. 471–2; Bernard H. M. Vlekke, *Nusantara: a History of Indonesia* (The Hague: W. Van Hoeve, 1965) p. 298.
32. '"The Rescuer" Manuscript: a Key to Conrad's Development – and Decline', *Harvard Library Bulletin*, 10 (1956) 335–6.
33. *Malay Sketches* (London: John Lane, 1895); rpt. in *Stories and Sketches by Sir Frank Swettenham* (Kuala Lumpur: Oxford University Press, 1967) p. 17.
34. Ibid., p. 18.
35. Ibid., pp. 103–4.
36. Juliet McLauchlan, 'Almayer and Willems – "How not to be"', *Conradiana*, 11 (1979) 138.
37. 'To Miss Aniela Zagorska', 12 Feb. 1923, Letter 88, *Conrad's Polish Background*, p. 287.
38. In recognition of his descent a Syed is allowed to wear a green turban. Burton explains: 'The green turban is an innovation in El Islam. In some countries it is confined to the Sayyids. In others it is worn as a mark of distinction by pilgrims' (Burton, II, 259n.). In *Almayer's Folly* it is Lakamba (not a Syed) who wears the green turban. Swettenham talks of the 'Famous Seyyid' as having a black head-dress (*Stories and Sketches*, p. 46) so it may not have been the practice in the Far East. That Conrad knew of the Syed's connection with green is shown by his statement in *The Shadow-Line*: 'An Arab owned her, and a Syed at that. Hence the green border on the flag' (*SL*, 4).
39. Qur'ān 5:7.
40. *Stories and Sketches*, p. 114.
41. 'Conrad to Miss Watson', 27 June 1897, *LL*, I, 206.

5: IDOLS AND EDIFICES

1. R. C. Brashers, 'Conrad, Marlow and Gautama Buddha: On Structure and theme in "Heart of Darkness"', *Conradiana*, 1, no. 3 (1969) 63–71.
2. '"Heart of Darkness": a Bodhisattva Scenario', pp. 43–4.

3. 'Narrative Presence: The Illusion of Language in "Heart of Darkness"', *Studies in the Novel*, 6 (1974) 337.
4. 'Conrad's East: Time, History, Action, and MAYA', *Texas Studies in Literature and Language*, 7 (1965–66), 280–1.
5. 'Eastern Logic', pp. 241 and 247.
6. 'A Further Comment on "Heart of Darkness"', *Modern Fiction Studies*, 3 (1957–58) 359.
7. Stein, 'Conrad's East', p. 276.
8. *Amiel's Journal*, 2 vols, trans. Mrs Humphry Ward (London: Macmillan, 1885) I, 41. In translation, the passage (with the epigraph in italics) reads as follows:

> Thou too sawest undulating in the distance the ravishing hills of the Promised Land, and it was thy fate nevertheless to lay thy weary bones in a grave dug in the desert! – *Which of us has not his promised land, his day of ecstasy and his death in exile?* What a pale counterfeit is real life of the life we see in glimpses, and how these flaming lightnings of our prophetic youth make the twilight of our dull monotonous manhood more dark and dreary.

9. Bonney, 'Eastern Logic', p. 230.
10. *Castles in Spain and Other Screeds* (London: Heinemann, 1927) p. 91. One could also mention that Amiel discusses Schopenhauer in his *Journal* (II, 69–74).
11. *Conrad's 'Heart of Darkness': a Critical and Contextual Discussion* (Milan: Mursia International, 1977) p. 158.
12. '"Heart of Darkness" and the Problem of Emptiness', *Studies in Short Fiction*, 9 (1972) 399.
13. 'Conrad's "Falk": Manuscript and Meaning', *Modern Language Quarterly*, 26 (1965) 280.
14. Ibid., p. 280n.
15. Ibid., pp. 280–1.
16. 'Beyond the Threshold in Conrad's "Heart of Darkness"', *Texas Studies in Literature and Language*, 11 (1969) 1022.
17. 'A Further Note on the Function of the Frame in "Heart of Darkness"', *Modern Fiction Studies*, 3 (1957) 170.
18. In an intriguing postscript to an essay on narrative form, Muriel Bradbrook suggests that in *Victory*, 'Conrad presents the conflict of Eastern mythology with Heyst's Western philosophy' and claims that 'at the mythological level *Victory* draws . . . upon the deeper faiths and rites of the region where it is set.' She sees Lena as embodying 'that eternal struggle of light and darkness, the subject of the Javanese or Balinese dance, the conflict between Goodness unarmed and the Sea Demon with his followers'. To this end, 'the Balinese Kriis dance symbolises the struggle enacted in Lena's contest for Ricardo's knife. The ironic victory of Eastern mysticism over deathly Nihilism culminates in the Brahmin funeral rite of purification by fire' ('Narrative Form in Conrad and Lowry' in *Joseph Conrad: A Commemoration*, ed. Norman Sherry

[London: Macmillan, 1976], pp. 141–2). In this view, Eastern mysticism (or Hinduism, at least) would become a positive force here but it would have been interesting to see a more detailed application; one that incorporated Ricardo's 'bonze-like attitude,' for example.

19. 26 Aug. 1898, Letter 24, *Conrad to Cunninghame Graham*, p. 101.

6: CONRAD'S CHRISTIANS

1. Wednesday 1908, *LL*, 77.
2. *Joseph Conrad as I Knew Him* (London: Heinemann, 1926) p. 29.
3. 11 Nov. 1901, *LL*, I, 301.
4. This may, in fact, be Father Beron himself since there is a similarity of description (*cf. N*, 138 and 371).
5. It is interesting to note that Thaddeus Bobrowski's account of this episode makes no mention of the priest ('Memoirs' II, 489–90; *Conrad Under Familial Eyes*, p. 73).
6. 6 Dec. 1897, Letter 3, *Conrad to Cunninghame Graham*, p. 49.

7: DEVIL AND SOUL

1. John Lester, 'Conrad's Narrators in *The Nigger of the "Narcissus"'*, *Conradiana*, 12 (1980) 163–72.
2. This connection between the devil and the ego is implicit in the teachings of most religions and explicit in the most recent, the Bahá'í Faith, whose Founder, Bahá'u'lláh, speaks of 'the Satan of self' (*The Kitáb-í-Iqán: The Book of Certitude*, trans. Shoghi Effendi [London: Bahá'í Publishing Trust, 1946], p. 72).
3. 'To R. B. Cunninghame Graham', 8 Feb. 1899, Letter 31, *Conrad to Cunninghame Graham*, p. 117.
4. *Congo Diary and Other Uncollected Pieces*, ed. Zdzisław Najder (Garden City, New York: Doubleday, 1978) p. 75. Lawrence Graver also relates the egoism/altruism implications of this letter to Conrad's fiction in *Conrad's Shorter Fiction* (University of California Press, 1969) pp. 44ff.
5. Wednesday to Friday 1904, *LL*, I, 329.
6. Ian Watt suggests 'mania' as a possible meaning for 'folly' when discussing *Almayer's Folly*, pointing out that Conrad would have been aware of the connotations of the word in French (*Conrad in the Nineteenth Century* [London: Chatto & Windus, 1980], p. 65).
7. 21 Dec. 1903, Zdzisław Najder, 'Conrad's Casement Letters,' *Polish Perspectives* (Dec. 1974) p. 29.
8. The references to Mephistopheles are religious via literature and the Faust legend rather than religious through biblical allusions. An over-reaching ego is, of course, at the centre of that legend.
9. Rosenfeld, p. 149; Harriet Gilliam, 'The Daemonic in Conrad's *Under Western Eyes*', *Conradiana*, 9 (1977) 219.

10. 'To E. L. Sanderson', 31 Dec. 1917, *LL*, II, 198.
11. *Models of Mind*, pp. 8–23.
12. Arthur Schopenhauer, *The World as Will and Idea*, 3 vols, trans. R. B. Haldane and J. Kemp (London: Routledge & Kegan Paul, 1883) II, 412; quoted in Patrick Gardiner, *Schopenhauer* (Harmondsworth: Penguin, 1963) p. 151.
13. *Parerga and Paralipomena*, 2 vols, trans. E. F. J. Payne (Oxford: Clarendon Press, 1974) II, 48.
14. *World*, I, 130; quoted in Gardiner, p. 159.
15. *On the Basis of Morality*, trans. E. F. J. Payne (Indianapolis: Bobbs-Merrill, 1965) p. 145.
16. Schopenhauer, *World*, II, 421; quoted in Gardiner, p. 166.
17. *Models of Mind*, p. 43.
18. James W. Parins et al, *A Concordance to Conrad's Lord Jim* (New York: Garland, 1976) pp. 151–82.
19. *Parerga and Paralipomena*, II, 162.
20. Ibid., I, 20.
21. Ibid., I, 114.
22. Ibid., I, 306–7.
23. 'Marlow's Descent into Hell', *Nineteenth Century Fiction*, 9 (1955) 291.
24. Schopenhauer, *Essay on the Freedom of the Will*, trans. Konstantin Kolenda (Indianapolis: Bobbs-Merrill, 1960) p. 17.
25. 'To John Galsworthy', Monday 1919, *LL*, II, 220.
26. 23 Dec. 1920, Letter 75, *Conrad to Cunninghame Graham*, p. 190.

8: THE PURPOSES OF CONRAD'S RELIGIOUS IMAGERY

1. 'Conrad's "Typhoon" and the Book of Genesis', p. 100.
2. 'MacWhirr and the Testimony of the Human Voice,' *Conradiana*, 7 (1975) 47.
3. Conrad produces a similar image of the 'last day' in his essay on Henry James where he writes of the artist as 'the imaginative man who would be moved to speak on the eve of that day without to-morrow' (*NLL*, 13–14). The apocalypse described in this essay is a scientific one as opposed to the more biblical aspects of the references in 'Typhoon', but the implication is that man's voice represents life since, for the artist, 'silence is like death' (*NLL*, 14). MacWhirr's voice can thus be taken, similarly, as a symbol of life on the ship, illustrating his defiance of the elements that are threatening to overwhelm him.
4. 25 Oct., *Letters from Conrad*, p. 52.
5. '"Peace that Passeth Understanding"', p. 83.
6. Ibid., p. 85.
7. Ibid., p. 88.
8. Ibid., p. 89.
9. Ibid., p. 90.
10. Ibid., p. 90.
11. Ibid., p. 88.

12. For a survey of a development of this myth, see Michael Cherniavsky, '"Holy Russia": a Study in the History of an Idea', *American Historical Review*, 63 (1958) 617–37.

13. 'Creature and Creator in *Under Western Eyes*', *Conradiana*, 8 (1976) 246.

14. *The Forsyte Saga*, p. 224.

15. 'To Sidney Colvin', 28 Dec. 1908, *LL*, II, 92.

16. 'To R. B. Cunninghame Graham', 4 Jan. 1900, Letter 36, *Conrad to Cunninghame Graham*, p. 129.

17. 'To Edward Garnett', 11 Oct. 1897, *Letters from Conrad*, p. 101.

18. Purdy, 'Peace', p. 85.

19. Wiley, p. 35.

20. *Conrad: The Psychologist as Artist* (Edinburgh: Oliver & Boyd, 1968) p. 34.

21. 'Theodore Parker', (1867), in *Culture and Anarchy with . . . Some Literary Essays*, ed. R. H. Super, *Complete Prose Works* V (Ann Arbor: University of Michigan Press, 1965) p. 83; quoted in Buckley, *The Triumph of Time*, p. 47.

22. *Ecce Homo* (1865; Boston, 1896) p. 3; quoted in Buckley, p. 47.

23. Quoted in Buckley, p. 81.

24. 2 Nov. 1895, *LL*, I, 184.

25. 'To Edward Garnett', 24 Jan. 1898, *Letters from Conrad*, p. 120.

26. 'To Edward Garnett', 11 Oct. 1897, ibid., p. 98.

27. *Conrad: The Moral World of the Novelist* (London: Paul Elek, 1978) p. 54.

28. Stanley Tick, 'The Gods of *Nostromo*', *Modern Fiction Studies*, 10 (1964) 19.

29. Quoted in Emily K. Izsak, '*Under Western Eyes* and the Problems of Serial Publication', *Review of English Studies*, 23:92 (Nov. 1972) 439.

30. Tolstoy's works include *Resurrection* and *The Power of Darkness*.

31. Quoted in Izsak, p. 442.

32. Philippe Villiers de l'Isle-Adam, *Axel*, trans. June Guicharnaud (Englewood Cliffs, N. J.: Prentice-Hall, 1970) p. 183.

33. 'Conrad's Axel', *Studies in Philology*, 48 (1951) 106.

34. Villiers de l'Isle-Adam, p. 86.

35. Andreach, p. 96.

9: CONCLUSION

1. 11 Nov. 1901, *LL*, I, 301.

2. Rosenfeld, pp. 173–6.

Selected Bibliography

I BIBLIOGRAPHIES

Ehrsam, Theodore G. (comp.), *A Bibliography of Joseph Conrad* (Metuchen, N J: The Scarecrow Press, 1969).
Teets, Bruce E. and Helmut E. Gerber (comps and eds), *Joseph Conrad: an Annotated Bibliography of Writings About Him* (Northern Illinois University Press, 1971).

(NB   An annual update of these bibliographies is maintained in the journal, *Conradiana*.)

II PRIMARY SOURCES

A. Works by Joseph Conrad

Collected Edition of the Works of Joseph Conrad, 21 vols (London: Dent, 1946–54).
Congo Diary and Other Uncollected Pieces, ed. Zdzisław Najder (New York: Doubleday, 1978).
Conrad's Polish Background: Letters to and from Polish Friends, ed. Zdzisław Najder, trans. Halina Carroll (London: Oxford University Press, 1964).
Joseph Conrad: Letters to William Blackwood and David S. Meldrum, ed. William Blackburn (Durham, N. C.: Duke University Press, 1958).
Joseph Conrad's Letters to R. B. Cunninghame Graham, ed. C. T. Watts (Cambridge University Press, 1969).
Joseph Conrad: Life and Letters, ed. G. Jean-Aubry, 2 vols (London: Heinemann, 1927).
Letters from Conrad 1895 to 1924, ed. Edward Garnett (London: The Nonesuch Press, 1928).
Letters: Joseph Conrad to Richard Curle, ed. Richard Curle (1928; rpt. New York: Folcroft Library, 1973).

Letters of Joseph Conrad to Marguerite Poradowska 1890–1920, trans. and ed. John A. Gee and Paul J. Sturm (1940; rpt. Port Washington, N. Y.: Kennikat Press, 1973).
'The Rescuer' Manuscript, Ashley-Wise Collection, 4787, British Museum, London.
The Sisters, ed. U. Mursia (Milan: U. Mursia, 1968).

B. Fiction, Drama and Poetry

Galsworthy, John, *The Forsyte Saga* (London: Heinemann, 1924).
Mickiewicz, Adam, *Forefathers*, trans. Count Potocki of Montalk (London: Polish Culture Foundation, 1968).
——, *Konrad Wallenrod and Other Writings*, trans. Jewell Parish, Dorothea Prall Radin, George Rapall Noyes *et al.* (University of California Press, 1925).
——, *Pan Tadeusz*, trans. George Rapall Noyes (London: Dent, 1930).
Słowacki, Juliusz, *Anhelli*, trans. Dorothea Prall Radin, ed. George Rapall Noyes (London: Allen & Unwin, 1930).
Tolstoy, Leo, 'The Kreutzer Sonata' in *The Devil and Cognate Tales*, trans. Aylmer Maude (London: Oxford University Press, 1934).
Villiers de l'Isle Adam, Philippe A., *Axel*, trans. J. Guicharnaud (Englewood Cliffs, NJ: Prentice-Hall, 1970).

C. Non-Fiction

Amiel, Henri F., *Amiel's Journal: the Journal Intime of Henri-Frederic Amiel*, trans. Mrs Humphry Ward, 2 vols (London: Macmillan, 1885).
Bahá'u'lláh, *The Kitáb-í-Iqán: The Book of Certitude*, trans. Shoghi Effendi (London: Bahá'í Publishing Trust, 1946).
Bickmore, Albert S., *Travels in the East Indian Archipelago* (London: John Murray, 1868).
Browne, Edward Granville, *A Year Amongst the Persians* (1893; rpt. London: A. & C. Black, 1970).
Burton, Richard F., *Personal Narrative of a Pilgrimage to El-Medinah and Meccah*, 3 vols (London: Longmans, 1855–56).
Graham, R. B. Cunninghame, *Mogreb-El-Acksa: a Journey in Morocco* (London: Heinemann, 1898).
Najder, Zdzisław, ed., *Conrad Under Familial Eyes*, trans. Halina Carroll-Najder (Cambridge University Press, 1983).

Nietzsche, Friedrich, *Beyond Good and Evil*, trans. R. J. Hollindale (Harmondsworth: Penguin, 1973).

Schopenhauer, Arthur, *Essay on the Freedom of the Will*, trans. Konstantin Kolenda (Indianapolis: Bobbs-Merrill, 1960).

——, *On the Basis of Morality*, trans. E. F. J. Payne (Indianapolis: Bobbs-Merrill, 1965).

——, *Parerga and Paralipomena: Short Philosophical Essays*, 2 vols, trans. E. F. J. Payne (Oxford: Clarendon Press, 1974).

Swettenham, Sir Frank, *Stories and Sketches*, ed. W. R. Roff (Kuala Lumpur: Oxford University Press, 1967).

Wallace, Alfred Russel, *The Malay Archipelago*, 2 vols (London: Macmillan, 1869).

III SECONDARY SOURCES

A. Critical Works

Allen, Jerry, *The Sea Years of Joseph Conrad* (New York: Doubleday, 1965).

Andreach, Robert J., *The Slain and Resurrected God: Conrad, Ford and the Christian Myth* (New York University Press, 1970).

Baines, Jocelyn, *Joseph Conrad: a Critical Biography* (London: Weidenfeld & Nicolson, 1959).

Boyle, Ted. E., *Symbol and Meaning in the Fiction of Joseph Conrad* (The Hague: Mouton, 1965).

Bradbrooke, M. C., 'Narrative Form in Conrad and Lowry' in *Joseph Conrad: a Commemoration, Papers from the 1974 International Conference on Conrad*, ed. Norman Sherry (London: Macmillan, 1976) pp. 129–42.

Braybrooke, Patrick, *Some Victorian and Georgian Catholics: Their Art and Outlook* (1932; rpt. New York: Books for Libraries Press, 1969).

Buckley, Jerome Hamilton, *The Triumph of Time: a Study of the Victorian Concepts of Time, History, Progress and Decadence* (Cambridge, Mass.: Harvard University Press, 1966).

Busza, Andrzej, *Conrad's Polish Literary Background and Some Illustrations of the Influence of Polish Literature on His Work, Antemurale* 10 (Rome: Institutum Historicum Polonicum, 1966) pp. 109–255 [separately published monograph].

Conrad, Jessie, *Joseph Conrad and His Circle* (London: Jarrolds, 1935).

——, *Joseph Conrad as I Knew Him* (London: Heinemann, 1926).

Conrad, John, *Joseph Conrad: Times Remembered* (Cambridge University Press, 1981).

Cox, C. B., *Joseph Conrad: the Modern Imagination* (London: Dent, 1974).

Daleski, H. M., *Joseph Conrad: the Way of Dispossession* (London: Faber, 1977).

Frye, Northrop, *Anatomy of Criticism: Four Essays* (Princeton University Press, 1957).

Gardiner, Patrick, *Schopenhauer* (Harmondsworth: Penguin, 1963).

Gekoski, R. A., *Conrad: the Moral World of the Novelist* (London: Paul Elek, 1978).

Gillon, Adam, *Conrad and Shakespeare and Other Essays* (New York: Astra Books, 1976).

Graver, Lawrence, *Conrad's Short Fiction* (University of California Press, 1969).

Guerard, Albert J., *Conrad the Novelist* (Cambridge, Mass.: Harvard University Press, 1966).

Gurko, Leo, *Joseph Conrad: Giant in Exile* (New York: Macmillan, 1962).

Hay, Eloise Knapp, *The Political Novels of Joseph Conrad* (University of Chicago Press, 1963).

Hodges, R. R., *The Dual Heritage of Joseph Conrad* (The Hague: Mouton, 1967).

Johnson, Bruce, *Conrad's Models of Mind* (University of Minnesota, 1971).

Karl, Frederick R., *Joseph Conrad: The Three Lives* (London: Faber, 1979).

Kirschner, Paul, *Conrad: the Psychologist as Artist* (Edinburgh: Oliver & Boyd, 1968).

Kridl, Manfred, *A Survey of Polish Literature and Culture*, trans. O. Scherer-Virski (New York: Columbia University Press, 1956).

Meyer, Bernard C., *Joseph Conrad: a Psychoanalytic Biography* (Princeton University Press, 1970).

Morf, Gustav, *The Polish Heritage of Joseph Conrad* (1930; New York: Haskell House, 1965).

——, *The Polish Shades and Ghosts of Joseph Conrad* (New York: Astra Books, 1976).

Moseley, Edwin M., *Pseudonyms of Christ in the Modern Novel: Motifs and Methods* (University of Pittsburgh Press, 1963).

Parins, J. W., R. J. Dilligan and Todd K. Bender, *A Concordance to*

Conrad's Lord Jim: Verbal Index, Word Frequency Table and Field of Reference (New York: Garland, 1976).

Reynolds, M. E., *Memories of John Galsworthy* (London: Robert Hale, 1936).

Rosenfeld, Claire, *Paradise of Snakes: an Archetypal Analysis of Conrad's Political Novels* (University of Chicago Press, 1967).

Saveson, John E., *Conrad: the Later Novelist* (Amsterdam: Rodopi N. V., 1974).

Sherry, Norman, *Conrad and His World* (London: Thames & Hudson, 1972).

——, *Conrad's Eastern World* (London: Cambridge University Press, 1966).

——, *Conrad's Western World* (London: Cambridge University Press, 1971).

Spence, G. W., *Tolstoy the Ascetic* (Edinburgh: Oliver & Boyd, 1967).

Starkie, Enid, *From Gautier to Eliot: The Influence of France on English Literature 1851–1939* (London: Hutchinson, 1960).

Walcutt, Charles Child, *Man's Changing Mask: Models and Methods of Characterization in Fiction* (University of Minnesota Press, 1966).

Watt, Ian, *Conrad in the Nineteenth Century* (London: Chatto & Windus, 1980).

Watts, Cedric, *Conrad's 'Heart of Darkness': a Critical and Contextual Discussion* (Milan: Mursia International, 1977).

White, John J., *Mythology in the Modern Novel: a Study of Prefigurative Techniques* (Princeton University Press, 1971).

Wiley, Paul L., *Conrad's Measure of Man* (1954; New York: Gordian Press, 1970).

B. Historical Works

Arnold, S. and M. Zychowski, *Outline History of Poland* (Warsaw: Polonia Publishing House, n.d.).

Brown, John P., *The Darvishes or Oriental Spiritualism* (1868; London: Frank Cass, 1968).

Buckley, Charles Burton, *An Anecdotal History of Old Times in Singapore* (1902; rpt. Kuala Lumpur: University of Malaya Press, 1965).

Burton, Sir Richard F., *The Jew, the Gypsy and El Islam* (London: Hutchinson, 1898).

Halecki, Oskar, *A History of Poland* (1942; London: Dent, 1955).

Hales, E. E. Y., *Revolution and Papacy 1769–1846* (London: Eyre and Spottiswoode, 1960).

Heyer, Friedrich, *The Catholic Church from 1648 to 1870* (London: A. and C. Black, 1969).

Leslie, R. F., *Reform and Insurrection in Russian Poland 1856–1865* (London: Athlone Press, 1963).

Longford, Elizabeth, *A Pilgrimage of Passion: The Life of Wilfred Scawen Blunt* (London: Weidenfeld and Nicolson, 1979).

Muir, Sir William, *The Life of Muhammad* (1861; Edinburgh: John Grant, 1912).

Reddaway, W. F., J. H. Penson, O. Halecki, R. Dyboski and others, eds, *The Cambridge History of Poland from Augustus II to Pilsudski (1697–1935)* (Cambridge University Press, 1941).

Slade, Ruth, *King Leopold's Congo: Aspects of the Development of Race Relations in the Congo Independent State* (London: Oxford University Press, 1962).

Stobbart, J. W. H., *Islam and Its Founder* (London: Society for Promoting Christian Knowledge, 1878).

Vlekke, Bernard H. M., *Nusantara: A History of the East Indian Archipelago* (1943; The Hague: W. Van Hoeve, 1965).

C. Articles and Reviews

Bonney, William W., 'Eastern Logic Under My Western Eyes: Conrad, Schopenhauer and the Orient,' *Conradiana*, 10 (1978) 225–52.

Burgess, C. F., 'Conrad's Catholicism,' *Conradiana*, 15 (1983) 111–26.

Cherniavsky, Michael, '"Holy Russia": a Study in the History of an Idea', *American Historical Review*, 63 (1958) 617–37.

Feder, Lillian, 'Marlow's Descent into Hell', *Nineteenth Century Fiction*, 9 (1955) 280–92.

Gatch, Katherine Hayes, 'Conrad's Axel', *Studies in Philology*, 48 (1951) 92–106.

Gilliam, Harriet, 'The Daemonic in Conrad's *Under Western Eyes*', *Conradiana*, 9 (1977) 219–36.

Godshalk, William Leigh, 'Kurtz as Diabolical Christ,' *Discourse*, 12 (1969) 100–7.

Gross, Seymour, 'A Further Note on the Function of the Frame in "Heart of Darkness"', *Modern Fiction Studies*, 2 (1957) 167–70.

Izsak, Emily K., '*Under Western Eyes* and the Problems of Serial Publication', *Review of English Studies*, 23 (1972) 429–44.

Johnson, Bruce, '"Heart of Darkness" and the Problem of Emptiness', *Studies in Short Fiction*, 9 (1972) 387–400.

——, 'Conrad's "Falk": Manuscript and Meaning', *Modern Language Quarterly*, 26 (1965) 267–84.

Ketterer, David, 'Beyond the Threshold in Conrad's "Heart of Darkness"', *Texas Studies in Literature and Language*, 11 (1969) 1013–22.

Lester, John, 'Conrad's Narrators in *The Nigger of the "Narcissus"*', *Conradiana*, 12 (1980) 163–72.

McLaughlan, Juliet, 'Almayer and Willems: "How Not to Be"', *Conradiana*, 9 (1979) 113–43.

Matthews, James W., 'Ironic Symbolism in Conrad's "Youth"', *Studies in Short Fiction*, 11 (1973) 117–23.

Moser, Thomas, '"The Rescuer" Manuscript: a Key to Conrad's Development – and Decline', *Harvard Library Bulletin*, 10 (1956) 325–55.

Najder, Zdzisław, 'Conrad in Love', *Polish Perspectives* (Nov. 1972) pp. 26–42.

——, 'Conrad's Casement Letters', *Polish Perspectives* (Dec. 1974) pp. 25–30.

Purdy, Dwight H., 'Creature and Creator in *Under Western Eyes*', *Conradiana*, 8 (1976) 241–6.

——, '"Peace that Passeth Understanding": The Professor's English Bible in *Under Western Eyes*', *Conradiana*, 13 (1981) 83–93.

Renner, Stanley, 'Kurtz, Christ and the Darkness of "Heart of Darkness"', *Renascence*, 28, no. 2 (Winter 1976) 95–104.

Ryan, John K., 'Conrad's Catholicism Questioned,' *America*, 19 Apr. 1924, p. 14.

Stein, William Bysshe, 'Conrad's East: Time, History, Action and MAYA', *Texas Studies in Literature and Language*, 7 (1965) 265–83.

——, '"Heart of Darkness": a Bodhisattva Scenario,' *Conradiana*, 2, no. 2 (1970) 39–52.

——, 'The Eastern Matrix of Conrad's Art', *Conradiana*, 1, no. 2 (1968) 1–14.

Tick, Stanley, 'The Gods of *Nostromo*', *Modern Fiction Studies*, 10 (1964) 15–26.

van Marle, Hans, 'Conrad and Richard Burton on Islam', *Conradiana*, 17 (1985) 137–42.

Walsh, Dennis M., 'Conrad's "Typhoon" and the Book of Genesis', *Studies in Short Fiction*, 11 (1974) 99–101.

Wasserman, Jerry, 'Narrative Presence: The Illusion of Language in "Heart of Darkness"', *Studies in the Novel*, 6 (1974) 327–38.

Watt, Ian, 'Conrad Criticism and *The Nigger of the "Narcissus"*', *Nineteenth Century Fiction*, 12 (1958) 257–83.

Wegelin, C., 'MacWhirr and the Testimony of the Human Voice', *Conradiana*, 7 (1975) 45–50.

Index